THE ZEN
OF GARDENING

IN THE HIGH AND ARID WEST

TIPS, TOOLS, AND TECHNIQUES

DAVID WANN

Fulcrum Publishing
Golden, Colorado

Library of Congress Cataloging-in-Publication Data

Wann, David.
The zen of gardening in the high & arid West : tips, tools, and techniques / David Wann.
    p. cm.
Includes bibliographical references and index.
ISBN 1-55591-457-8 (pbk. : alk. paper)
1. Gardening—West (U.S.) 2. Arid regions—West (U.S.)
3. Gardening—Philosophy. 4. Zen Buddhism. I. Title: Zen of gardening in the high and arid West. II. Title.
SB451.34.W47 W36 2003
635'.0978'09154—dc21
                        2002151254

Editorial: Marlene Blessing, Ellen Wheat, Daniel Forrest-Bank
Design: Anne Clark
Interior illustrations: Marjorie Leggitt, Leggitt Design
Cover photograph: Anne Herman
Back cover photograph: Edee Gail
Map: Marge Mueller, Gray Mouse Graphics

Printed in Canada
0 9 8 7 6 5 4 3 2 1

Fulcrum Publishing
16100 Table Mountain Parkway, Suite 300
Golden, Colorado 80403
(800) 992-2908 • (303) 277-1623
www.fulcrum-books.com

Contents

SECTION III

STRATEGIC GARDENING
• HOW TO GROW PESTO, SALSA, AND CHERRY PIE •

SECTION IV

Ornamentals for the West
· FLOWERS, TREES, AND SHRUBS
THAT TAKE A LICKING AND KEEP ON TICKING ·

SECTION V

ZEN MASTERS OF THE WEST
· HARVESTING 500 YEARS OF
WESTERN GARDENING EXPERIENCE ·

ACKNOWLEDGMENTS

I'm very grateful to Marlene Blessing, Ellen Wheat, Dan Forrest-Bank, Anne Clark, and other folks at Fulcrum Publishing, who made this book possible. I also want to thank Mona Neeley and Donna Norris at *Colorado Country Life* magazine, where much of this material was first published.

This book is dedicated to my neighbors in Harmony Village, to Susan, and to all the masters of western gardening who have inspired me and laid down a pathway the rest of us can follow.

THE HIGH AND ARID WEST

INTRODUCTION: THE ZEN OF GARDENING

WRITING A GARDENING BOOK and working in a garden are like yin and yang, opposite and intertwining. At the computer, you focus on a narrow stream of rationality, instructing brain cells to pick and arrange beautiful bouquets of garden thoughts. But out in the garden, you let your brain cells go loose like dogs chasing sticks in a park, instructing your senses and your intuition to take over.

The knowledge you harvest from the garden is eventually stored in some root cellar or freezer in your brain, and as a garden writer, you pull it out when you need it. But the fact is, you first gather the information with your *hands* and your senses. Gardening, like sex, is hands-on.

So if you will, think of this book as produce I harvested with my own hands. One of my main goals here is to persuade thousands of readers that gardening is more exciting than TV, shopping, or even writing books. The more gardeners that inhabit this country, the better chance we'll have of creating a new, improved American Dream. I hope to somehow convince you that gardening is more hip than a Porsche convertible or an Armani dress. Believe it or not, it's even more fun than working out! Instead of resorting to the Tummy Tightener, you exercise your abs while stretching to plant a row of Swiss chard. Instead of listening to pounding Jazzercise music, you get the no worries, no hurries calls of meadowlarks, robins, and red-winged blackbirds.

Instead of spending $65 on a dinner for two, you spend 65 cents for that day's portion of seeds. While many forms of recreation cost hours of work to buy, gardening *pays*. You get hours of pleasure and satisfaction, free. You get pleasurable, sensuous products from it, like juicy heirloom tomatoes and exotic Oriental poppy blossoms.

And while you're in the garden, your credit card is out of service. So overall, gardening is a very shrewd investment. The work isn't easy, but it's creative and has a purpose, which is important to me. As much as any other activity, gardening *makes sense*.

It provides many of the qualities I want my life to include—adventure, challenge, mental stimulation, physical exercise, and tangible, edible rewards.

I have to admit that writing this book has been even more of a kick than commuting to work at rush hour for an all-morning staff meeting. Every summer morning, I'd go out to the garden to gather more material, more produce, for the book. Usually I'd become hopelessly sidetracked and spend mindless hours on things that needed to be done, arriving back at my desk somewhere around dinnertime. (Okay, the truth is out—I'd rather garden than write about gardening.) But the writing was much easier in the winter, because it was more fun to hunker down in front of my computer, like an expectant father, than shovel snow.

I have another confession to make, right up front. I'm not a Zen Master. But the community garden and orchard I'm helping to establish in Golden, Colorado, has in a sense been a Zen exercise in mindfulness, discipline, and the joy of being right in the moment. Give me an 80-degree day and a blank earth canvas—a well-prepared garden bed—and I can tune out just about any static the world can serve up.

If gardening at its best is an exercise in being connected to the rhythms and vibrations of daily life, some of the expert growers I know do indeed resemble Zen Masters. They've learned that gardening can calm the storms of mental chaos by reconnecting mind with nature. In a sense, these masters of horticulture skillfully walk a tightrope, balancing the visible and invisible worlds above and below the soil. In Zen-like gardening, it's not just the "getting done" that's important, but the "being present." These masters of gardening approach their work with a full palette of senses and a mind that stays on track. They garden in the present as well as in the future, knowing that the garden itself is the ultimate product, and that it will take years of focus to bring it into biological balance.

When I asked Master Gardener Lana Porter what she likes best about gardening, she told me, "I like what it does for my head.

Sometimes, when I'm watering a healthy crop, or planting seeds, or cultivating between rows, I'm not thinking anything at all—a radical switch from my previous life as an overworked bureaucrat." She came to her senses eight or ten years ago, choosing a pathway to mental clarity in her gardens. "People tell me I should take care of my crops more efficiently—with irrigation systems on timers, designer fertilizers and pesticides—so I could spend less time out here. But that way of growing disconnects the grower from the garden. The whole point is to spend *more* time taking care of the plants and less time in front of the TV."

She added, "I like the opportunity to take care of one little chunk of the Earth, and to feel like I'm in control of at least one thing in my life."

Like Lana, I'm on a pathway that leads to human/horticultural mastery, but by no means am I a "Zen Master" yet. That's why, in this book, I've included interviews with some of the fastest trowels in the West. Together, we've weathered lots of trials and errors, and we're confident this book will help you avoid some of the errors.

I hope, too, that the book stimulates you to create and feel the connections in your own gardens. Connections among people, plants, pests, organic produce, health, communities, and habitats. Ideally, a garden is a cycle of events in which the gardener grows, along with the soil and the crops. Food from the garden and bright, fragrant flower blossoms invigorate the gardener to grow more food and blossoms, a perpetual cycle of delight.

In the first section of the book, "How to Grow a Gardener," I admit that yes, I do have a problem—an addiction to gardening. But first, I jettison years of pent-up frustration over the fickleness of western weather. Think of the book's opening essays as group therapy—the literary equivalent of screaming into our pillows! Anyone who's ever tried drought gardening in the western states of Colorado, Utah, high-elevation New Mexico, Wyoming, Montana, the Dakotas, Idaho, northern California, northeastern Arizona, the

Oklahoma panhandle, eastern Washington/Oregon, and western Kansas/Nebraska will be able to relate.

By no means am I suggesting that all gardeners follow the same pathway into the garden that I did. Each gardener needs to find her or his own way. But maybe "How to Grow a Gardener" will give readers a little direction, and inspiration.

"The Tools of the Trade" is more about mental tools than metal tools. More about the software of ecology than the hardware of hoes and rakes. However, in "Strategic Gardening," I'm on my knees, offering down-to-earth advice about how to coax vegetables and fruits from a sun-parched garden. Much of the wisdom in "Strategic Gardening" grew out of trials and errors I've encountered in the last six years, trying to create a market-sized community garden from ground zero—a bulldozed, sun-baked chunk of Colorado.

"Ornamentals for the West" is a celebration honoring trees, shrubs, and flowers that take a licking and keep on ticking. Who says plants need warm nights or water?

In "Zen Masters of the West," I summarize more than 500 years of western gardening wisdom, reporting what I learned from dozens of experts in their own gardens. I'm confident you'll find their observations invaluable. The fact they are still at it not only proves that gardening is possible here, but that you may be able to do it without making a complete fool of yourself. We strongly urge you to give it a try.

The first step is to deal with the cruelty of geography. There's an invisible line that separates gardeners of the high, arid West from eastern gardeners. Known in geography jargon as the 100th meridian, it cuts the layer cake of Kansas and Nebraska in half, roughly separating the primordial short grass prairie—where rainfall is typically a distant memory—from the tall grass prairie, where gardens are essentially automatic.

East of The Line, farmers grow corn, a tall grass, and west of The Line, they grow wheat, a short grass. Except, of course, in the abundant coastal regions of Washington, Oregon, and California. (These rain-blessed regions are not a focus of this book.)

Okay, okay, I may be exaggerating a little here, but it's indisputable that on topographical maps, east is green and the arid West (where I garden) is brown. From an airplane in midsummer, it's the same two-toned story, unless you happen to fly over a brief blush of green at the foot of the Rockies right after a three-day, flood-thirsty monsoon. So we're talking biology and meteorology here, not just hearsay. Scientific fact, not just precipitation envy.

The truth is, as God's chosen gardeners—both back east and on the West Coast—sip iced tea on front porches shaded by climbing roses, they have only to watch steady, gentle rains soak into rich, dark soil. Summertime, and the livin' is easy! Rarely do they resort to dragging their sprinklers and hoses out of the garage, though they do have to swat more bugs per minute than we do, a small consolation. They also pull more weeds per square foot, but those weeds usually have wimpy surface roots that give up without a fight, unlike some western weeds whose thick, fibrous taproots are best unearthed by gravediggers with backhoes or geologists packing explosives.

We gardeners of the High Plains and mountains are meteorologically and topographically challenged, that's the long and short of it. "The wildest weather on the planet," western landscape expert Jim Knopf calls the Front (easternmost) Range of Colorado. "Arctic fronts collide with tropical air masses here, creating an ever-changing house of horrors."

About 150 years ago, U.S. officials inscribed a box over 100,000 square miles of the territory I currently live in, and named it Colorado. Average elevation, 6,800 feet. Average annual precipitation, about 15 inches, including the most frequent hailstorms in the United States. Average organic content of native soil, less than half a percent. They concluded it was futile to try growing anything in this box, shaking their heads sympathetically. (Eventually, of course, they inscribed "no grow" boxes over most of the Sunbelt, mountain, and High Plains landscape.) In 1805, Lewis and Clark reported to President Thomas Jefferson and colleagues back east that it took undaunted courage to even set foot west of The Line.

The truth is, the horticultural zones written about in this book—mostly USDA Zones 4, 5, and sometimes 6—are often Twilight Zones of frustration. ("Imagine a piece of land," drones Rod Serling, "where nothing wants to grow....") The techniques included here are designed to keep you out of the Twilight Zone, if you live at elevations of 4,000 feet up to 9,000 feet or so, and if you're water challenged like me.

Writes Marc Reisner in *Cadillac Desert*, "A drought lasting three weeks can terrorize an eastern farmer, but a drought of five months is, to an (inland) California farmer, a normal state of affairs.... One does not really conquer a place like this. One inhabits it like an occupying army and makes at best, an uneasy truce with it."

Cheyenne, Wyoming, the fourth windiest city in the country and the most hail-ridden (ten hails per year), is a good example of the challenges we face. This city of 50,000 brave citizens began as a place to pump Crow Creek water into the steam engines of freight trains hauling coal back east. Not that there's a whole lot of water there to pump; in 1867, one of the city's first citizens, Nannie Steel, counted twelve trees in downtown Cheyenne. Nevertheless, horticulturist Shane Smith, longtime director of the Cheyenne Botanic Garden, loves Cheyenne *because* of its imperfections. For one thing, its fluky weather and barren landscape make it a place where few people would ever agree to live.

"If you find a place with a flaw or two, you'll be home in minutes, while the people in the so-called perfect places are still stuck in traffic," Smith concludes, with the air of a student cutting class.

Robin Chotzinoff looks at it from a slightly different perspective. In the book *People with Dirty Hands,* she writes, "I love the Colorado Plains because they remind me of the ocean. But I hate them for being so empty." Like me, Chotzinoff grew up in New York state, where the ground is green and the sky is gray. Like mine, her words celebrate the small but very sweet victories we high-elevation gardeners win over unpredictable, Mars-like conditions.

Chotzinoff captures the essence of dry western gardening when she explores a cemetery in a low-income section of Denver, where long-abandoned rose bushes have proven they're survivors. When no one's looking, she clips cuttings from these persistent diamonds-in-the-rough, admiring their self-reliance and stubbornness. "You never find anything interesting on a rich person's grave," she concludes. "Too much perpetual care." In the arid West, plants rarely get too much care, because nature won't allow it.

Another easterner with a long historical shadow, Civil War hero and explorer John Wesley Powell, went so far as to pronounce the West largely *unfit for human habitation*. Fortunately, we've proven him wrong, haven't we? Here we stand, shell-shocked grins on our faces, dinged-up shovels in our hands, and feet firmly planted on barren, rocky soil!

The question is, are we heroic or pitiful?

Well, either way, here we come! Like the neglected, super-hardy roses in Denver's rundown cemeteries, we just get stronger and more determined by bizarre weather and one-bean soup soil. We develop thick, red-necked skins, and somehow we emerge proudly with bouquets of flowers and bushel baskets of vegetables. If we keep at it for more than a few decades, we each stand a chance of becoming unshakable masters of horticulture—Zen Masters, if you will. When hailstones the size of river rock shred the lettuce a few hours before a dinner party, our first inclination may be to throw childish tantrums and vow never to garden again, but instead we lace up our boots and get out the seeds.

The truth is, we've come too far to give up. By pooling all available information, maybe we can make a go of it. That's what this book is—a meeting of the minds. This is the beginnings of a strategy that can empower each of us to hold our heads a little higher as we walk home from the garden, even if the lettuce *has* been reduced to slug bait and the garden fence and all it encloses *have* been sandblasted by prevailing winds.

Ladies and gentlemen, this is a book about dignity.

In *Gardening in the Mountain West,* Barbara Hyde methodically makes the most of western climatic conditions with evergreen wind-breaks, soil-building compost, and water-retaining mulches. Always the optimist, she envisions the maturation of western soils—in some distant geologic era. "Most mountain soils are not soils yet," she explains, "but a gritty material that will weather gradually as eons pass to first become sand; then a slightly smaller particle, silt; and finally the smallest of soil particles, clay." (So, come back in 100,000 years?)

As ground-breaker George Kelly did a half century earlier in *Rocky Mountain Horticulture,* Hyde provides valuable, time-tested lists of flowers, vegetables, and trees that thrive in western conditions. In the manner of a Red Cross nurse, she imagines western gardeners anxiously riffling through the index of her books "with muddy fingers, to find a needed bit of information that will mend the troubled plant."

Lauren Springer and Rob Proctor's bedside manners may be less poetic but no less empathetic, especially when it comes to perennial flowers. In *Passionate Gardening,* coauthor Proctor confides, "The challenge is to make a series of experiments look like a garden." The director of horticulture at Denver Botanic Gardens admits, "I'm in zone denial, refusing to recognize the limitations imposed by the almighty USDA Zone Map. Certainly, there's value in evaluating plant hardiness by minimum winter temperatures, but there's much more to it than that."

Indeed there is, since winter temperatures west of The Line sometimes swing freakishly up and down fifty degrees in a single afternoon. And spring's no better, Proctor observes. "Poets may write sonnets about sweet, lovely spring, but the season here can turn on the gardener like a mad dog."

When it comes to facing the grim reaper of water scarcity, he counsels that ironically, novice western gardeners kill more plants by drowning than by drought. "In clay soils," Proctor writes, "too much kindness results in waterlogged soil, rot, and a quick death." Coauthor Lauren Springer is also a proponent of tough love in the flowerbed. Every bit the experimenter that Proctor is, Springer has "tried many a plant, some in the manured part of the gardens and others in unamended areas. I'm amazed by how many prefer the unadulterated soil."

Readers, take note! This is a central tenet of our Zen-like strategy for the high and dry West—ride the horse in the direction it plans to go. In rich soil, Springer observes, "some plants grow quickly to overly large, lush dimensions and generally die after the first winter or in the following year." Instead of encouraging the puffy, vulnerable tissue of rapid growth, Springer and Proctor tutor their plants that life here is unpredictable and harsh, and that growth should be steady, wind savvy, and deliberate. Certainly, vitality is a must, but no extra points for prima donna lushness, here. Proctor and Springer never promise a rose garden, not even to the roses.

Colorado native John Cretti, long the region's "Mr. Green Thumb" and now a KHOW radio host, is optimistic. He knows that the West's unique challenges can be converted into botanical opportunities. (We just need to know as much as he does.) "Discover the lay of the land and the diversity of our native plants," he counsels in *Colorado Gardener's Guide*. "Take advantage of the natural and human-created microclimates around your home." Years ago, when I was a Master Gardener in Cretti's Extension Service office, I'd hear him counsel, "Start small and grow with confidence. Let your landscape evolve along with your knowledge, skills, and interests."

In other words, look before you leap. Think big, but start small.

Before you stake out garden square footage that may claim first call on your life, find out if you have the undaunted courage to endure what the arid West's climate and soils serve up. For the most part, I agree with Cretti. I say if you're a Zen Master or—like most of us—just students, go for it.

How to Grow a Gardener
· IN ONE SHORT LIFETIME OR LESS ·

SYMPTOMS OF GARDEN FEVER
· THUMBS WITH A TINGE OF GREEN ·

MY FIRST TASTE of gardening came when I was three or four years old, right in the middle of a botanically challenged century, in which engineered un-planting had become standard practice. My dad and I spent a day transplanting a cottonwood tree from a nearby swamp into the front yard of our brand new suburban home in Illinois. I remember feeling humbled by that tree once it got its roots and started bolting skyward like a plume of fireworks. Forty-five years after we left the house, my father wondered whether that cottonwood was still there, and partly because his days were numbered, I got on the Internet and found a librarian willing to take a picture of the little house at 206 Nashua. She called back asking, "It's a little brown house with a huge tree in the yard, right?" I carried her photographs with me on my last visit with my dad. The look we exchanged said, Life goes on.

It occurs to me that maybe my thumb was greenish even as a boy. And also, that careers in ecology usually begin when a mentor leads us into a greenhouse, a chunk of wilderness, or a wetland.

In college, I remember painting an impressionistic picture of a seedling with enthusiastic new leaves, maybe announcing to the world that the "artist" was ready to undergo rapid growth himself. I had a few naturalistic epiphanies in my college years, one of which was an early morning walk in the foggy Indiana countryside. As cattle grazed serenely on lush green grass, and the sun came up over the sycamore trees, I suddenly perceived the nakedness of life, like a living patchwork quilt. "I see it!" I exclaimed to my dog (who also saw it). "Everything's connected to everything else."

Later, on a semester overseas, I had another *Aha!* experience as I walked barefoot in Hampstead Heath in London, mud squishing between my toes. I realized in a flash of insight that mud isn't really dirty—it's the essence of clean, the place where life truly begins and ends.

But my garden fever really kicked in a few years later, when my wife and I got onboard the "back to the land" movement and bought a ramshackle, miniature log cabin in the foothills outside of Denver. We built an A-frame solar greenhouse from logs harvested right in our neighborhood. It was about 30 feet long including a storage compartment with four 55-gallon drums painted black to catch and then slowly release the sun's energy at night. The greenhouse was enclosed by a layer of 10-mil plastic with two layers of interwoven chicken wire around it. The idea was that in a severe gust of wind, the plastic could neither blow in nor out.

The tomatoes I planted in that greenhouse didn't really prosper because of the shady exposure right at the base of a massive Colorado blue spruce. Plus, we were up at 7,000 feet in altitude, and even on summer nights you usually needed a jacket. We got great vines but little fruit, and a year or so later the greenhouse came down. But I'd caught the bug, and my thumbs slowly began to fade to greenish. I'll never forget how good that tomato foliage smelled. I'd break off a few leaves and rub them between my fingers so the fragrance would stay with me. Part gardener, part hornworm.

For the next few years, from our well-shaded property on the north side of the mountain, I studied the sun's course across the neighbor's meadow on the other side of the dirt road. Like a beautiful woman, it basked in sunlight all day long. I couldn't help but notice the vigorous crop of native vegetation. Two little drainage streams flowed through the property on either side of the would-be garden. Like a wolf, I watched the meadow change from one bouquet of wildflowers to another, right into late summer.

Meanwhile, my shady yard did all right with strawberries and lettuce and shade-tolerant flowers like columbines and foxglove, but beans and other sun lovers just went through the motions, with little to offer at the end of a season. My first few seasons, in fact, were pitiful because of what I later termed "watermelon syndrome"—ignorance of what would grow in a cold-air sink of a valley, a mile and a third above sea level.

I didn't realize it those first few years, but the damp, hard-packed soil I first tried to grow crops in was lacking two of the most critical elements of a good garden—air and drainage. And the sandy soil uphill from the wet patch was sorely lacking a third critical element, organic matter to hold moisture and to time-release nutrients. I soon solved both shortcomings with fanatical applications of hay, peat moss, mushroom compost, kitchen scraps composted and enriched by chickens, horse and sheep manure, pine needle mold, alfalfa feed pellets, corn cobs scavenged from a Denver farm, bags of leaves, rock phosphate, soybean meal, cottonseed meal, fish meal, bonemeal, and even hair from the local barbershop.

Sharecropping the First Garden

Even before I'd realized that a typical symptom of addiction to organic gardening is the fleeting urge to eat rich composted humus directly (I've never actually done it), I knew I had to garden on that plot of sunny meadow across the road. The land had been part of the Marsh Farm in the middle 1800s, then Civil War General Parmalee's homestead. A 1926 photograph hanging in the Post Office showed that same little meadow with the two little streams, the same elevated mini-mesa, and across the road, some of the lumber and logs that went into our cabin.

I longed to get my shovel into it.

After a few neighborly conversations with the owners of the land about the Fourth of July parade or their grandchildren, I finally asked if there was any way I could rent that unused chunk of meadow. And for ten years, that 35 x 30-foot plot was my high-elevation experimental laboratory. Right from the start it was clear that peas, carrots, broccoli, potatoes, onions, salad greens, radishes, rhubarb, and strawberries would survive the cold nights, desiccating winds, and jack-in-the-box frosts and hailstorms. It was equally apparent that cucumbers, peppers, eggplant, and lima beans were flatlanders. You could grow them in a good year, but you had to know what you were doing.

Over the years, corn—the king of fresh produce—and tomatoes, surely the queen, also proved fickle. The earliest varieties of each consistently produced lush foliage, but it was a crapshoot whether I'd get bumper crops or green tomatoes and white, immature corn kernels.

Late in my foothills gardening years, I documented that with some pampering a half-dozen winter squash plants could produce bushels of storable, vitamin-packed produce. So in good years we harvested the Native American trilogy of corn, beans, and squash. I had good luck with 'Ebony' acorn squash, which would stretch inquisitively along the fence in search of a rain forest. I also grew vineless 'Bush Table Queen' and 'Golden Nugget' varieties.

There was nothing that quite matched the pleasure of poking around in early fall, greeting dangling squash-faces that continued to smile for a few months on the root cellar shelf. Unless it was the pleasure of harvesting the first crunchy radishes and spinach from one cold frame and early crisp romaine lettuce from the one right next door. Or maybe the taste of the first tangy, almost-ripe strawberry, announcing the arrival of shortcake and strawberry daiquiri season.

In my foothills gardens, I used little plastic tunnels, or "cloches," that were far more successful than my shady solar greenhouse had been. I bent lengths of thick wire into arches and fastened them together with a 1 x 2-foot piece of wood with holes drilled in it—a mini "ridgepole." Where Zen came into it was remaining dispassionate as fierce night winds whipped and tattered the cloches, leaving the emerging crop exposed to both frost and nibbling, furry fiends. But overall, the tunnels worked wonders. One of my most useful strategies was watering the tunneled beds in the morning, then letting them crust over on top in the afternoon sun so slugs couldn't slime their way to my prized spinach or baby broccoli plants after dark.

Another invention was the bottomless one-gallon apple cider jug. In springtime, I'd score the bottoms of the hoarded jugs with a special scoring wheel (like a miniature pizza cutter), soak a string in gasoline, and wrap it around the scoring. Then I'd set the string on fire for a few seconds and quickly submerge the jug in a snow bank. The bottom would clink off miraculously! I had a whole fleet of jugs to cover plants on spring nights and then take off in the morning—or on colder days, just unscrew the lids. During severe hailstorms in the middle of summer, I'd race to the garden carrying four or five jugs, trying to spare my babies, the second-planting seedlings, from hail that pelted not only their helpless leaves but my helpless head.

A WAY WITH PLANTS

Some of my friends tell me they have "black thumbs," and that each ill-fated horticultural effort results in the botanical equivalent of assisted suicide ("Away with plants!"). But let these black thumbs experience one proud success—a philodendron that vines up the office wall, or a Type A tomato plant that yields half a bushel of juicy beefsteaks—and they'll start to notice slight changes in the appearance of their thumbs. At the bank or grocery store, clerks will begin to ask what happened. "Oh, nothing," the born-agains will reply, modestly. "I guess I just have a way with plants."

And the more transformations they witness, for example, of barren soil to organic black humus, the greener those modest thumbs will become. The more bright little seedlings they transfer meticulously from rickety wooden flat to rich earth, and the more abundant their humus-rich potato patches become, the more hopelessly lost they'll be. They'll begin waking up at five in the morning to chase deer out of the melons, and start turning down free trips to Costa Rica because they need to be home with their germinating seeds.

Ah, my friends, such a fate befell me. From one skimpy row of peas planted next to our foothills garage, I descended into an obsession with plants. I read everything I could get my hands on, from *Farmers of Forty Centuries* and *The Encyclopedia of Organic Gardening* to *Biodynamic Gardening* and *How to Grow More Vegetables*. From Rudolph Steiner to Sir Albert Howard to David Pimental and back again. It paid off, because after ten years of hands-on education in a high-altitude garden, I became a complete addict, going into withdrawal in winter months when the garden was sleeping.

HEALTH, WHOLENESS, A SOURCE OF DELIGHT

I'd become hooked on being the broker between a plant's genetic potential and a garden's assets—one of which was a growing bank of knowledge in my head. Since I worked swing shift during those early gardening years, I'd spend hours each morning making compost and transplanting seedlings. I began to be a nut about what I ate, feeling the cycle of energy that flowed through the garden. Reading a pivotal book by Wendell Berry, *The Unsettling of America: Culture and Agriculture,* I knew exactly what he meant when he wrote, "In gardening one works with the body to feed the body. The work, if it is knowledgeable, makes for excellent food. And it makes one hungry. The work thus makes eating nourishing and joyful, not consumptive, and keeps the eater from getting fat and weak. This is health, wholeness, a source of delight."

I must have loved the work, or else the slugs would have beaten me back. In the early years, I'd watch for the emergence of the peas or carrots, and assume I'd screwed something up, because seedlings would only come up here and there, if at all. Then I visited the garden after hours one evening to close a cold frame, and guess who I discovered, happy as clams without shells, feasting on tender, delectable pea sprouts?

You could drive by that garden on a damp evening in late May and make out my dim outline, with a miner's helmet flashlight strapped on my head, illuminating the battlefield. I don't know how many thousand slimy slugs I sent to mollusk heaven, but I do know that if slugs had been nickels rather than chicken feed, my coffee cans full of them would have been a down payment for a small farm in Tuscany.

In the throes of a passion teetering on fanaticism, I began to experiment with esoteric practices like those found in biodynamic literature. Among other things, I was instructed to place deer guts in the compost pile. When you think about it, it does make intuitive sense that there would be microbes in deer innards that specialize in decomposing cellulose and other organic leftovers, but where do you get a good, fresh deer bladder these days? Instead of having to explain my need to deer hunters (which I may do, ultimately), I incorporated a list of basic ingredients reputed to stimulate a compost pile—I think it was dandelion, chamomile, yarrow, stinging nettles, valerian, and oak bark—and I have to admit, my compost pile was legendary that year. (But was it because I fanatically turned the pile about every fifteen minutes, or was it the herbs?)

Every spring, as snow melted enthusiastically off the roof of our log cabin, my life would begin again, as the sap rose back into my limbs and brain cells. I'd offer (no, insist on) interminable tours to family members, pointing out the miraculous resurgence of perennials, the newly planted rows of peas and radishes. I wrote garden columns for the local paper, and became a Master Gardener by taking the required intensive course and serving as a volunteer at the Extension Office. When people would bring in dead plants and ask what had killed them, or call and ask what flowers would thrive in their shady backyards, I tried to access the crammed information like a college student in a final.

I gave my best shot at supplying what Master Gardeners are supposed to supply: a blend of science, botanical forensics, and empathetic handholding. Consulting the office's bookshelf and fact sheets, I blithely advised people what to do with their bluegrass lawns even though the only practical experience I'd ever had was mowing the family lawn as a kid. The yard that surrounded our own mountain cabin was native grasses, weeds, and my own virgin plantings, and in general I tended to turn my nose up at the thirstiness and aristocracy of lawns. I remember commenting to a friend about all the time spent to fertilize, reseed, water, and mow the lawn, whose final product is typically bagged up and taken to the landfill.

What I'm saying, reader, is that somewhere around 1980, I applied for and was accepted into the society of plant nuts. I began to be an agricultural activist, passionately researching not only what happened in my own garden, but also in the collective, planetary garden. I discovered that pesticide use had increased at least thirteenfold since mid-century, yet pest damage remained about the same. That American society was spending $4 billion for those pesticides, but twice that in hidden costs like fishery losses, groundwater contamination, bird losses, and pesticide resistance. That bees, called "flying $50 bills" by grateful farmers, were routinely being poisoned by farm chemicals.

And that the average age of the American farmer is 60-something. Who's learning the trade well enough to feed the rest of us?

According to industrial ecologist Robert Ayres, humans now annually produce more fertilizer synthetically than nature herself. But the truth is that the father of synthetic fertilizer, German Justis von Liebig, died feeling very queasy about his historic "discovery" that plants needed three basic nutrients—nitrogen, phosphorus, and potassium. He realized too late that plants need dozens of micronutrients, just like people do. The soil had been supplying these trace elements naturally, but was being mined out, eroded, and left as spoil. In 1843, in his twilight years, the father of modern agriculture wrote, "I had sinned against the wisdom of our creator. I wanted to improve his handiwork, and in my blindness, I believed that in this wonderful chain of laws, which ties life to the surface of the earth and always keeps it rejuvenated, there might be a link missing that had to be replaced by me—this weak powerless nothing." Oops.

But the wheels were already in motion. Most farmers were already addicted.

LESSONS FROM AMERICA'S MASTER FARMERS
· WHEN GANDHI SAYS "GO" ·

AS MAHATMA GANDHI OBSERVED: Speed is irrelevant if you're headed in the wrong direction. My intensive, self-paced research told me that, mesmerized by yield, American agriculture was arrogantly headed in the wrong direction and destroying itself in the process. I knew intuitively that we needed the passion of farmers like Michael Ableman, who in the book *On Good Land* writes, "For me, farming is like falling in love. Both are means of perpetuating the species."

I harvested the opportunity of a lifetime when I found funding to produce a television program I called *Sustaining America's*

Agriculture: High Tech and Horse-Sense, narrated by actor and wine-maker Raymond Burr. By studying the methods of the country's best farmers, I learned principles that apply in both garden and field.

The grantors wanted me to steer clear of the then-controversial term "organic," but truthfully that was precisely the kind of grower we sought out and interviewed, we just didn't use the term. Instead, the script referred to "what one farmer calls 'just damn good farming.'" The film crew and I traveled thousands of miles on the skyways, highways, and dirt roads of America, touring farms in Virginia, Florida, Iowa, Nebraska, California, Colorado, Kansas, Delaware, Illinois, and Pennsylvania. With great curiosity, I asked the farmers about anything I wanted to know, acting as if I already knew the answers but the lay audience did not. What a bright and sunny learning experience!

Nebraska farmer John Fleming had been practicing his craft for half a century, and you could see it in the vitality of his crops. An aura of health—a glow of vigor—hovered over his few-hundred-acre rolling farm. We followed him with a camera as he fertilized his fields with the best fertilizer of all—his footsteps—and we soaked up wisdom as we walked. "You know, good farming is not like baking a cake from a box," he explained. "We've been working at this for fifty years, and we're just starting to get it right."

Fleming's face may have been dappled with melanoma, but the front hallway of his house was covered with agricultural awards he'd won from the Soil Conservation Service and the Nebraska Department of Agriculture. His immaculate red barn was straight out of a Grant Wood painting, and twelve kids had all attended college on the bounty of his well-tended farm.

He offered proof that contour plowing and cover crops conserved both soil and water. "Our neighbor tried for years to get a decent well on his property, but he kept coming up dry. Then he finally comes over near our fence line, sinks a well and gets fifty gallons a minute. I told him we'd been saving it with good farming since before he was born."

You could *feel* the difference between that farm and any ordinary farm. We felt the same magic standing beside another Zen Master in Penn's Creek, Pennsylvania, where Walnut Acres mail-order organic farm was located. Back in the forties, Paul Keene had met Gandhi and told him about his passion for growing. "He told me and my new bride to go back to America and get after it." (My guess is, when Gandhi said "go," you went.) With a team of horses and $200, Keene began to create a work of art—his farm—that by 1990 was worth $6 million a year—even though it was "just organic."

Virginia farmer Lewis Ashton practices sustainable farming on land that was ceded to his ancestors by King George in the 1660s. He showed us large-scale composting techniques and "strip farming" in which blocks of corn were surrounded by sculpted grassy waterways that prevent erosion. Ashton had learned to account for every molecule of nutrient, timing fertilizer applications precisely so nutrients were available exactly when needed.

In Iowa, expert growers learn from each other in an organization called the Practical Farmers of Iowa. In our TV program, agronomist Rick Cruse lectures from one of their fields, pointing out the virtues of a new way of arranging crops. An expert pheasant hunter, Cruse had observed that pheasants were more abundant in fields that grew more than a single crop. He began researching and promoting a concept he called "strip intercropping," in which corn, beans, and small grains were planted four to six rows wide and rotated from year to year. "The outside rows of corn," he explained, "have higher yields because they get more sunlight. The soybeans replace nitrogen taken up by the previous year's corn crop, and the oats or other small grains have all the water and sunlight they need because they're planted earlier in the season, before either the corn or beans...."

That day it sunk in, the way a soaking spring rain does, how agriculture at its best is a living system, not a factory.

Long, multicolored, gleaming strips followed the rolling contours of Tom Franzen's farm as if Emerald City lay somewhere in the distance, just over the rainbow. The cameraman climbed Franzen's silo to get incredible footage of a farm designed for diversity. There is no better example of the human/nature balance than a farm or garden that meets most of its own needs!

The techniques used by the Practical Farmers reminded me of "biointensive" gardening techniques I was beginning to use in my garden back home. For example, the heavy, compacting wheels of farm equipment always rolled in the same pathways, in effect creating raised beds like mine, except they stretched from one end of the farm to the other. This reflected the ancient master gardening practice of keeping the soil loose and airy by never walking in a garden bed. Another of the farmers' techniques, ridge tillage, optimized interactions among sunlight, soil, and water. The elevated mounds in which crops were planted provided a warm spring seedbed, good drainage, and the incorporation of oxygen, just as a raised bed does.

As I traveled the country talking with masters of agriculture, it became clear to me how complex and profound well-practiced agriculture really is. When I'd ask one of these masters how he grew a certain crop, invariably he or she would pause and tell us, "It depends." To practice a craft as complex as agriculture, you had to be mindful of what crop preceded the current crop, how much rain had fallen in recent months, and whether the soil was full of life or mined out by years of monoculture. You had to know when to plant and when to hold off, and which variety of seed would perform best in this bioregion. You had to know which crops liked to grow next to each other, and how to create a biological balance that controlled pest populations. There's no one right way to grow a crop—it depends.

At The Land Institute in Salina, Kansas, I followed futurist Wes Jackson's footsteps right into another personal epiphany. I understood at the gut level that nature and evolution really do know best. Sure, there have been some errors, but with so many trials having been performed, things are pretty well in balance. Or at least they were, before an industrial/commercial paradigm became dominant. Maybe we can regain that balance.

Jackson's lifelong mission is to literally cut against the grain of our prevailing paradigm, by farming with the flows of nature. Studying the way ecological succession works, he hopes to tap into the richness that occurs in climax phases such as a Kansas prairie. A mature ecosystem is characterized by a diverse community of deep-rooted perennial plants, with the ability to hold nutrients in place and recycle them endlessly. Jackson argues that conventional agriculture, as practiced for millennia, is still immature, because its currency of exchange is mostly *annual* species that thrive in disrupted, simplified ecosystems.

"People are primarily grass seed eaters," he begins, "and secondarily legume seed eaters. These seeds (grains such as wheat and soybeans) are annuals selected historically to grow best in monocultures. Farmers till the soil yearly to plant grains, leaving it bare, vulnerable to wind and rain. Tons of topsoil wash into our rivers, and a lot ends up in the oceans.

"In the Great Plains, the natural vegetation is prairie—mixed communities of grasses, legumes, and other plant families—that once supported large numbers of animals, and human life. Our goal is to create prairie-like grain fields, combinations we call herbaceous perennial seed-producing *polycultures*.

"We think these domestic prairies would secure the soil, cope successfully with insects and disease, and utilize water in an optimum way."

The Land Institute's work flows with the currents of natural succession. By painstakingly breeding (not genetically engineering) perennial crops such as Illinois bundleflower, Jackson and his colleagues intend to provide higher grain yields every year without sacrificing the grounded, persistent qualities of perenniality.

As I stood next to Jackson on the Kansas prairie, I understood in a flash *how* diversity supplies time-tested solutions. It's whatever makes it in a given situation. In a dry year, certain species will continue to thrive because their roots reach deeper. They'll keep the system in play until rain comes, when their surface biomass is utilized by species with shorter roots. Some species supply nitrogen, some attract pests, others repel pests. Some species survive prairie wildfires successfully because they are capable of regenerating from the roots. Overall, a diverse system of farming can naturally supply everything the system needs. For every challenge, there's a solution incorporated into the system, in contrast to "factory farming" that supplies short-term solutions in the form of chemicals and energy-intensive plowing, harvesting, and processing.

In another flash of insight, I realized that inspired agriculture and horticulture are more about *balance* and *permanence* than yield. The end products are important, yes, but not as important as the equilibrium of the system itself. In the strip-intercropping pattern of growing, crops didn't need to be fertilized as heavily or sprayed with pesticides because the system itself provided the needed services. The innovative farmers who used this method didn't alter the acreage of each crop they grew, they just added information, growing the crops a bit more like nature does.

Peach grower Paul Buxman was notorious in the Fresno, California, area as "the guy who didn't spray pesticides." We knew that because when we were still an hour's drive away from his orchard, we asked a few other growers if they knew him. Their assertion was that by not spraying, he was breeding pests that would later plague *their* orchards. Buxman asserted something quite different: that his forty acres of trees were under biological control, and that their fields could be, too, if they learned to trust nature's balance.

Paul Buxman was determined to grow with little or no pesticides because he'd lost his son to leukemia. He couldn't prove conclusively it was the chemicals that caused it, but he wasn't going to take any chances with the rest of his family.

When we drove up to his house, it was plain this was no ordinary operation. There were large stands of bright orange, red, and blue wildflowers surrounding each of his fields, which he planted and maintained to keep the beneficial bugs happy. "Most of the beneficial insects have a diet of meat and potatoes," he explained. "The meat are the pests, of course, and the potatoes are the nectar that wildflowers and fruit blossoms supply. Nothing against vegetarianism," he said with a smile, "but when it comes to growing fruit, you want carnivores out there."

Buxman pulled a Swiss Army knife out of his pocket and opened the magnifying glass. "This is like a Consumer Reports of pest control," he said, examining a plant with the lens. "This tells you if you really have a problem or not. By knowing the habits of about twenty-five insects—both pest and predator—I can find out if the orchard is still in balance."

It's not that Buxman never has pest damage, but that a small amount of damage is tolerable. By not using expensive pesticides, he saves money overall and also avoids killing beneficial insects by mistake.

As he mowed (but didn't plow under) weeds that he lets grow between his peach trees, he explained, "Some of my fellow growers insist that weed mulching won't work—that weeds rob water from the trees. But I've observed that by turning these weeds under, I build up the organic content of my soil, which captures and *holds* moisture." Mulching between trees with native grasses and weeds also provides diversity that helps maintain populations of beneficial insects.

Iowa corn, soybean, and hog farmer Dick Thompson was a masterful teacher as well as farmer, hosting frequent Field Days on his immaculate farm. His pigs were a good example of his farming philosophies. Each pig family was in hog heaven, with its own little cabin in a sunny field, instead of being crowded together in a concentration camp. "We feed them probiotics, like the *Lactobacillus* you find in yogurt, instead of antibiotics," he told us.

Thompson treated each field of corn, beans, and vegetables with the same respect he gave his pigs. We felt compelled to take a little of his farm with us. We harvested enough sweet corn for our little film crew, wrapped it tightly in tin foil with a little butter and salt, and tucked it securely onto the van's hot engine. A few hundred miles later we, too, were in hog heaven!

My self-education about gardening has taken me into the fields of an organic farm in New Zealand, where my son and I volunteered; the lush rice paddies of Vietnam, where horticulture is a high art and water buffaloes are in charge; and the truck farms of southern France, where gardening is not something you have but something you do, expertly. I've also observed the shipshape farms of the Amish, explored ancient irrigation systems of the Anasazi, and traveled throughout the arid West, always on the lookout for how and where things grow.

I've read gardening and farming books by the bushel, as if they were detective novels. But when it comes to growing things, the most valuable education is definitely the hands-on knowledge. From year to year, a plant person builds a foundation of basic skills by being out there, doing one experiment after another. I buy seeds in bulk from a store that packages them without the glitzy colors and sells them for prices that don't put me in debt. So I experiment; if I lose a few seeds, it's worth it.

I'm also getting better at saving seeds and bulbs. I gladly accept offers from neighbors and friends for cuttings and divided perennials. And I've gradually increased my own stock of perennials by transplanting the offspring of overzealous crops like raspberries, strawberries, horseradish, and asparagus. Like a bank account, the wealth of the garden is slowly building, and with it, my knowledge of how to survive as a western gardener.

There are many aspects of horticulture I'm still a novice at, like Latin names, for example. As opposed to being just a bunch of hieroglyphics, botanical terminology (taxonomy) enables a grower to be very specific about the needs and the performance of plants. For example, there's a world of difference between *Phlox paniculata*, an upright perennial that grows to about two feet, and *Phlox subulata*, a flowering ground cover. My rationalization about not studying plant names has always been that the most essential information involves the *behavior* of a plant rather than its name. Every year, I forget the names of wildflowers I see on the trail, but I'm familiar with their faces. I know I'll find a certain flower in full sunlight and dry soil and another plant peeking out from a shady, protected area. That's the real knowledge, I tell myself.

Still, if I want to eventually become a Zen-like horticultural master, I'll need to learn more about taxonomy. Eventually, I'll be able to make the connection between each plant and the family it came from, because that can tell me a lot about what it will put up with. To know, for example, that purple coneflower and winecup are Great Plains natives enables me to focus my attention in a drought year. The natives will persist far more readily than plants that came from the tropics and subtropics, such as squash and tomatoes.

THE POLITICS OF GARDENING
· PRODUCTIVE GARDENS, PRODUCTIVE LIVES ·

IN MY SELF-EDUCATION about horticulture, I came across a fable called *The Man Who Planted Hope and Grew Happiness,* by Jean Giono. It's a story about a guy who singlehandedly reforests a large district of southern France and brings nature back into balance. I thought of myself as a protégé of that character, stitching the earth back together with comfrey hedges and native perennials.

About the same time, I read *Diet for a Small Planet,* by Francis Moore Lappé, about the need for humans to eat lower on the food chain. (If the whole world insists on consuming at American levels, we'll need five more planets.) I began to question the sanity of an economy in which 800,000 farms were abandoned between 1969 and 1999, according to U.S. Census statistics, leaving a 1 percent minority of boardroom corporate "farmers" supplying half of U.S. food production. In my own tiny garden plots, I wanted to be more like Walnut Acres and Arrowhead Mills than the Phillip Morris, Kraft, and Con-Agra operations Frances Moore Lappé describes in *Hope's Edge*. I wanted to be more like the small growers who together market $1 billion worth of produce at farmers markets and roadside produce stands.

Gardening became an important piece of my personal politics. I wondered why we limit ourselves to twelve basic foods (like rice, wheat, corn, potatoes, beans, bananas, coffee, etc.) when more than 20,000 edible species are available to us. Why the average morsel of food travels 1,300 miles to get to our dinner tables. And why, when all the machinery, fuel, chemicals, irrigation, processing, and distribution are figured in, we spend ten calories to get one calorie of food value. As Joan Dye Gussow observes in *This Organic Life*, "The water content of luxury foods (for example, 88 percent of a peach is water) means we're burning a lot of petroleum to ship cold water around.... Tomatoes are even more watery than peaches. Keeping all that water cool as it moves north from Florida or east from California is helping warm the planet."

Diet is not only critical for personal health, but also for planetary health. According to the authors of the book *Eating for the Earth*, it now costs $50 per acre per year in the United States to clean up after modern agriculture—to remove pesticides from drinking water, repair soil erosion, and deal with air pollution. Write Linda Riebel and Ken Jacobsen, "This *doesn't* include costs for damage to our health, the reduced effectiveness of antibiotics, or loss of diversity."

We may have the fastest, cheapest food in the world, as a percentage of income, but we also have the most expensive health care. What's the connection? One out of every twelve U.S. health-care dollars is spent coping with diabetes, Francis Moore Lappé reports in *Hope's Edge*, yet we continue to spend $10 billion a year on food advertising, very little of which promotes unrefined grains or organic produce!

The word "companion" literally means "with bread." Writes Lappé, "Embedded in family life and in cultural and religious ritual, food has always been our most direct, intimate tie to a nurturing earth as well as a primary means of bonding with each other. Food has helped us know *where* we are and *who* we are."

With these kinds of convictions in mind, I began to feed my soil, observing life, death, and resurrection with my own eyes. I learned how to balance the greens with the browns in my compost pile, and eventually put a small flock of chickens in charge of composting, Phase I. After a few years of observation, I learned to serve up eight or ten times as much straw, leaves, and sawdust (browns) as plant leftovers and kitchen scraps (greens), to get dark, crumbly humus. Poultry manure is especially high in nitrogen, and the chickens' constant scratching, pecking, and fluffing transformed huge piles of plant matter into the best compost on the planet.

I began to feel healthier than I ever had before, and the proof was right there on my face, flushed with energy. I knew literally at the gut level that organic gardening is not just about what we *don't do* (such as spray pesticides and fertilize with packaged powders) but what we *do*, such as feed the soil, rotate crops, and create biological balance.

Certainly, it's true that the U.S. Food and Drug Administration routinely finds disturbing levels of residues of carcinogenic, neurotoxic, and endocrine-disrupting pesticides in 30 to 40 percent of the food it samples. And that when scientists like Harry Leichweis, a chemist at General Mills, analyze organic foods with a mass spectrometer, those percentages of harmful ingredients fall toward zero. But I was discovering that there's much more to it than that.

Organic produce, taken as a category, simply has more vitality in it than conventional produce because of how it's grown. The soil it comes from has more life in it, which means that nutrients reach crops more effectively, since soil organisms deliver nutrients to the root zone as if essential minerals were pizza pie. The organic grower, using mechanical cultivation to control weeds and prepare seedbeds, is more likely to provide plenty of air in the root zone, and more likely to use a knowledgeable rotation of crops that boosts the soil's immune system. And the aboveground living environment is intentionally more diverse, resulting in a crop less badgered by disease and pests. Organic produce delivers health because diversity and balance flow through it.

I'm not a certified nutritionist, but thirty years of cause-and-effect observation have convinced me that my body is happier, calmer, and more energized eating food that comes from healthy soil. In my early days of gardening, I also began to taste the difference. I knew with my own senses what biochemical analysis later verified—that per unit of produce, food grown in healthy soil contains less water and more nutrients.

In a *New York Times* article (May 13, 2001), writer Michael Pollan interviewed John Diener, a California farmer who grows the same crops both conventionally and organically. Writes Pollan, "He said he knew that his organic crops were 'better,' not just because they hadn't been doused with pesticide. When he takes his tomatoes to the cannery, the organic crop reliably receives higher Brix scores—a measure of the sugars in fruits and vegetables. It seems that crops grown on nitrogen fertilizer take up considerably more water, thereby diluting their nutrients, sugars, and flavors. The same biochemical process could explain why many people—including the many chefs who swear by organic ingredients—believe organic produce simply tastes better. With less water in it, the flavor and nutrients of a floret of organic broccoli will be more concentrated than one grown with chemical fertilizers."

The *Journal of Alternative and Complementary Medicine* reported that the average amount of vitamin C is 27 percent higher in organic crops compared to conventional ones. Iron is 21 percent higher on average, and calcium 26 percent higher.

According to anthropologist Claude Levi-Strauss, ancient tribes referred to foods as "good to think" or "bad to think." It occurs to me that if anonymous supermarket food is too often a thoughtless noun, produce from a well-tended garden is much more like a high-energy verb.

WHAT GOOD IS A GARDEN?
· DECOMPOSING LIFE'S STRUGGLES ·

IN THE GARDEN, life's struggles, snags, and snafus decompose into rich, black earth. Idiotic interest rates, nagging bills, and the slow-motion speed of bureaucracy may be out of my immediate control, but in the garden, I see and feel things happening—things that are real, not just white-knuckle policies and commercial blabber. As I plant seedlings or hoe a sturdy crop of basil, none of "the operators are currently busy helping other customers." The operators (bees, worms, and ladybugs) are all busy helping me, and they never put me on hold, either, because we're all in it together. What's in my best interest is also in their best interest.

In the garden I can touch, smell, see, and taste where I live. I know about Golden, Colorado, partly by making horticultural deals with it. I learn what it can provide, and what I can coax from it, as my knowledge and skill continue to expand. In the garden, life and death dance before my eyes every day, and I come to a better under-standing of my own health and mortality. The garden literally brings me back to my senses.

A few years ago, I watched my friend, Zen grower Lana Porter, come back to her senses. The garden she works is far more than just a lush, reclaimed vacant lot—it's a biological extension of her self, and it's a way of life. "I eat very well out of this garden just about all year round," she says, "and the organic produce gives me energy to grow more produce and get *more* energy. It's a cycle of health that has literally cut my everyday expenses in half. My grocery bills are lower, my health bills are lower, I don't need to pay for exercise, and my transportation costs are lower because I don't have to travel so much to amuse myself."

When the garden becomes a lifestyle, we begin to rethink where we spend our time, energy, and money. We go out to eat less, partly because what comes out of the garden is superior to what comes out of a typical restaurant's kitchen, and partly because we just want to keep working in the strawberry bed or planting the broccoli seedlings. It occurs to us in a flash of insight that time isn't money—it's *life*. So we don't really get it when friends ask us if growing a certain crop is "worth the time," since carrots or onions are so cheap at the supermarket. When we're asked that question, we wonder, What else would we do with the time? Watch TV? You can't feel the soil on a silver-blue screen. Surf the Internet? You can't smell the flowers or hear meadowlarks calling back and forth as you work. Drive to the mall? You can't move slowly and deliberately on a highway, or pause to examine the orange pollen on the legs of a bumblebee.

Still, if it's tangible, quantifiable value our friends need, we can get them that as well. In *Coming Home to Eat,* Gary Nabhan tells about three neighbors who kept logs measuring all costs and returns from their two home gardens for three years running. "Although Tom, Dave, and Nancy liberally irrigated their desert gardens, the market value of the vegetables they produced was more than ten times what they paid for tap water, and three times their total costs for water, manure, tools, and seeds," Nabhan writes. "Even though water was their largest single gardening expense, they reaped between $7 and $9 worth of vegetables for every dollar they spent on water. Devoting just two to three hours a week to sowing, manuring, watering, weeding, and harvesting, they produced $150 to $180 worth of vegetables each year, harvesting a broad mix of greens, beans, beets, fruits, or shoots no matter what the season."

The other day I came across a website that offers visitors a unique, and somewhat creepy, opportunity to water a plant remotely with a computer-generated command. The plant could be partly *yours,* because you could view it on your computer screen and water it robotically. That poor plant must have drowned in the first few days, from overwatering, yet this piece of "art" was poignant, reminding me of the robots (Huey, Louey, and Dewey) in the movie *Silent Running,* who maintained the space station greenhouse long after the humans had died. I believe we need to be intimately connected with plants, or risk becoming robots ourselves.

Gary Nabhan asks, "Just what exactly is it that we want to have cross our lips, to roll off our tongues, down our throats, to fill our nostrils with hardly described fragrances, to slide to a brief halt within our bellies, to mix with our own gastric juices, to be transformed and conjured into something new by the myriad microbes in our guts, to migrate across our stomach linings, to surge into our bloodstreams, and to be carried along with insulin for one last ride, and then to be lodged within our very own bodies? What do we want to be made of?"

There are larger costs than the money we give the clerk at the supermarket. Writes Joan Gussow in *This Organic Life,* "Welfare is one of the long-term fallouts of the agricultural industrialization that drove many poor southern blacks off the land where they grew food, into urban dependence.... Groundwater depletion (encouraged by subsidies), water polluted with nitrogen fertilizers and pesticides, soil erosion, and salinization are other uncounted costs of food production...."

In other words, if we want to help the environment, we need to think about where our food comes from and how it is grown. We need to examine the full effects of our lifestyles. New Mexico grower Stanley Crawford converses with many customers at farmers markets, who often ask him if his produce is organic. He told me he's often tempted to ask in return, "Is your *life* organic? What about the money you pay me with? Is it organically earned?"

Certainly, we are far more than what we eat, but in a world so disconnected from its roots, the source of our food can be a great place to experience our own germination as activists. It may be true that we can't all go back to living on farms, since there probably isn't enough great land left for that. (Much of it is buried under billions of tons of concrete and asphalt.) But we *can* all go back to the garden, whether that garden is in our own yard or on a plot of land owned in common by a neighborhood.

RECIPES FOR A COMMUNITY GARDEN
· NEIGHBORHOODS, SKILLS, AND HEALTH ·

As I SIT AT MY DESK working on this chapter, the world seems to be swirling around me, testing my focus, bumping my self-discipline offline. About fifty yards from the back edge of the community garden—a hundred yards from my desk—a 100-acre catastrophe is being born, in the breach position. Earthmovers, backhoes, and tractors are groaning, backup beeping, smoking, scraping, excavating, piling, and otherwise shaping hole sixteen of a soon-to-be golf course.

Another energy-stripping distraction is steady winds of up to fifty miles per hour that have swept through our valley in the past week like tornadoes-in-training, sucking up dust clouds from the construction site and mixing them with clouds of smoke from a forest fire that's roasting a rural residential neighborhood on the outskirts of Denver.

As if all this were not enough, weather forecasters are calling for up to five inches of *snow* by tomorrow morning, May 24, so I've just spent half an hour covering baby tomato plants with inverted plastic plant pots, draped with old, ragged blankets. From hot and bone dry one day to cold and wet the next, a situation like those Thomas Cooper writes about in *Odd Lots*. "Hardiness is not an issue for the plant but the gardener, whose nerves are vulnerable to disturbances day and night."

But there's one saving grace from this vantage point at my desk—the emerging garden that's a central focus of this book. Six years into its creation as a would-be horticultural work of art, the garden is gliding into summer under full sails, never mind all the chaos with the golf course and the bizarre weather.

After hundreds of hours of work on hardpan, High Plains desert dirt, the soil is now black and spongy, the shrubs and perennial flowers are becoming established, the windbreak of Siberian peashrubs curves around the garden's perimeter like a sculpture, and eighteen fruit trees are now taller than baby giraffes. Even if a freeze takes the tomatoes and experimental artichokes tomorrow morning, there are second-string replacements in the cold frame, waiting to get in the game.

Creating a garden from scratch is a little like carving a huge sculpture out of hardwood. You'll bet your weekends and evenings you can make it look like a beautiful woman, and every week you carve a few more sensuous curves out of the slab. But the fact is, no one has ever seen the statue, except on paper—not even you. The person with the vision—the wood carver—often feels a little crazy, trying to describe what the garden will look like. And trying to describe little signs and indicators of progress, like 6 inches more growth on the adolescent apple trees.

When the garden is a community garden whose produce is shared by a whole neighborhood, the challenge is to somehow convince your neighbors—fellow gardeners and co-funders—that you know what you're doing. Even though you've secretly acknowledged it will be ten years before Aphrodite appears, if all goes as planned.

In our garden, I've been the primary wood carver and soil digger for the first phase of the garden, but planting and harvesting events are becoming more popular every year, and many community meals (we have them about once a week) have been graced with organic produce right from the neighborhood garden, fertilized with compost from everyone's kitchen.

A few years ago I stood in front of the space where a perennial flowerbed would be, trying to describe the sculpture's latent beauty to Linda, a woman with a green-tinged thumb. "It seems like bright orange and yellow daylilies should go right here in the corner," I suggested, "so they'll be visible from the common house..."

A few years earlier, twenty-seven families and households had formed an association to create a community-by-design in Golden, Colorado. We firmly believe that neighborhoods can be more friendly, productive, and diverse. When we moved into Harmony Village, the community garden existed only as a generic square on the site plan. But did it ever have good bones: lots of cottonwood, river birch, and box elder trees growing along two creeks; foothills directly to the west; a mesa with a prominent butte to the east; 100 acres of open space to the south; and our very distinctive adobe-style neighborhood to the north. This would be a pleasant place to work, whether you were a red-winged blackbird or a scarecrow come to life (which is sometimes the way I feel, as I throw fistfuls of gravel at bunnies the first thing in the morning).

My self-appointed mission was clear, if somewhat ambitious: to sculpt a world-class work of art from hardpan dirt. Because the garden's original topsoil had been scraped away to meet drainage and grading requirements, the first and most daunting challenge was to rebuild it, like a squirrel rebuilds his nest after a fire.

I figured that in an arid location like ours, the bulldozer had—in half an hour or less—scraped away a thousand years of soil building. How many gazillion microbes and crawlers had given their lives to build that foot and a half of soil? I optimistically hoped to undo the bulldozer's handiwork in less than a decade. To get the ball rolling, we decided to allocate $600 to purchase a semitrailer truckload of finished compost to incorporate into the rocky, sandy subsoil. I remember a particularly frustrating spring day in the emerging garden, trying to coax just a few more inches of depth from the rototiller. Only by the third year did we begin to see worms in the soil and vitality in the crops.

Now, in the seventh year of the emerging garden, we're really getting somewhere. Neighbors bring houseguests out to walk past the garden because it's finally starting to look like more than a construction site. Each bed has a story to tell. Just as bright eyes and rosy cheeks indicate the health of a child, the shiny dark spinach leaves and disease-free snap beans that thrive in our garden indicate the improving health of our soil.

As chief gardener and compost turner, I began to get appreciative comments from neighbors in about the fifth year, when our fruit trees were no longer stick figures and the asparagus bed had become a dense thicket of healthy-looking ferns. "Next year," I predicted, "we'll have our first Festival of Spears. And we should be able to harvest enough asparagus from then on to supply two or three common meals, every year."

About once a week, our neighborhood shares a meal in the common house, a building we own cooperatively. We even have a large cast-iron bell that rings to announce meals—usually attended by thirty or forty people. At those common meals, I showcase the steady progress of our soil, expertise, and critter-confounding fences.

On the morning of a common meal, I usually harvest and clean the produce at its peak, and my neighbors tell me they taste the difference between our salads and wimpy store-bought salad. Bob, the neighborhood's expert weekend carpenter, designed and built a small fleet of solar-heated cold frames that provide two large bowls of greens at least eight times during the winter months. During the summer months, beds of lettuce, spinach, arugula, carrots, green onions, and sorrel stay cool and productive under shade cloths, next to healthy green tomato plants. Spring and fall are prime salad seasons, when greens aren't beat up by heat or cold.

In the early years, the most popular crop of all seemed to be the winter rye we plant every fall to build the soil, because with a little supplemental watering, it stays green through the winter, making the garden look like a park by comparison with the common green that looks like a desert. Sometimes, I have to remind neighbors that the grass is not meant for walking on, since that compacts the soil. We try to hand dig the rye under at least a month before we plant, incorporating fall-hoarded leaves and a little compost at the same time. We've also planted sacrificial stands of buckwheat, white clover, and alfalfa, with great results.

Every year there are more people in the garden, growing a favorite tomato variety or pumpkins for autumn carving. This year, Rick and Wanda's tomatillo plot was something new, over next to the artichokes I grew experimentally. John's traveling onion patch is beginning to claim a larger territory, also. (The seed heads establish new plants, which we use for green onions.) With so many people sharing a garden, the number of gifts from friends outside the neighborhood increases: divided perennials, abandoned rhubarb, and out-of-control horseradish have all found new homes in the garden.

Last week, a boxful of hundreds of film canisters appeared mysteriously on my front porch, along with eight or ten new one-gallon jugs for storing solar heat (and coolness in the summer) in the cold frames. Each film canister already has a drainage hole punched in it, making it an interesting possibility for starting tomato and pepper seedlings. (The question is, will the seedlings come out of the canisters without damaging the roots? We'll find out.) Another recent contribution was a 200-foot roll of black plastic screening for use as shade cloth. (I'm also going to try it as mulch for squash plants this year.)

Seeds and seedlings always have a way of showing up early in the spring after spring fever has struck the neighborhood. But the most valuable contributions are the table scraps from both individual and common house kitchens. Just about everyone has a plastic designer composting bucket, and every week each bucket is emptied into the compost pile. A generous layer of leaves over each bucketful provides carbon that biologically balances the nitrogen-rich scraps. We routinely pull compost out of the third bin, then rotate each of the other bins toward the final product. I really can't recall anything much cuter than one of the neighborhood girls, Lianne, pulling a wagon loaded with buckets (at twenty-five cents apiece) out to the compost, then standing on a log to empty them.

Our current composting techniques have eliminated the fruit fly infestations that discouraged participation when we first began. Back then the black plastic containers we used released swarms of flies when we'd take the lids off, like something out of a horror movie. "I'm not going near the compost," I heard one neighbor tell another. Now, even when citrus peels that attract fruit flies are part of the mix, we don't have to hold our breath when we dump the compost, or run to escape clouds of swarming flies. I think the open air enables predators to get at them, keeping populations down to begin with. Houdini, the neighborhood black cat, makes another key contribution as chief mouse and bunny chaser.

I used to get calls whenever a herd of deer was tromping in the garden, foraging for 'Bright Lights' chard or 'Sungold' cherry tomatoes. But these days, neighbors are likely to chase them out themselves. One concerned friend, John, made a red plywood boomerang for each household near the garden, but the truth is, deer have a wry sense of humor. I got fed up and dogged one deer into a thicket of thistles hundreds of feet from the garden. It took me quite a bit longer to get through the tall, prickly mess than it did the deer, and when I got to the other side, she seemed to be waiting for me, with a little deer smile on her face. The only sure deer deterrent is the seven-foot-tall game fence that we'll eventually construct around the garden's perimeters. Then the deer can be as cute as they want for the kids, without getting pelted and cursed by grumpy, outraged gardeners.

Large-scale plantings of garlic and basil at the edges of the garden seem to discourage both deer and rabbits, and I've also successfully planted decoy crops of hot mustard right next to vulnerable rows of lettuce. This year we're going to ask each of the cooking teams to "adopt-a-sauce," to make sure basil, garlic, cilantro, parsley, horseradish, hot peppers, tomatoes, and onions are all harvested at their peaks. One group will make pesto, another salsa, a third tomato sauce, and a fourth horseradish sauce.

At an upscale restaurant the other night, I made intriguing arrangements for the bumper crop we typically get from our rows of basil. When the owner of the place came past our table, I asked if he were in the market for locally grown herbs. "We buy more than a hundred pounds a week," he told me, giving me his business card. Who knows, maybe this is the start of a cottage industry that will eventually supplement someone's retirement check.

Community gardens are like any other garden, except their harvests can be a bit more educational, just for fun. Neighborhood kids learn where peanuts come from (even if this crop does miserably in our

High Plains garden). One by one, community residents learn that their thumbs do have a greenish tinge. When favorite crops are brought successfully to the table, a genuine sense of accomplishment comes with it. And on a summer evening, when three or four neighbors pull weeds in the strawberry patch, discussions take place that wouldn't have happened otherwise—especially in living rooms with blue, blaring TVs on.

In the first six years of our garden, we've watched bare-root shrubs like western sand cherry and Nanking cherry—bought from the state forestry office for sixty cents apiece—grow into sturdy windbreaks and edible landscaping. We've learned, hands-on, what grows in our climate-challenged corner of Colorado. We've seen wastes become food again, and we've felt the cycle of nature in our bodies as expended energy becomes energy again, in the form of great-tasting produce.

But the sculpture of a beautiful woman is still taking shape. To be truthful, she still looks more like a Rocky Mountain juniper than a statue of Aphrodite.

Our horticultural goals for the near future include getting chickens and bees. Because of an active coyote population, we'll have to keep the chickens penned up, but we plan to experiment with "chicken tractors" (movable pens) that will weed and fertilize one chunk of garden after another. We hope bees will pollinate our assortment of fruit trees and store a little Harmony honey in the process.

We're also in the last stages of acquiring water rights in the agricultural ditch that runs right between the garden and the orchard. We formed a private corporation of fifteen households that bought one or more $200 shares of stock. Instead of paying close to $3 per thousand gallons for potable, chemically treated water, we'll pump from a channeled tributary of Clear Creek with a solar-powered irrigation system.

We're slowly learning important lessons about sustainable growing, such as "use what's already there" instead of purchasing inputs in expensive packages and bottles. We're learning that gardens grow people, and knowledge, and that the most important produce coming from a garden is the garden itself.

BOTANICAL ARCHEOLOGY
· GARDENING IN THE PRESENT ·

LAST SUMMER I TOURED the ruins of my first garden in the foothills, abandoned years earlier. I'd planted my first row of peas there, as warm Chinook winds melted snow off the roofs of our well house and garage. As I poked around in that first garden, I learned some humbling things about gardening in the arid West. Western gardens are not forever. Where I'd once harvested bright orange carrots and dark green lettuce, a smug stand of prickly thistles had taken over. (I'd always suspected they would.)

Sure, the lilacs, raspberries, irises, horseradish, and comfrey had survived for years on their own, their roots burrowing into the crumbly organic soil I'd served up by the wheelbarrow load. And it was a vigorous enough stand of thistles that now colonized the landscape, bearing testimony to all the manure, leaves, hay, and grass clippings that still enriched the plot. But you had to know there had been a garden there, or you might not have seen it.

Standing next to the abandoned garden, I recalled hand-mowing waist-high sheaves of grass that surrounded the garden as twilight fell, ecstatic about its future value as compost. I recalled the great satisfaction of snaking a garden hose through the culvert that ran under the dirt road, so I could siphon water from our surface well into the garden without even turning the pump on. In my mind's eye, I could see my daughter Libby eating snap peas off vines taller than she was. And there I stood, leaning on a shovel and talking to a passing neighbor about the current year's crops.

Fond memories indeed, but the truth is, gardening happens best in the present, where you hear the bees buzzing and smell the honeysuckle they're after. The present, where your grape vine heroically resists wilt after three weeks of drought, and where your acorn squash tastes as sweet as a freshly baked cinnamon bun. If you try to transcend the present to create a perpetual living sculpture on what is naturally dry land prairie? No way.

The best you can hope for, I think, is to spend many delightful, mindless hours out there—feeling, smelling, and touching the seasons, and trying heroically to keep things alive until rainy days return. Anytime you look at your watch and what seemed like twenty minutes was actually two hours, you know you're in the right place. In days past, Americans talked about stopping to smell the roses, but now, sadly, we give ourselves only the time to "wake up and smell the coffee." Fortunately, when you let time go loose in the garden, you've escaped the fearful, guilt-ridden clutches of deadlines, and instead given yourself a lifeline.

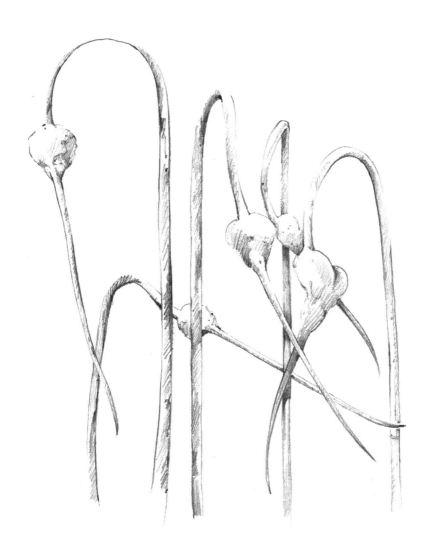

THE TOOLS OF THE TRADE
· RECONNECTING BODY AND SOIL ·

BUILDING SOIL IN THE DEAD OF WINTER
· NO REST FOR A WEARY GARDENER ·

STEAM RISES OFF the compost pile as I turn the top layer. If the microbes in the pile stay on schedule, I'll have rich, dark compost by March or April, at the latest. It's a sunny January day, and I plan to spend the afternoon gardening. (If I'd gone skiing in the mountains instead, I probably would have pulled a muscle in my shoveling leg.) I glance over at a bright green swath of winter rye growing in front of the cold frame. Although the grass blades froze solid during the arctic-like freeze, they thawed out without a complaint, surviving without any protection.

Unceremoniously, I empty a bag of hair clippings I got at the barbershop into the pile. They come out in a skull-shaped clump, causing an instinctive recoil in me. I feel better after taking a pitchfork and spreading the high-protein clippings throughout the pile— converting the skull into harmless food for the pile's hungry masses.

Certainly, it's not high season in the garden, but with a little plan- ning, many High Plains winters are an ideal time to improve your soil. For starters, you can have your soil tested (contact your local Extension Office for details). You can grow cold-hardy cover crops all winter, and when the soil's not frozen or too wet for digging, you can incorporate organic ingredients like leaves, manure, and hay that you stockpiled in the fall. By feeding and fluffing up the soil in existing plots, you're composting right where the crops will grow next summer. Which saves you the trouble of carting compost to the garden.

I've discovered that digging leaves into the soil is a great way to keep it loose and workable throughout winter. As time and weather permit, I go out and re-dig each plot two or three times in the cold months. Each time I dig, I see fewer leaves and more loamy soil. As spring warms the soil, all that's left is earth and earthworms.

One of my favorite sports is leaf scavenging. I like to stockpile a hundred or more bags of leaves in the fall, then use them all winter for compost and the following summer for mulch. I have thousands of assistants throughout the metro area, who rake their lawns and stuff the leaves into huge plastic bags. They feel the same sense of urgency about raking and getting rid of their leaves that I do about collecting them. So by the time I've tossed a few dozen bags into the pickup, a lot of guilt has disappeared on both sides. Once I know the trash pick-up schedule, I can cruise the alleys and curbsides and harvest thirty or forty bags in about half an hour. Last fall I calculated that our surrounding neighborhood is at least a 2,000-bag resource, making leaf harvesting a snap as long as we stay alert about when they're being raked.

I love it when bags are filled with multicolored leaves and a little grass thatch—raked on a dry day so the bags are light. Oak and maple leaves are especially valuable because they add acidity to the West's generally alkaline soils.

Manure runs are a little more work, but with a much higher return in nutrients per volume. I make deals with local horse owners, who sometimes load tractor buckets into my pickup truck, just to be rid of it. Horse manure (or better yet, poultry manure) should be used in moderation in the compost pile or garden, because it's high in salt. And I never grow crops in soil fertilized with fresh manure— because of both high temperatures and health risks. By digging it under in the fall and winter, along with layers of leaves, I give it a season to decompose.

Another winter workhorse in most parts of the arid West is ryegrass. Planted in October, a variety known as "winter rye" will send roots deep into the soil (reputedly up to ten or more feet), remaining bright green until springtime if watered or snowed on a few times. This year I planted vetch and clover in with the rye, and all three are doing great. In the spring, I'll rototill the cover crops under and plant alfalfa during the growing season. Then next year, I'll be planting potatoes and beans in soil that was once too hard-packed for rototiller blades to penetrate. What really got the process going was a season's worth of grass clippings, layered on the future plot—courtesy of a local landscaping company. After spreading a layer of manure on top of the clippings, I deep-watered the ingredients a few times. Within a few weeks, the soil softened up enough to get a seedbed ready for the cover crops.

Notice how much credit I take for transforming the soil. I can get away with that because the real heroes—billions of microbes and tiny organisms—are too small to protest. But if I had microscopic vision, I'd see with my own eyes how leaves, manure, and other organic materials are converted into rich humus.

What a great horror movie it would make! One species of bacteria breaks down nutrients, a second species processes those products into a form that plants can use. A colony of fungi glues soil particles together, creating air spaces and loose soil in the process. Legions of one-celled protozoa eat bacteria, releasing nitrogen into the root zone, and other species colonize the roots of plants in the bean family (legumes), pulling nitrogen right out of the air to serve up to their host plants.

Good soil functions like an immune system. As long as there's enough to eat, the beneficial organisms thrive, keeping the bad organisms in check. But when overdoses of chemicals and a shortage of organic material kill off the good bugs, the bad bugs come after your plants.

To be a good gardener, then, is to be a shrewd manager. You're not just a garden geek, you're a CEO with quintillions of employees. The mission is huge pumpkins, tomatoes that titillate your taste buds, and honeysuckle blossoms you can smell all the way down the block; and the best strategy to meet that mission is to keep feeding the soil, including surprise bonuses delivered in the middle of winter.

WHAT EXACTLY IS SOIL?

IT's SUNDAY AFTERNOON, and the construction crew that's building a golf course out beyond the garden is probably home watching a golf tournament on TV. Like a kid raiding the refrigerator after bedtime, I sneak onto the site with a pair of buckets and a shovel. I can't let a seam of dark black topsoil go unappreciated. Instead, I'll invite ten or fifteen bucketsful into my compost pile, where its wild, teeming populations of microbes will be warmly welcomed.

As I fill another pair of buckets, I fall into a reverie about the history of the soil. First deposited as rock dust in an ancient floodplain, the soil contains petrified dinosaur manure, a valuable addition to any garden. I know this for a fact because the whole area was once thick with dinosaurs. (Hence, the name Fossil Trace Golf Course.) I fast-forward to herds of bison, grazing on the old riverbed. I'm grateful for their nitrogen and phosphorus contributions, too. Then I'm in the recent past, standing on a field of corn and soybeans. A large silo on the hill above me is a relic of those farming days, as is a huge, lone cotton-wood tree that received enough moisture from irrigation to grow eighty feet tall.

These are macro events that have occurred at roughly human scale over the eons. Even *T. rex* was closer to my size than the bacteria that double in population within an hour when conditions are right. In fact, in a single bucket of floodplain humus, there are more living organisms than there are people on Earth. It's easy for me to imagine a bison herd, but when it comes to teeming herds of bacteria, I'm pretty much clueless. Writes Evan Eisenberg in *The Ecology of Eden*, "The soil is a flea market, an economic free-for-all in which every scrap of merchandise—second-hand, seventh-hand, busted, salvaged, patched—is mined for its last ounce of value."

In *Gardening for the Future of the Earth*, John Jeavons uses a similar analogy. "The root actually 'bargains' with the humus, exchanging some of its positively charged hydrogen ions for calcium, magnesium, manganese, copper, zinc, and other charged nutrient ions bound to the surface of the humus." Like you and me at the farmers market, the plants choose which nutrients they need to balance their own inner chemistry.

What's accomplished by all this bargaining and bartering is soil that drains well yet holds moisture, that contains enzymes and acids to break down bits of rock dust, that has a sort of immune system complete with antibiotics and growth hormones, that captures, holds, dispenses, and recycles nutrients in a continuous cycle. Like a sponge, a good humus retains six times its own weight in water, and binds up toxic elements like heavy metals so they aren't absorbed by crops.

In their amusing book, *Gardening: A Gardener's Dictionary*, Henry Beard and Roy McKie suggest letting a child play in the garden to find out what soil texture you have. "Inspect the results. Is it a castle, a tasteful little ashtray, or a messy mud pie? That's really all there is to it." The fact is, we don't need to be soil scientists to have good gardens. We just need to know enough to keep the soil workers happy, by supplying the essentials: air, water, and food.

The relationship of a grower with his or her soil can border on fanaticism. When you begin to understand that there's a whole universe of organisms in a small vegetable plot, it humbles you. For Wendell Berry, soil is a sacrament, a miracle of death and rebirth. "The soil is full of dead animals and plants, bodies that have passed through other bodies," he writes. It may seem like a creepy notion at first, but when you realize it's the way of the world, you let go and just trust it, somewhat the way an airline pilot trusts the technology of flight.

COVER IT!
• MULCHES AND COVER CROPS •

FOR THE WESTERN GARDENER, mulches and green manures (cover crops) are like aces and kings in a poker hand. When the driest season in a century smacks us in the face, as it has in Colorado recently, your stockpile of mulching materials and the organic content of your soil—bolstered over the years by green manures—are what keep your crops in the game. Mulches and cover crops are both composed of biological mass, either once-living or still-living, used to optimize soil conditions.

Mulches, which consist of dead plant material like compost, leaves, spoiled hay, grass clippings, and pine needles, keep moisture in the root zone and also control weeds that would otherwise steal water from the crop. With lower water evaporation rates, soil moisture remains ideal, which makes nutrient uptake more effective.

Mulches also moderate soil temperatures, keeping the grow zone cool in the summer and warm in the winter. In the summer, the insulating qualities provided by mulch help protect roots from heat stress, resulting in stronger, healthier plants. In the winter, a layer of mulch protects the roots of perennial plants by keeping the soil from freezing and thawing.

My favorite mulch, especially for acid-loving crops like potatoes, is pine needles, which I scavenge from schoolyards and parks in the late fall. (The trick is to catch the grounds crew in the act of raking.) During our windy winters, other mulches like leaves, straw, and wood chips are blown into the next county, but pine needles stay put. When garlic shoots first emerge in early spring, I lay a thick layer of pine needles on top to keep the soil temperature constant. As May temperatures shoot up in the daytime, the pine needles also keep the root zone cool and the garlic happy.

Here are a few things to keep in mind about mulches:

- Never use material from the crop that is to be protected. For example, don't use potato vines from last year's crop to mulch this year's potatoes, because the old vines might transmit disease.

- Use a light-colored mulch during the summer and early fall to reflect heat. Use a dark-colored mulch in winter and early spring to help warm the soil to permit earlier planting and hasten early growth.
- Older grass clippings, leaves, and sawdust laid down as a mulch can cause a temporary nitrogen deficiency in the soil, as soil microbes tap into soil nitrogen to break down the vegetation. Add a source of nitrogen, such as well-rotted manure, before you lay down the mulch.

Soil scientists refer to the "carbon-to-nitrogen ratio" as a key indicator of whether an organic material will add nitrogen or cause a deficiency of it. The carbon-nitrogen ratio of sawdust is 400 to 1, for example, while the C-N ratio for a cover crop like sweet clover is only 12 to 1. This is why cover crops are a valuable card to have in your poker hand.

Cover crops are living plant crops and are most valuable when they are incorporated into the soil, where they build soil structure and provide nutrients for upcoming crops. Instead of buying and bringing home bags or truckloads of compost or manure, bring home some seeds to plant a "green manure" crop.

The added organic matter from cover crops increases populations of beneficial soil microorganisms and earthworms, and also increases the soil's ability to hold water. An active, diverse community of organisms such as bacteria, actinomycetes, fungi, centipedes, springtails, mites, millipedes, spiders, beetles, and earthworms performs many critical functions, including:

- producing vitamins and other growth-enhancing compounds;
- increasing plant uptake of soil phosphorus;
- controlling outbreaks of soil pathogens;
- releasing carbon dioxide that is then absorbed by plants to form new plant tissue;

Types of Mulches: Their Advantages and Disadvantages

Mulch Type	Advantages	Disadvantages	General Comments
Organic mulches			
Cocoa-bean hulls	Long lasting, dark brown color.	Compactable, forming a crusty surface. (Harmless if stirred to break crust.) Expensive.	Molds may form on surface.
Crushed corncobs	Uniform in color.	May retain too much moisture at surface or compact if kept wet.	Cobs dyed various colors. Availability limited in some areas.
Grass clippings	Readily available.	Must be applied loosely, in thin layers to reduce matting.	Allow grass to dry before applying as a mulch.
Hops	Attractive color. Nonflammable.	Disagreeable odor until dry.	May be available from local brewery.
Leaves (composted)	Readily available.	Not very attractive. May become matted.	Good soil amendment.
Leaves (fresh dried)	Readily available.	Not very attractive. May blow away. Fire hazard. Wet leaves compact into slimy mats.	Most appropriate in naturalized gardens or shrub masses.
Manure (strawy)	Usually available.	Unpleasant odor. Weed seeds.	Better soil amendment than mulch. Should be aged and/or heat treated.
Newspaper	Readily available.	Don't use color inserts or red ink.	Use 3 to 6 sheets thick and cover with organic mulches.
Peat (sphagnum)	Usually available in bulk amounts.	May crust on surface. May blow away.	The only acid-forming peat, but even this is variable with source. Best used as a soil amendment, not as a mulch.
Pine needles	Attractive. Do not compact.	Difficult to obtain in quantity. Can be a fire hazard.	Best for winter protection of fall-transplanted material.
Shredded bark, bark chips, chunk bark	Long lasting, attractive (chips more attractive than fine shreds).	Cost relatively high. Shredded bark may compact.	Use for informal walkways.
Straw	Readily available.	Blows easily. Highly flammable. Weed seeds often present.	Best used as a temporary mulch around plants needing protection in winter. Anchor with wire mesh.
Wood chips, shavings, pole peelings, recycled shingles	Long lasting. Readily available.	Texture and color not uniform.	Rustic but usually attractive. Will not compact readily.
Inorganic, inert mulches			
Clay aggregates (heat treated)	Gray/brown colors available. Lighter than gravel, easier to transport. Weed-free.	Expensive.	Brand names available (Turface, Terragreen).
Weed-barrier fabrics	Reduces weeds. Allows air and water penetration. Long lasting if covered with mulch. Easy to apply.	Some may be costly. Most deteriorate in sunlight unless covered with another mulch material such as wood chips.	A good substitute for black plastics.
Gravel, stone	Available in colors to match or complement the architecture. Inexpensive.	Will not prevent growth of some weedy grasses.	Use black polyethylene beneath to prevent weeds.

Adapted from *Mulches for Home Grounds*, by J. R. Feucht, Cooperative Extension landscape plants specialist.

• creating more soil aeration and distributing nutrients by continuous tunneling and burrowing. (Think of all the miles traveled by these busy, uncountable critters!)

There are several kinds of cover crops. The first kind is grasses and leafy plants like rye, winter wheat, buckwheat, barley, oats, millet, and brassicas (kale, radish.) These are generally fast growing and provide lots of biomass to aerate the soil and build soil structure when they are turned under.

The second kind of cover crop is the legume, which pulls nitrogen right out of the air and into the soil. Some legumes, like alfalfa, clover, and vetch, are multiseason crops, providing nutrients as they grow and also whenever they are turned under. Some cover crops such as alfalfa have roots that reach down into the subsoil up to eight feet, bringing valuable hard-to-reach nutrients up to the soil surface as the crops are harvested. You can sow cover-crop seeds like clover and winter rye in the fall and turn them under in the spring, or sow more tender seeds like buckwheat and millet in the spring and turn them under in time to plant fall crops like spinach, lettuce, radishes, and broccoli.

Both kinds of cover crops can become "too much of a good thing" if they are allowed to go to seed. So either mow or turn under cover crops before they seed.

Sometimes mulches can be cover crops, and cover crops can be mulches. This year, instead of planting alfalfa and clover in certain parts of my garden, as planned, I've "planted" a cover crop of grass clippings. I'm careful to dry each layer out and add air as I spread the clippings out, which prevents matting and fast-acting, stinky decomposition. Then I spread another layer of fresh clippings on top, stockpiling dried mulch for use around crops and at the same time, feeding the soil with the bottom layers of clippings. This fall, I'll add a thick layer of horse manure to the clippings I haven't used as mulch, and in the spring, I'll dig the whole bed under, feeding next year's crops with this year's mulch.

Green Manures for the West	Comments
Annual ryegrass	Overall an easy crop to establish.
Perennial ryegrass	Faster establishment than other perennials; extensive root system.
Winter rye	Can grow at low pH and at cool temperatures.
Oats	Requires good soil drainage, but tolerates low pH.
Winter wheat	Requires fertile soil; avoid wet or low pH soil.
Sweet clover	Better with high pH than other clovers.
White clover	Good for low pH soil, treat with inoculant.
Buckwheat	Do not allow to mature, or reseeding will occur.
Barley	Likes pH of 7–8.

Similarly, cover crops can be mulches when they are planted right under another main crop, such as melons, squash, or tomatoes. In fact, recent USDA research demonstrated that tomatoes planted in a cover crop of hairy vetch had fewer insect problems and were twice as productive as tomatoes grown without the cover crop. Vetch, a legume, fed nitrogen to the tomatoes' roots, kept the crop cool and weed-free. In general, cover crops also reduce soil loss from wind and water erosion.

When you begin to garden holistically, feeding the soil rather than just the crop, you begin to work with materials that are close at hand and that don't require heavy inputs of energy, like powdered fertilizers do. You begin to realize that cover crops and mulches are like aces in the hole.

A Menu of Organic Fertilizers
· GOURMET TREATS TO BUILD YOUR SOIL ·

IF YOU CHOOSE to become an organic grower, you'll inevitably become a broker in a stock market of materials that were once living, from alfalfa meal to horse manure to oak leaves. The strange thing is, it will begin to seem very normal. Once you get hooked on the rightness of it, you'll be in select company, with Thomas Lipton, who invented

Sources of Organic Fertilizer	
Alfalfa meal	Supplies organic matter, high in nitrogen
Bat guano	High in nitrogen
Bloodmeal	High in nitrogen
Bluegrass hay	Good balance of nitrogen, phosphorus, potassium (NPK)
Cow manure	Good food for the beneficial soil organisms
Coffee grounds	High in nitrogen
Compost, homemade	High in NPK, trace elements
Eggshells	High in calcium
Epsom salts	High in magnesium, sulfur
Feather meal	High in nitrogen
Fescue hay	Good balance of NPK
Fish emulsion	High in nitrogen, sulfur
Fish meal	High in nitrogen
Flowers of sulfur	Lowers pH, 99 percent sulfur
Granite meal	High in potassium
Greensand	High in potassium
Gypsum	Lowers pH, adds calcium
Hairy vetch	Good green manure for winter crop
Kelp meal	Contains 60 trace elements
Oak leaves	High in potassium
Peat moss	Good for organic matter, lowers pH
Pig manure	High in nitrogen
Poultry manure	High in nitrogen, phosphorus
Rock phosphate	High in phosphorus
Sawdust	Adds organic matter if well rotted
Sheep manure	High in nitrogen, potassium
Soybean meal	High in nitrogen
Sweet clover	Organic matter
Wood ashes	High in potassium, raises pH
Worm castings	Contains 11 trace elements

the tea bag as he soaked manure in burlap bags to make liquid fertilizer; with Thomas Jefferson, recycling all the household scraps into Monticello's gardens; and with Leo Tolstoy, mowing hay for compost with a scythe for the sheer joy of it.

It won't matter anymore if your neighbors think you're weird, because you'll have a new, elevated status as a liaison between life and death. Your badge is the smudge of compost on your gardening jacket, a badge you wear proudly.

The idea of organic fertilizers is to feed the soil, then let the soil feed the crop. The Master Gardener simply learns how to get out of the way and let nature do the work.

WHAT NATIVES KNOW
· THE RIGHT PLANTS FOR THE RIGHT PLACES ·

ZEN MASTER LAUREN SPRINGER repeatedly sings the praises of native plants in *The Undaunted Garden*. "After a particularly vicious hailstorm one late July, I stood forlorn among the icy white golf balls, green tatters, and slush, immobilized and sickened by what fifteen horrible minutes can wreak on a garden." But in the days that followed, Springer discovered a silver lining in her beds of native plants. "Calliopsis, mealy-cup sage, prairie coneflower all originate from regions prone to hail. Their leaves were either too fine and narrow to be torn to smithereens, or they were pliable enough to bend with the impact, or in some cases, they were so strong and leathery that the hailstones slid or bounced right off them."

Arizona author and grower Gary Nabhan describes another victorious proving-out of natives in *Coming Home to Eat*. He had eagerly brought back squash seeds from cousins in the old country, but discovered they were genetically out of place in Tucson: "The withering stems all emanated from the bushy zucchini plants from seed I had brought back from Lebanon. They were infested with squash-vine borers. Their thin, brittle stems offered no resistance to the caterpillars, which sucked the remaining life out of them. In contrast the thick, hairy stems of the native O'odham squash had dealt with caterpillar invasions for centuries by enclosing each developing larva in a gall-like growth, while the vines continued to spread, root, and fruit. Even if the caterpillars did serious damage to one stretch of a vine, the O'odham squash had the capacity to send down roots at several nodes, and their entire mandala of vines seldom succumbed to the assault."

I heartily second the observations of Springer and Nabhan. I'm right in the middle of a spring as dry as the ashes of nearby forest fires, and I've watched one native plant after another dutifully awaken, emerge from beneath a blanket of leaf mulch, and get ready for another season, like the all-stars of spring training.

READING THE SIGNS
· GARDENING ON BOTH SIDES OF THE BRAIN ·

MY GUESS IS THAT in the world's vast population of gardeners, there are many who would rather not have to test their soil. I once got a great soil-testing kit for a Christmas present, and over the years, the various chemicals dried up and the instructions were lost or else decomposed to ash. I never once used it. Similarly, for the same reasons my sock drawer is not always shipshape organized, I'd rather not keep a logbook. I'm not saying this is the proper way to do it, just that for me, it's tempting to garden by the seat of my pants if I can get away with it. In this unfocused approach, knowledge and awareness come to me, the gardener, effortlessly and intuitively, like a playful cat coming home for dinner.

However, in the real world, most gardeners come to grips with the fact that we can't really have a successful garden while our brains are on auto. Sooner or later, we do begin to keep a log, so we can remember what variety of cucumber did so well and when the first frost hit the year before last—a year very similar to this one. Sooner or later, we admit that if we don't know what's in our soil, we also won't know what's causing poor yields and wimpy displays of flowers.

But maybe there's middle ground between rational and intuitive approaches to gardening. Maybe a detailed, fact-crammed log of each gardening season—the more rational way to steer a garden—can be supplemented by a less formal but no less informed reading of nature's signs. Maybe we can test the soil intuitively by observing the vigor of our crops. In this more intuitive, less rigorous approach, a gardener's strategy is to blend in with the life teeming in the garden, and try to make sense of the patterns. You don't actually have to look like a corn stalk or a chunk of manure to be warmly accepted in the garden. You just have to show each plant the respect it deserves, and listen to what it has to say.

Case in point: When's the right time to plant potatoes? A person could answer that question in various ways: by throwing a dart at the calendar; by paging through her loose-leaf logbook, complete with snapshots of each bed; or by consulting the cottonwood trees. A new rule of thumb begins to take shape: when cottonwoods bud, plant the spuds.

Weeds have something to tell us too, if we choose to listen. When *Taraxacum officinale* (dandelion) emerges from the soil, we should have our spinach transplants ready to go in the ground, that's a fact. And if the dandelions appear stunted, some weed readers would advise that the soil needs phosphorus. A heavy infestation of dandelions, they say, is indicative of clay soil and acidity, just as a field of yarrow may indicate low levels of potassium.

The leaves of garden crops are indicators, too. Not only are they solar collectors, but also expressions of relative well-being. The potatoes we planted in consultation with the cottonwoods tell us they are deficient in potassium because their leaves are dull, without any sign of purple or bronze coloration, and with leaves that curl forward.

If a gardener keeps his eyes and ears open, there's more than enough information available to drive him nuts. One of these mornings, he'll catch it out of the corner of his eye: limp snap bean leaves signaling "water me, scatterbrain" by semaphore.

SIXTEEN RULES OF THUMB FOR ZEN GARDENERS OF THE WEST
· MINDFULNESS IN THE GARDEN ·

I'VE BEEN AT IT now for about twenty-five years, and learned a lot about the two basic kinds of gardens. You can have a partnership with your garden that's based on wisdom, contentment, and health, or you can default to a fool's garden by not paying attention. You can bring great energy to the work—energy that's replenished with healthy food, insights, and brilliant blossoms, or you can bring sprays, powders, genetic engineering, and other high-tech methods to make the work "easy" and the produce impressive-looking. The rules of thumb listed here apply to the first kind of garden.

Go easy on yourself. Gardening is best practiced without shame, doubt, regret, envy, or dread. The only good garden is a no-guilt garden. Diane Ackerman phrases it well in her book *Cultivating Delight*: "Some gardeners seem unable to fully enjoy their gardens, so caught up are they in the latest skirmish with mildew or beetle. Weeding can attain the status of a holy war. My philosophy is: Forget winning, cultivate delight."

If at first you don't succeed, keep planting. Wipe the slate clean by burying the evidence or hauling it to the compost pile. Your Brussels sprouts may be covered with aphids from stem to stern, but nobody needs to know that. The spinach looks anemic? Now you see it, now you don't. Lupine seeds never came up? Plant right over 'em. If they do finally emerge, maybe a few have won the right to grow between rows.

Think like a plant. Plants aren't engineers, and they don't know anything about last frost dates, inches of rain, or number of days to maturity. They just want to grow. Put them in the right places, and learn to read the signs of their vitality. Use your intuition. Weave together crop history, weather, plant vitality, and a cupful of compost to meet a plant's needs. Learn to ask, "If I were a deep-rooted Nanking cherry, drooping a little after a freeze but trying to keep my sense of humor, wouldn't I want the mulch pulled back to warm the soil up?"

Get your hands dirty. So dirty you'll need a scrub brush to get them clean again. Rather than wondering if the soil is moist under a sun-baked surface, poke your finger in there. In the book *People with Dirty Hands,* Robin Chotzinoff writes, "I prefer to write about gardeners, because they are so much more interesting than real people." And so much more real than squeaky-clean people.

Garden strategically. As you stretch your abs across three rows to weed the icicle radishes, think about salad. As you dig a wheelbarrow full of compost to mulch each strawberry plant, think about shortcake. Begin to practice strategic gardening by growing the right crops at the right time to make one of your favorite recipes. What a deal, to have basil, garlic, and a touch of parsley ready to go all at the same time, to make pesto!

Practice "tough love." Your plants need to be ready for the challenges of the West. Don't baby them. For example, if you've started lettuce seedlings indoors, put them outside in the daytime whenever it's warmer than 38 or 40 degrees. They need to know how bright the sun is here, and they need to start getting enough natural light to avoid becoming leggy as they stretch for light. As soon as nighttime temperatures remain well above freezing, leave the seedlings outside all night. How else are they going to learn how fast temperatures plunge in a high and dry climate, after dark?

Garden with all your senses. You may not be able to see a billion microbes in a handful of soil or smell subtle chemical messages constantly being sent from plant to plant, but you can see a glow on the leaves of a healthy stand of chard. You can smell the richness of a well-rotted bucket of compost, taste the season's first crunchy snow peas, and feel the feathery leaves of an asparagus plant. Instead of wondering if a bed needs water, get your fingers into it, like a dipstick, to check for moisture.

Become a rainmaker. I've watched it happen, again and again—this dance between the sky and the earth. And somehow human vocal chords can find the right frequency to release stored-up electricity and pressure in the sky. Or so it seems. After a long dry spell, during which your garden hose is more like a fire hose, lightning and thunder respond especially well to a throaty, earthy incantation: "C'mon, rain!" It's like you're daring the skies to open up, on behalf of the soil, the crops, and your own sanity. And what the heck, even if your theatrics don't deliver a drop of moisture that particular afternoon, the fact that you're standing on the back porch in your underwear, sniffing the breezes and scanning the skies, means you're hooked. One way or another, those crops will get water.

Harvest the intangibles. This may be the most important rule of all. It's not just food we're after, but knowledge, serenity, and calmness—what I call "spacetime." Remember that what gardens do best is help gardeners grow. At the end of a season, you may not have cantaloupes (the squirrels got all fifteen of them), but you had the satisfaction of knowing how to grow them and bringing them to ripeness. You've got the right tools, you just need to operate a better melon bed next year, with a more effective squirrel barrier.

Watch the gardens of your neighbors. Pay particular attention to the older folks to find out what grows best in your neighborhood, and what doesn't. I remember conversations I had with white-haired professional landscapers as they worked in their own yards. Longtime residents of what used to be the countryside's farmhouse but is now surrounded by neat rows of suburban houses, they kneeled in lush, handcrafted beds, leaving paving stones behind themselves so the rest of us can find the way.

Fertilize the soil, not just the plant. Gardens aren't factories, they're ecosystems that are constantly at work. Mulching a tired-looking crop with rich compost brings health not only to that current crop, but also to the surrounding soil and therefore the crop that follows it, and the system as a whole.

Develop a sense of timing. Prioritize tasks so that when the garlic rows need hoeing and aerating, or the broccoli needs to be sprayed with *Bt* to prevent cabbage worm infestations, you're on it. When the cabbage moths are flying, get out the mister, mister. Pruning the apple trees can wait. After a good rain, the weeds pull up easily, and liquid fertilizer stays in the root zone. Mulch packed around the fruit trees will hold in the moisture you've just captured. It's all about timing.

Never make the same mistake twice. (In my case, never make it more than half a dozen times.) As insurance against repetitious errors, keep a logbook. Or at least tell your spouse or gardening colleague about the initial mistake, so if you do it again (and again), you can blame it on them.

Remember that gardening is a race we should never expect to really win. We can appear to be in the lead from time to time, however. That is, if we're willing to neglect the housekeeping, our careers, and our personal hygiene.

Experiment. For example, hang CDs from a tree limb to startle the deer, or try stapling a picture of my face on a wooden stake and pounding it into the besieged beds. Who knows, it might just work.

Remember that the best garden ever is always in the future. Garden for the future as well as the present. Build next year's soil, nurture the trees and perennials for future years.

THE SECRET LIVES OF PLANTS:
SEX AND DEATH IN THE GARDEN

WHEN IT COMES TO the behavior and ecology of plants, most of us are pitifully unsuspecting as we perform our list of garden chores. We don't have any real understanding of who's eating who, whose blossoms are considered to have the most sex appeal, and who's sending messages to whom. We sense in a vague way that, both above and below the soil, the entire garden is vibrating with life and constant motion. In fact, this is a primary reason we like to be there—because all the things that are happening somehow give us energy. We just don't know exactly what they are. When it comes to specific activities that occur in these microscopic, multidimensional worlds, we don't have a clue.

And maybe that's a good thing, after all. How would you like to be at the scale of a spider mite as he strips off huge slabs of leafy tissue, chomps on them, then looks around for a bite of meat? In any square inch of the garden, a microscopic "Jurassic Park" is unfolding, except with a much larger cast than in the movie. As war is waged and love trysts are consummated all around us, we continue to pleasantly putz in the flowerbed, obliviously deadheading the cosmos, so to speak.

When it comes to sex, our presence in the garden is a little like being a dog in a bedroom where lovemaking is going on. In a way, we intrude on plants' secret lives, barely noticing age-old rituals as they unfold—incredibly intricate mating rituals that have developed over millions of years (at the same time that our thumbs were evolving, then beginning to turn green). Wonderfully fragrant molecules waft in the air, chemically calculated to attract pollinators to consummate transactions between the stamen of one plant and the pistil of another. So powerful are these molecules that they seem sexy even in another kingdom—the animal kingdom. Some of our most exotic perfumes are fabricated from rose or jasmine overtones, as if we, too, are capable of botanic arousal. In a very real way, spring is a biological elixir partly because it smells so sexy! (In what way do humans reciprocate?)

Another drama that unfolds as we work obliviously is intense chemical warfare between plants and predators. "Plants can't move, so they stand their ground with bad tasting and dangerous compounds like strychnine in the bark," writes Diane Ackerman in *A Natural History of the Senses.*

Most of the spices, whose heady aromas we are drawn to, repel insects and animals. We are enjoying the plant's war machine.

And most plants have allies strategically located throughout the garden or landscape, which release chemical messages when they are being attacked. For example, when an elm tree is attacked by elm leaf beetles, its chemical messages alert other trees in the grove to produce toxic compounds before the attackers land on *their* leaves.

Not only do plants make love and war right in front of our noses, they also have fevers and clairvoyant encounters. Using high-resolution infrared cameras, scientists detected elevated temperatures on tobacco leaves infected with tobacco mosaic virus. Russian scientists even attached lie detectors to the leaves of plants, and claim to have documented a fear response when experimenters thought about harming the plant.

Maybe it's as Michael Pollan hypothesizes in *The Botany of Desire:* plants only keep us around to make sure their numbers increase, even if it means being eaten in the final Act.

SECTION III

Strategic Gardening
· HOW TO GROW PESTO, SALSA, AND CHERRY PIE ·

SANDLOTS AND GARDEN PLOTS
· THE BEST-LAID PLANS ·

WHEN I WAS A KID playing sandlot football games, we'd huddle over sketches, stick-drawn in the playground dirt. "Go deep," the quarterback would instruct, "then cut back, full speed, and I'll hit you with a bullet pass." Every spring, when I begin to plan and then plant a season's garden, I remember those grade school huddles. "Go deep," I tell the roots of an Asian cucumber transplant. "Climb the trellis I'm planting you next to that I just spent three hours screwing together," I tell the vines. I can always picture exactly what the trellis will look like, after the cucumber vigorously executes the strategy.

But let's face it, in sandlot football games there are always wobbly spirals that result in interceptions. And it's the same in every garden. Even in big-league gardens there are weeds, wilts, and cabbageworms. In the game plan, the roots go deep but in reality, they have a hard time penetrating the defensive line of compacted soil. So our strategies need to be flexible, spontaneous, and creative. We need to have backup plans and second-string seedlings ready to jump in and replace wounded first-string plants. We need to plant more beans than we could ever eat because the bunnies will get some of them and blight will take its share, too. We need to maintain an inventory of shade cloth for hellish summer days and moldy old blankets for fluke frosts.

We need vials of organic snake oil to beat the bugs and containers of seaweed and alfalfa pellets to invigorate our champion tomato plants. We need a sense of humor, and most of all, a sense of humility. After all, we're trying to manage millions of variables as if there were only four or five. Let's face it, the odds of implementing our initial strategies are pretty small. However, if the strategy reinvents itself daily to fit changing conditions, everyone's a winner.

How to Become a Seed-Starting Maniac
• All it takes is time and care •

Tired of waiting for the garden in your backyard to look like the garden in your head? Well then, come to Blooms R Us and take home three or four truckloads of seedlings. For less than $2,000, you can have an instant garden!

Or, if the *process* of gardening is as valuable to you as the product, try bringing your own seedlings into the world. If you have the patience and the space, try starting seeds indoors to produce seedling transplants. Surely, this is one of the most valuable skills in a western gardener's repertoire.

In sparse climates like ours, sowing seeds directly in the garden is like spending an afternoon in a casino—you may get lucky, you may not. Seeds dry up too easily or get washed away by gully washers. And they also take up space while they germinate and then try to bulk up for the roller coaster of weather challenges that lie ahead.

On the other hand, if you plant seeds indoors in customized, ideal conditions, you can transplant vigorous, hardened-off seedlings into your beds just at the right time (you hope). "Hardening off" means gradually exposing seedlings to colder temperatures and brighter sunlight.

As adolescents rather than babies, seedlings no longer have the innocent, fragrant, just-germinated tenderness that sends bugs, bunnies, and slugs into ecstatic feeding frenzies. Homegrown seedlings have sturdy root systems, and enough leaves to be able to lose a few and still make it. Jackpot! One flat at a time, at your own pace, you can add lush little squares to the crazy quilt out there in the backyard. What was, yesterday, only a freshly dug bed is today a recognizable bowl-to-be of salad or a color coordinated bed of native perennials. Nice work, and you did it yourself.

Having an inventory of seedlings gives you flexibility to replace a harvested crop right away, giving the new crop a head start on both weather and weeds. And by starting your own seedlings, you can grow the varieties you want, instead of just what the garden center has. Tired of paying garden-center prices for 'Big Boy' tomatoes? Start your own 'Brandywine' or 'Sungold' cherry tomatoes for the price of a seed packet.

By planting your own seeds, you get to watch seedlings emerge right before your eyes, surely one of the most rewarding aspects of gardening. Certain aspects of your life may be overly complicated, but the seeds keep it simple. With the care and touch of a master surgeon, you learn by doing what seedlings need. The primary principle is "try a technique, and see how it works." Secondary principles are: Don't let your potting soil dry out (but don't let it get soggy, either). Space seeds 1 to 2 inches apart so they don't compete for nutrients and light. Thin seedlings when necessary, and be ruthless in your selection of the most vigorous sprouts. Thin quickly and without regret by pinching stems between index finger and thumb or cutting with scissors. Fertilize seedlings with compost tea, diluted seaweed, or fish emulsion about every ten days. Then let there be light—lots of it.

Seed master John Jeavons brings a touch of Buddhism to the ritual of planting seeds. "Think like a seed," he writes, in *How to Grow More Vegetables*. "Ask yourself what a seed needs in nature—air, warmth, moisture, soil nutrients, microorganisms. As a seed, you need these things, at least, along with other plants, birds, insects, spiders, frogs, and chickens. You need an entire microcosm of the world."

Always remember that seeds have their own agendas. They germinate in different temperature and light conditions. Some seeds, like lettuce, dill, and savory, need light to germinate, so they don't like being buried. Other seeds, such as spinach, asparagus, and beets, like to be soaked overnight before being sown. Some seeds, like parsley and rhubarb, have hard coats that need to be sandpapered or at least rubbed together before sowing. Some seeds take *months* to germinate. Cool-season crops like cabbages, carrots, and onions will germinate in soil temperatures as low as 50 degrees F., but warm-season species

> **Basic Equipment for Becoming a Master of Seed Starting**
>
> • Patience.
>
> • A few good recipes for potting soils that simulate the homelands of your favorite crops and flowers.
>
> • A good source of light to prevent seedlings from becoming spindly, miniature beanstalks.
>
> • A spoon and a hand trowel to transplant your babies into larger and larger flats.
>
> • Flats to start the seeds in, and several sizes of pots to transplant them into.

like tomatoes, peppers, and beans need soil temperatures to be at least 60 degrees. Try using lukewarm tap water to warm the soil and encourage germination.

This spring I successfully started and transplanted about twenty-five different flats of lettuce, tomatoes, artichokes, peppers, broccoli, and wildflowers while two stray flats of seeds from faraway places just sat there. Banana seeds from a tree in Vietnam and Silver Fern tree seeds from New Zealand may be extremely slow germinators, or maybe I've lost them—at this point, it's hard to tell. In any case, they're off in one corner of my living room/greenhouse/messy space, which I tiled instead of carpeted so it would be more plant-friendly. (The question is, how people-friendly is it? Can someone please finance my greenhouse?) Sunlight warms the tiles and radiates heat, and water that inevitably drips on the tiles is not a major concern. I also have a tabletop fountain made out of copper pipes that puts at least half a gallon of humidity in the air every day in the summer, which germinating seeds love.

I confess I often purchase a favorite seed starting mix, Fertilome, which contains lots of peat and vermiculite (a water-holding product made from mica), as well as enough incorporated organic fertilizer to give seedlings a healthy start. But I also use homemade potting mixtures that are roughly one-half finished compost and one-half garden bed soil. Another simple mix is equal parts sifted compost, sharp (gritty) sand, and turf loam, a compost made from clumps of sod. For a more elaborate, balanced organic mix, combine and mix the following ingredients in a bucket or wheelbarrow: 8 quarts compost, 6 quarts sphagnum peat, 6 quarts vermiculite, ¼ cup bonemeal, ¼ cup kelp meal, and ¼ cup blood meal. These natural ingredients are available in many garden centers, though you may have to mail order the kelp meal.

I plant seeds in plastic flats (about 11 by 22 by 3 inches) that last three or four years before cracking, because I like their translucent, tight-fitting lids that hold in the humidity to encourage germination. For seedlings that will remain in the flat for longer than a month, I use deeper containers. I have a small fleet of homemade wooden flats (redwood or cedar work best), and a third-string assemblage of Tupperware containers, cookie sheets, and antique Coca-cola flats that sort different seed crops into neat collections of square plastic pots made from plastic juice bottles. I cut them in half with a scissors and poke drainage holes in the bottoms with a sharp stab of a paring knife (I still have all my fingers). These little square pots fit into rectangular flats very efficiently.

I'm intrigued by the idea of pots made from compressed soil blocks or sheets of newspaper, but haven't had much experience with either of those. Garden supply houses sell presses and molds to homemake your own pots, but in the case of soil blocks, you need to use very fibrous soil.

It's a good idea to premoisten your potting soil before planting. This prevents seeds from being carried down into loose soil by a first watering.

There are many mysteries of seed starting that reaffirm one's confidence in natural design. Folded up within the seed coats is everything a seed requires to become a mature plant. The unfolding of all that stored-up information and cargo is nothing less than a miracle! There's no doubt that seeds communicate with each other, below the ground. Using chemical messages, the seeds "observe" while early germinators make their move. Then, by chemical and thermal consensus, they go for it by the dozen, mutually stimulated by growth hormones each seed releases. At some level, their energetic communications are part of the fever we feel in the spring.

Another significant stimulant is the moon. According to biodynamic growers, the best time to plant both quick and slow germinators is two days before the new moon and up to seven days after the new moon. This makes intuitive sense, because the seeds can soak up moisture and then be affected by lunar tides that occur even in the soil. During the new moon, the Earth's gravitational pull is at its peak, since the moon's pull is weak. This helps root development. As the moon waxes, leaf growth is stimulated by an increasingly stronger lunar pull as well as increased moonlight.

When's the second-best time to plant seeds? Whenever you get forty-five minutes and need a productive diversion.

One of my standard operating procedures is to get flats out in natural sunshine as soon as sprouting occurs. Even on cold, sunny days (above 40 degrees F. or so), the ground warms up enough in protected areas to keep seedlings happy. I have a south-facing alcove out my back door that eventually will become a greenhouse, but in the meantime is a seedling nursery. In a microclimate like this, the ambient temperature can be ten or twenty degrees warmer. Flats go out on sunny spring mornings and come back in before dark, full of solar energy that keeps them from "bolting," or becoming spindly. Even in the heat of summer, my alcove is a great place for seeding. I cover seeded, watered flats with a 30-percent shade cloth, and come back in three or four days. Seedlings need at least fourteen hours of light a day to grow vigorous roots and leaves.

Studies have demonstrated that an increase of 2 percent to 4 percent in root vigor can double or triple yields. When I visited his garden in Willits, California, John Jeavons told me a story about the connection between plant roots and overall vitality. "A biodynamic gardener once had a row of broccoli plants. Only two plants had aphids on them, and both were quite infested. The two plants were dug up, and the gardener discovered that the roots were damaged and stunted. The healthy broccoli, with vigorous roots, went untouched by the insects, while nature eliminated the unhealthy plants."

Species like beans, radishes, carrots, and squash aren't fond of having their roots messed with, so it's best not to start them in pots but rather directly in the ground. The vigor of other seedlings is actually increased by being transplanted into larger pots before final transplanting into the garden. This includes members of the cabbage family (except Chinese cabbage), lettuce and most greens, tomatoes and peppers, and many herbs and flowers.

A good time to transplant your seedlings is after they develop their second set of true leaves. Hold the seedling by the leaves or cradle the root ball, because the stem is more vulnerable to permanent damage. Transplant in the evening to give the plant some "downtime" for adjusting, and water the roots after firmly planting the seedlings in rich, fresh potting soil. When transplanting into the garden, consider covering the newcomers with inverted one-gallon pots while the plants re-establish their roots.

I've replaced the standard windowsills in my sunny living room with ten-inch-wide sills to accommodate seed flats, but even these sunlit shelves are only a backup location, since seedlings begin to stretch after a few days. For happy, sturdy seedlings, practice tough love. As long as it's sunny and not windy, get flats of newly sprouted seeds outside as soon as possible. If this just isn't possible, you can get good results from suspending a shop-type fluorescent light two to four inches above seedlings. The tubes don't have to be "full-spectrum." Off-the-shelf tubes work just as well. I know, it sounds like way too much light and it seems a little unnatural, but it does work. Rig up the light so you can raise it as the seedlings grow. To make the setup totally convenient, put the light on a timer, set for about fourteen hours. I don't use this technique, but I've seen it work often enough to recommend it if natural sunlight isn't available.

What if, despite your great intentions, your seeds don't come up? The odds are good that your problem is one of the following:

• Old seeds that have lost their vigor
• Seeds that were sown too deeply

- Soil was not firmed around seeds
- Soil temperature was too high or too low
- Too much water
- Not enough water
- Soil-borne diseases like damping off, a white, furry-looking fungus that grows in wet soil.

The best way to learn which mistake(s) you're making is to keep planting, observing what does work. Seeds are cheap and, after lots of trials and errors, you'll acquire a "second nature" about what your seedlings need—when to water, fertilize, transplant, and cheerlead them—indicating that you've become a seed starter. Way to go!

In It for the Pie
· FRUIT TREES AND FLY-FISHING ·

"THE BEST TIME to plant a fruit tree," the saying goes, "is fifteen years ago, and the second best time is now." With that sentiment in mind, I set out a few seasons ago to plant a mini-orchard on the edge of our community garden.

My first observation is that waiting for fruit trees to mature is like fishing. You watch patiently as the trees grow as tall as your teenager, then over the course of the next few years, they become the height of his favorite basketball star. Finally, after five or six years of no-yield fishing, you've got a bite—of a crisp 'Gala' apple! At last, the care and attention that went into each tree seem justified.

I confess that day has not yet dawned in our community orchard. But at least we've gotten eighteen trees in the ground, in reasonably neat rows that confer a sense of orderliness and potential each time I'm out there. I throw the irrigation hose around as if I were fly-fishing for apples, confident that in a few more years my efforts will bear fruit.

Already, I've learned that in Colorado, the challenge of fruit is largely the challenge of frost. Too often, March comes in like a lamb but goes out like a lion. And every time the lion roars, another branch full of blossoms shivers to death. Friends with mature trees tell me to expect apples every other year, sour cherries two out of three years, and peaches every third year. That's a sparse catch, compared to California or New Zealand yields. So, why do we do it?

Simple—because we love pie!

For the sake of homemade pie and fresh fruit right off the tree, my neighbors and I carefully located our orchard in an area that's well protected from frost. We hope. It slopes downhill slightly, from west to east; it has a frost barrier of mature honey locusts on two sides and has an agricultural ditch between the foothills—where frost typically comes from—and the trees. Frost tends to flow like water, and our hope is to siphon that cold air into the ditch and let it drain away harmlessly.

Our orchard has plums, sour cherries, pears, peaches, and apples, but the target crop is definitely apples. The next additions to our apple holdings will be 'Bechtel' and 'Snowdrift' crabapple trees, which are good midseason pollinators for many different varieties of apple. I like the idea of pollinating with a touch of wildness. The crabapples were there long before Adam and Eve. I'm also prepared to go out next spring with an artist's paintbrush tied to the end of a long stick, and manually cross-pollinate in case the bees are still sleeping.

A lot of the artistry in producing a continuing supply of apple pies is selection of varieties. Simply put, you select disease-resistant strains whose blossom times overlap. A few of the varieties that are currently popular, like 'Gala', 'Jonathan', and 'Golden Delicious', are susceptible to fire blight, while 'Red Delicious', 'Liberty', 'Wealthy', and 'Freedom' varieties are less so. To find charts that tell you more about which varieties to plant in your area, call your local extension agent, or do a search on the web with keywords like "disease resistant apples" and "apple pollination."

Last week I harvested twenty-six years of experience at White Buffalo Orchard in Paonia, Colorado, where Wayne Talmadge has been growing 'Gala', 'McIntosh', 'Golden', and 'Red Delicious' apples since the late '70s. One of his recurring rules of thumb is that pampering an apple tree can lead to trouble, sort of like spoiling an only child. For example, fire blight, a bacterial disease that causes blossoms, shoots, and fruit to blacken and shrivel, gains a foothold in trees that are overnourished. "Fire blight shows up in warm, humid years after too much fertilizer has been applied," Talmadge told me. "The bacteria love to attack nitrogen-rich growth, so we feed our trees very moderately with fish powder and seaweed—just enough to keep their health in balance." Talmadge also grows alfalfa and clover between the trees, to put steady supplies of nitrogen into the soil.

So far, fire blight hasn't been a major problem at White Buffalo, mostly due to Talmadge's vigilance. "When it does show up, we cut off affected branches quickly," he said. "Otherwise we may end up with one big cut—six inches off the ground."

In contrast to fire blight, the codling moth thrives in dry weather. When I asked Talmadge about this proverbial "worm in the apple," he shook his head. "That's a big problem here," he said. "We try to use a cross-section of natural controls for the codling moth, but we always have at least a little damage."

One of his strategies is to disrupt the moth's mating season with pheromone traps. "Imagine a hundred phones ringing, and you're trying to figure out which one to answer," he explains. "That's what it's like to be a male codling moth trying to mate in a sea of pheromones." He also releases parasitic wasps—tiny predators that feast on moths. He puts out black light traps, which the moths are attracted to, and he sprays a newly developed virus that keeps moth populations in check. "For the home gardener," he said, "it looks like the virus is going to be the best way to go."

I asked him for tips on watering, an arboreal chore that sometimes mystifies me. If a tree looks less perky than usual, has it received too little water or too much? To make sure, I dig exploratory trowel holes around the tree. Since most of the roots are no more than eighteen inches deep, I look for signs of moisture in that zone. If it's dry, I soak the tree at low flow for half an hour or so. Talmadge reminded me that in Colorado, it's hard to overwater, especially in well-drained soils. "But again, you don't want to pamper the tree with too much water. If you overwater in the fall, the tree may drop its sap late and be more vulnerable to freezing." The rule of thumb there is to start watering around bloom time, and stop watering in September. "If you want a vigorous, healthy tree that bears well and resists disease, don't baby it," he summarizes.

PANNING FOR GARLIC
· A WESTERN GEM ·

IMAGINE IT—a garden crop that's unappealing to pests, including leaf-eating bugs, deer, rabbits, and most viruses. A crop that stores for at least half a year, is useful in many different kinds of cooking, and is great for your health. Sounds like a fantasy? Wait, we're not even through yet. Imagine a crop that also grows dependably in western soils and climates, and that—believe it or not—sometimes grows right through the snow, cold, and darkness of *winter.* Garlic!

Seeing me bent over a freshly dug garden row in the fall, with a bowl of garlic cloves ready to be planted, neighbors might take me for a prospector who'd lost his way. And in a sense, they'd be right. While it may be an exaggeration to say that homegrown garlic is worth its weight in gold, it's definitely a western gem—one of those few precious crops that's well worth the effort.

My success with garlic began just a few years ago. I'd always heard it was easy to grow, but a few past experiments with it hadn't worked. Maybe I planted the cloves too deeply, or maybe they'd gotten waterlogged in the spring. Whatever the cause, my bulbs were miniature, in perfect scale with elf recipes. Then a friend and I rented a cabin outside Steamboat Springs, Colorado, where Angelo, the proprietor, loves to grow a type of garlic called Rocambole. He gave me a sackful of garlic cloves that had been drying on his workbench, and told me a few of his secrets.

"With loamy, well-drained soil and enough water," he told me, "you can't miss." Maybe as a result of his Italian heritage, Angelo likes garlic so much that he presses it and spreads it on homemade bread, all by itself. I'd have to say, for an eighty year old, he's pretty lively—is it the garlic? Research indicates that in addition to keeping vampires at bay, garlic lowers cholesterol, helps prevent cancer, and lowers blood sugar. I confess I sometimes crunch a clove or two before bed, if it feels like unwelcome bacterial visitors have landed. This last-ditch remedy usually works, and I recently found out why. Garlic contains allicin, a powerful natural antibiotic that kills bacteria like staph, strep, and E. coli.

After seeing Angelo's great results, I went home and double-dug some beds for the seed-cloves he'd given me—two beds that were each about eighteen square feet. I dug in some black, loamy compost and about two pounds of rock phosphate, and on the same day that I planted tulip bulbs—about mid-October—I pushed fifty or sixty cloves 3 to 4 inches into the soil, spaced four inches apart, incanting Angelo's name as I watered them. The following June, I harvested two buckets of garlic bulbs that made the supermarket's look shriveled and wimpy. I'm told that supermarket garlic also has a much shorter shelf life than homegrown, because shipment time and refrigeration speed spoilage.

I traveled all the way to Dixon, New Mexico, to talk with Stanley Crawford, author of *A Garlic Testament*. Because the guidebooks didn't have the right information, Crawford had to discover by experimentation that the proper time to plant garlic in the arid West is late fall. He noticed that leftover bulbs from the previous year's crop sprouted early in the spring, and so he began planting in October. "At my altitude," he says, "garlic will spend most of its life under the ground, a good nine months of the year, and if the bulbs had their way they wouldn't come up for air at all." We tend to think that the mission of garlic, or any crop, is to come to our tables, when really its mission is just to grow.

Another Colorado garlic nut worth consulting is Walt Lyons, who grows garlic commercially on a little farm in "East Nowhere," east of Fort Collins. About ten years ago, he and his wife were looking for a crop to grow on their new farm. Says Walt, "We wanted something that would grow on only a small fraction of the land, would survive frequent windstorms, and not be bothered by the hail that often pelts the region. Colorado has all four seasons—often by noon—and we wanted something we could count on."

They decided to grow garlic and sell it on the Internet, so they wouldn't have to maintain a retail store. They've now tested fifty or sixty varieties, and are partial to "hardneck" varieties as opposed to the softneck types from California usually found in supermarkets. "Hardneck varieties grow in Siberia," Walt explains, "and they seem to do pretty well here, too."

Hardneck varieties can be identified in the early summer garden by twisting, circular seed shoots or "scapes" that produce small bulblets. While these bulblets can be saved and planted for harvest in a year and a half, Walt suggests clipping the scapes instead and stir-frying them. "If you get them young enough, they're tender and mildly spicy—a real delicacy." (Clipping also increases the size of the bulbs underground.)

I asked him for his three most important tips for the grower who's never planted garlic before. "Add bonemeal or rock phosphate to the soil for good growth," he began. "Mulch the plants with straw or leaves in the winter, to minimize freezing and thawing that can damage roots. And don't be short on watering, especially in the winter. If the plants dry out you won't get good production."

Walt cuts back on watering a week or two before harvesting, so the bulbs won't rot. And he doesn't fertilize in the spring, instead relying on nutrients already in the soil. "We're lucky to have cows grazing right across the road," he says, "so we use lots of well-rotted manure from cows we know personally."

The way to tell when garlic is ready to harvest is when the leaves turn brown. Just when you think the whole crop is a failure, you pull up a few of the burned-out plants to compost them and discover bulbs the size of small limes, or in the case of elephant garlic, the size of oranges. "A lot of our customers like to grow elephant garlic, even though the taste is much milder, because it's so easy and produces such big bulbs," says Walt.

To get your garlic patch started, try a half-pound each of a few different varieties, with varying maturation times, storage quality, and tastes. Think of yourself as a prospector, in search of the plumpest, tastiest nuggets of garlic your soil can produce.

Don't Let Onions Make You Cry!
· AVOIDING HARVEST HEARTBREAK ·

THERE ARE AT LEAST three times onions can bring tears to your eyes. First, when you notice how much more expensive the sparsely filled seed packets are than they were back in the 1980s. Second, when you pull up a large, sturdy plant expecting to harvest a hardball-sized onion, but find a marble instead. And third, when you dice up the golf ball onion for stir-fry, with tears running down your cheeks. But be brave, reader—don't let onions get you down. Wipe away your tears, and read on.

1. To avoid the heartbreak of overpriced seed packets, try saving seeds from heirloom varieties, which (unlike hybrid seeds) will be genetically constant year after year. Experiment until you find an "open-pollinated" variety that makes the perfect hamburger onion or the best onion soup, and selectively breed a winner for your own garden conditions. Onions are a biennial, which means they produce seeds in their second year. So leave your plumpest blue-ribbon onions in place at the end of the season. Next year, when second-year plants are in bloom, cross-pollinate with another onion plant of the same variety, using a cue tip or an artist's paintbrush. Sounds like a lot of work, right? Then just buy the seeds, but be sure to

get "long day" varieties for Colorado—like 'Yellow Sweet Spanish', 'Walla Walla', and 'Ebenezer'.

2. To avoid *bulbus melancholia*—disappointment related to the harvesting of tiny onions—grow them in loose, well-drained soil with plenty of well-rotted compost or manure. Try growing onions from seeds or transplants rather than sets (small bulbs), which often produce more leaves than onion.

3. Avoiding tears when dicing onions requires a lot of skill and practice. There are as many remedies as there are for hiccups. In the quest for tearless onion dicing, chefs have been observed chewing bubble gum, holding burnt wooden matchsticks between their teeth, and burning candles while they dice. But like hiccups, the tears usually just keep coming. For guaranteed no-tears results, use scuba gear when you dice onions. (You won't need the flippers, of course.)

Why let onions ruin your day or your growing season? Just figure out what kind of onions you want to eat—red, white, yellow, or green (scallions)—and get started early in the season. You can start onion seeds indoors, eight weeks before you plant them outside. Since onions are extremely hardy and can be planted before the last spring frost, try starting seeds indoors in February. Transplant the seedlings when they are 3 inches tall, or if they get spindly before you can work the soil, prune them back. (Interestingly, each individual onion leaf creates food for another layer of the bulb.)

You can also buy transplants at the garden center, in bundles of fifty or sixty. Space the plants 4 to 5 inches apart in the row to produce large-sized bulbs, or space 2 to 2½ inches apart and harvest every other plant as a green onion. Allow 12 to 18 inches between rows, or space onions 6 to 8 inches apart in all directions in beds.

If you do use sets, *don't plant them too deep*. Unlike tulip or daffodil bulbs, onions like to be planted near the surface. The tops of the sets should barely be covered, with less than an inch of soil. Remember the Goldilocks principle when selecting the right sets to grow plump onions. The smaller bulbs may not fatten up, while the largest may produce mostly leaves, so plant bulbs that are just right—solid, fleshy, medium-sized sets. You can use the same spacing strategy for sets as for transplants: If you plant the small bulbs 2 inches apart, harvest every other plant as green onions, which will leave space for bulb development of the remaining sets.

The onion root maggot is about the only real pest this crop has in Colorado. Discourage it with soil that drains well and is fertile enough to harbor parasitic nematodes that go after the maggots. Deer and rabbits won't bother onions, so there's no risk planting them in unfenced areas. In fact, onions are so pest resistant that they are actually used in some organic pesticides. Weeds and wild grasses, on the other hand, don't show much aversion to onions and can rob nutrients from the developing bulbs. Because onions have shallow roots, it takes a little extra care when you cultivate around them to keep the bed free of weeds.

Green onions can be pulled anytime after the tops are 6 inches tall. They become stronger in flavor with age and increasing size, so when they're too large to eat raw in salads, use them for cooking. Mature garden onions are ready for harvesting when the green top withers, falls over, and starts to turn brown. This usually happens in mid to late summer. Don't overwater as the bulbs mature—they like to spend their last days fairly dry. In fact, Colorado is good onion territory because low humidity and high temperatures encourage good bulb formation.

Here's where the old-world artistry comes in. Lay mature onions (tops and all) in a single layer on newspaper, out of the sun, and let them cure for a few days. Then braid the tops together, and hang your crop in bunches in the shed or in the basement. If temperatures remain cool (50 to 60 degrees), the onions will still be ready to use on Thanksgiving and even into the New Year.

Do you feel better now?

MAKING YOUR YARD LOOK GOOD ENOUGH TO EAT
· EDIBLE LANDSCAPING FOR HIGH AND DRY YARDS ·

I REMEMBER A PEANUT BUTTER and *berry* sandwich I had a few summers ago while camping in Redstone, Colorado. Some very ripe serviceberries had somehow gone undetected by birds, right next to our shady campsite. We squeezed the pits out and put fresh berries and peanut butter on some good homemade bread. Survival at its finest. (We were "hunter-gatherers," since I first had to hunt for the peanut butter.) My mother is a hunter-gatherer, too, picking oranges and grapefruit off the citrus trees in her Tucson backyard for fresh-squeezed juice. It seems like a no-brainer: Why not let your landscaping feed you, without much effort on your part?

It may be true that citrus trees don't grow in Colorado, but I'll bet you didn't know that hardy kiwis sometimes do, in a protected area. There's a kiwi variety (*Actinidia arguta*) that comes from Russia, where it survives temperatures of -40 degrees F. And there are huckleberries, blackberries, elderberries, mulberries, currants, grapes, gooseberries, wild plums, chokecherries, sour cherries, and other shrubs and brambles that make neighborhood birds plump and self-assured—and sometimes even drunk. (Watch carefully—if a robin is unable to walk a straight line under a currant bush, it may have just eaten some overwintered, fermented berries.)

It may seem like I'm making fun of birds, but actually I get along pretty well with them, except for one small issue: They're eating my berries—constantly, merrily, and obliviously. If you have berries, you'll have birds and butterflies, dive-bombing and fluttering blissfully through *your* airspace. (You don't think birds make fun of *us*? Watch a sparrow peck a strawberry clean from the crown, then spy on you from a tree limb.) If you have fruit, better get used to hummingbirds zinging past your ear en route to the wild plums or the Red Lake currants.

It's hard not to be a little envious of birds' ecstasy, but maybe it's contagious. So if you think you can adapt to a Technicolor backyard splashed with colors, fragrances, and happy-bird songs, go ahead, plant an "edible landscape." Cut back on the amount of time you spend maintaining the lawn and spend it instead watering tomorrow's breakfast. I'm not suggesting that you get rid of your lawn completely, because lawns do work pretty well as ground covers. They do isolate the mud from the carpet. But they also consume a lot of resources, chemicals, and time, to produce a final product that's typically sent to the dump. Americans pamper 20 million acres of lawn that cumulatively consume millions of bags of fertilizer and reservoirs full of potable water. Each time we mow, it's the pollution equivalent of a 150-mile car trip, and keep this in mind: Every summer day in America, a would-be napper goes crazy from the sudden startup of a droning lawn mower, and next time, it's going to be *me*.

What if just one-fifth of your lawn became a mini-orchard, grape arbor, and fruit nursery?

You don't need to be an expert to grow fruit, you just need to envision your yard in a different way, and do a little research. By reallocating money for a few well-chosen varieties, and blowing off a few weekends, you can create a Garden of Eden in one corner of your yard that looks good enough to eat. (That's you, lying in a hammock strung from the grape arbor to the semidwarf apple tree, picking mulberries while you read Rosalind Creasy's *The Complete Book of Edible Landscaping*.)

Why not throw a few nonberry species into your landscape while you're at it? For example, prickly pear cactus, yucca, daylily, and piñon pine can all get comfortable on your plate, if you let them. If they seem too weird to eat, have a closer look at the exotic fruits now on display at your local supermarket—I saw one yesterday in the checkout line that looked like a cross between a gourd and a yellow, bumpy-quilled porcupine. Anything that looks that strange and still gets shipped around the world must taste pretty good. (I'm going back today to see if any are left.) Gourmet chef Jay McCarthy blends his way through 500 pounds of cactus "pears" a week to prepare a margarita he calls

"The Cactus." And certainly, any truly resourceful person has already harvested yucca pods in their infancy and roasted them like a potato, or stir-fried the huge, clustered white flowers that taste a little like apple.

However, in the opinion of Tom Gillan, longtime owner of the Native Nursery in Golden, there are some native berries you'd have to be starving to eat. Gillan, who has "traveled many Rocky Mountain miles," is not a fan of white-stemmed gooseberry pie. "The Europeans think gooseberry pie is a gourmet treat, but the piece I had was tart enough to bring tears to my eyes." About the showy-flowering thimbleberry, he comments, "Its botanical name is *Rubus deliciosus,* but the fruit is sometimes bitter enough to make you gag."

He recalls an Indian recipe that grinds sour wild berries into a semibitter pemmican, or else gruel, and stirs in mullein, Gamble's acorns, or yucca seed. That sounds a little dry, but chokecherry syrup—poured over rice cakes by the campfire or vanilla ice cream by the TV—now there's a real treat. "To make chokecherry or boysenberry pancake syrup," he explains, "you use a standard jelly recipe but only put in half the pectin." To harvest piñon nuts ($18 a pound in health food stores), Gillan puts a blanket or sheet under a tree loaded with pinecones, and shakes the tree. "You get about a 50/50 mix of seeds and cones, then you put the cones next to a fire or in the bright sun for an afternoon. You can roast the nuts or eat them raw if they're very fresh. They grow all over the southern part of Colorado and throughout New Mexico, high-altitude Utah, Nevada, and Arizona."

Gillan suspects silver buffaloberries might make as decent a wine as chokecherries and elderberries do, but he hasn't tried them yet. The most unusual element of Gillan's virtual, edible landscape is a species known as "devil's claw," with a seedpod that tastes like coconut. "Its forked pod is often used in southwestern flower arrangements," he explains. But what he gets most excited about eating are the unopened buds of the daylily. "Dip them in batter and deep-fry them like onion rings." he suggests. "You'll love them."

He shares a little berry-bush wisdom as I leave his nursery. "Don't plant berries near your patio, because they'll make a mess. Plant them on the peripheries of your yard."

Edible landscaping can provide many hours of weird eating, if that's what you're after. And if the exotic fruits and seeds of your labors disappear before you harvest them, well, nobody's going to starve—especially the wrens, magpies, and robins that ate them.

THE FESTIVAL OF SPEARS
· ASPARAGUS—MORE THAN JUST A PRETTY FERN ·

WHEN I WAS A KID, "exparaguts" was another one of those creepy vegetables from hell. The spears were visually impressive, because they looked like rocket ships, but I refused to consider them food. Maybe that's because I hadn't yet tasted spears that I'd grown myself and eaten real-time in the garden, right off the stalk—or steamed just slightly and served with olive oil and lemon juice.

In the last few years, I've planted more than a hundred crowns in the community garden, and this spring dozens of spears will launch our first annual neighborhood asparagus festival. If pampered with lots of compost, well-rotted manure, and peat moss, each plant will contribute half a pound of produce to the festival of spears.

Here are a few good reasons western gardeners should grow asparagus:

- It grows well in alkaline soils, which we have.
- It can stay in the same bed for up to thirty years
  (sometimes I wish I could).
- It's fairly expensive in supermarkets most of the year.
- It looks like rocket ships.

The only real downside to growing asparagus is the waiting period. Bringing an asparagus bed into peak productivity takes about as long as a mission to Mars. After preparing a loose, well-fertilized bed, you plant crowns about a foot apart, in rows about 3 to 4 feet apart. Then you wait. The first year, you get lots of ferns but just a few spindly spears, about the thickness of straws. Second year, the rule of thumb is finger-sized stalks, which you can harvest for a few weeks if you fertilize the bed after harvesting and promise to keep the weeds from taking over. But it's not until the third and fourth years that you begin to get gourmet spaceships about the diameter of magic markers.

In early spring, you need to be on asparagus alert, because the garden centers begin to get their crown supplies in, and supplies are limited. It's possible to grow asparagus from seed, but it's a lot of work to get the seeds to germinate. Start your bed from crowns, even if they do look like dried, gray tarantulas. You'll want to be an early customer at the garden center so you can select the fleshiest, most vigorous-looking crowns to transplant into your bed. You could mail order your own crowns, but I suggest selecting them yourself at the greenhouses so you can leave the losers behind.

New varieties like 'Jersey Giant', 'Jersey Prince', and 'Jersey Knight' are good yielders, and old reliable varieties like 'Waltham' and 'Mary Washington' have great disease resistance. But for a little more flavor, try a French variety called 'Larac'. If you can't plant the tarantulas right away, sprinkle them with a little water and cover them with sphagnum moss, or put them in a paper bag in the produce compartment of your refrigerator, for up to ten or twelve days.

Asparagus begins its spring wake-up when the soil is 50 degrees or so. Watch for the early dandelion blossoms or the swelling of cottonwood buds, then plant your asparagus along the north edge of the garden, where it won't shade other crops. Remember, a loose, rich bed is critical for several reasons: Asparagus can't tolerate waterlogged roots, and the roots can go as deep as ten feet if there's moisture that far down. So make it loose, and keep it that way, by never walking on the bed. Plant your tarantula crowns about 5 inches deep on individual mounds, spreading out the "legs" so they'll grow in all directions.

Mulch both before and after emergence of the spears. In early spring, mulch with leaves, grass clippings, or straw (without weed seeds) to keep the soil cool—so spears don't come up too soon in our erratic weather. Pull the mulch away when freezes seem to be over, but remulch between plants as spears emerge, to discourage weeds and hold in the moisture. Soak the bed deeply at least once a week throughout the summer.

Experts disagree on some of the fine points of growing asparagus. Some swear that harvesting spindly spears from two-year-old plants will decrease the vigor of the plants, but others insist it will actually stimulate further growth. Some counsel to cut spears below soil surface, others argue it may cause root rot.

Here's my advice: Sidestep the dueling green thumbs and find out what works best for you, by direct observation. In your own garden, you're the boss! What you really need to know is how the plants like to grow, and who eats them, besides us. Then you can devise your own strategies to reach that target annual yield of half a pound per plant. Here's the scoop on the physiology of asparagus: The spears are actually trying to be ferny foliage. If you don't harvest when the rockets are between 6 and 10 inches tall, ferns will begin to emerge and the stalks will become coarse and stringy.

Beware of asparagus beetles (one-fourth inch long, metallic blue-black bodies with red and white markings), whose job is to eat their fill of foliage and turn it brown. And brown foliage means fewer spears because of decreased root mass.

To keep your plants relatively free of asparagus beetles, stick your face into the ferns as often as possible. These fern-eating lowlifers don't seem to like being observed and threatened with handpicking. Or is it just *my* face they don't like? I'll tell you what—if you have beetle problems, give me a call and I'll send photographs of my face, to mount on garden stakes. Hmmm, maybe there's a business opportunity there....

How to Grow Strawberry Rhubarb Pie
• PLANNING A MEAL SIX MONTHS AHEAD •

IT'S A GOOD IDEA to plan meals ahead, right? And if you're six or seven months ahead, well, so much the better. Your dinner may not be in the oven, but at least it's in the *ground*. I call it strategic gardening—planning what crops you'll grow based on what recipes you'll use when cooking them.

Last year I knew I wanted homemade salsa, so I grew the cilantro, tomatoes, onions, garlic, and peppers for enough salsa to feed a roomful of hungry Broncos fans on the first day of the season in late August. It was a superbowl of salsa: I knew that by what wasn't left.

The other day I stood outside a barren-looking winter garden, telling a neighbor, "What you're looking at is a plot of strawberry rhubarb pie. You have to kind of squint a little, but it's a pie, all right," I said, nodding my head. I added, "If you're lucky, you'll get a piece of it."

"I just hope you don't burn the crust," she said.

All that separated us from that pie à la mode was a good effort from the team—the soil, the strawberry bed, the hedge of rhubarb around the strawberry bed, and me. I wasn't worried, since strawberries and rhubarb are both excellent crops in western gardens. They'll tolerate both frozen winters and hot summers, if you choose the right varieties, and if you treat them like dessert—the royalty of the garden. (Come to think of it, both species do have "crowns.")

The truth is, the life of a commercial strawberry is far less than regal. According to the U.S. Food and Drug Administration, strawberries rank No. 1 in pesticide residue among commonly eaten fruits and vegetables. Methyl bromide is routinely applied to strawberry fields, exposing both field-workers and consumers to a toxic chemical. Picking and shipping is also stressful if you're a berry—a race against time. Because strawberries are so perishable, they're packed and rushed to cooling facilities within thirty minutes of picking. Then hours later, they're on the road in energy-intensive refrigerated trucks, sometimes traveling thousands of miles from Mexico, Florida, California, or Oregon to the supermarket.

My own preference is a travel distance of 3 feet—from the plant to my mouth as I harvest them. I like fresh strawberries so much that I planted them in my small front yard instead of grass. Since they're in the shade of a few cottonwood trees, they don't get the eight hours of full sunlight they need to be heavy producers, but then they don't have to be mowed, either. The yard is an ivy-like mat that turns reddish orange in the fall. I feed these plants composted poultry manure shoveled in around each plant. I am willing to share the harvest with neighborhood kids, but I frustrate local squirrels by spreading reusable nylon netting over the beds.

We also planted several hundred plants in the vegetable garden, where sun and soil conditions are ideal. In late March, we dug in four bushels of compost per 1,000 square feet of bed before planting the bare-root strawberries (get them at garden stores for about ten cents apiece). We also added some bonemeal for healthy roots. A happy, well-fertilized plant can produce up to a quart of berries during the first fruiting year, but production usually declines each year, so I usually dig up a bed after three or four years.

I use the ever-bearing varieties because they tend to be hardier, and if a late spring frost kills the first blossoms, we'll still get a late summer or fall crop. 'Ogallala' and 'Fort Laramie' are good varieties for western gardens, as well as the new "day neutral" varieties 'Tribute', 'Tristar', and 'Fern'. I space the plants in a matted row system 2 feet apart in rows that are 4 feet apart, then let the runners fill in the rows. The first year, I pick the blossoms off to let the plants become more vigorous. Each fall, I cover the plants with a 2- or 3-inch straw or pine needle mulch, after daytime temperatures dip to freezing (around December 1 at mile-high elevations).

Strawberries don't have many enemies in the arid West, but vigilance is necessary to keep slugs from carving big, blissful holes in the berries. I've used diatomaceous earth, beer traps, wood scrap traps, wood ashes, and handpicking to control slugs, but I do resort to synthetic slug bait occasionally, keeping it away from animals. When discoloration appears in plants, I quickly remove them to avoid spreading yellows or red stele disease to the rest of the plants.

What about the other main ingredient of the pie, rhubarb? It too is an easily grown crop that's winter hardy and drought resistant. A well-fertilized plant can remain productive in one place for up to fifteen years. I successfully started the 'Victoria' variety from seed last year, but a more convenient way is to buy potted roots at garden stores in the spring. A word of caution—unless you get them (and strawberry roots) in April, supplies will run out, and you'll either have to wait until next spring or mail order them.

Rhubarb likes to grow in fertile, well-drained soils. Space rhubarb plants about 3 feet apart to ensure good production. As with strawberries, remove flower stalks and don't harvest the first year. After the plant is established in the second or third year, rhubarb can be coaxed into early production by covering the plants with clear plastic in the early spring, then cutting holes as the crown starts to grow. Harvest the stalks (not the mildly poisonous leaves) by breaking them off at soil level like celery stalks. The stalks will keep well in plastic bags in the refrigerator for up to three weeks, and can also be canned or frozen.

After four or five years of good growth, rhubarb roots can be divided to maintain vitality and get some new plants. Wait until early spring growth indicates good dividing points, then use a shovel to dig up clumps and replant them. You can grow either red- or green-stalked varieties. I prefer the green stalks for pie because they are more tart, offsetting the sweetness of strawberries. Can't you taste that pie already?

PLANTS THAT LIKE EACH OTHER
· COMPANIONS IN THE GROUND AND ON THE PLATE ·

WHEN TWO PEOPLE like to be around each other, we sometimes refer to it as "good chemistry." We know there's more to it than chemicals, but we're not willing to call it "magic." It's the same with plants. Some species seem to thrive in each other's company—gardeners call them "good companions"—but we don't have all the information about why this is so. We have observed that they suffer fewer pest attacks, grow more vigorously, and yield better. Sometimes they even taste better when they're in good company. The question is, how can companion planting be used so that music—not noise—comes out of our gardens?

While the hard science of companion planting will never be totally complete, we do have a long history of experience and observation to draw on. Gardeners have been experimenting with companion planting since at least 300 B.C., when Theophrastus started recording his observations in a journal. In the 1970s, ecologists Peter Atsatt and Dennis O'Dowd compiled data, performed experimentation, and began referring to "plant defense guilds" in which physical, chemical, and biological mechanisms combine to create a resilient plant community. They explained that interdependence among neighboring species extends far beyond garden borders, and takes place above and below the soil. The diversity in a resilient system jams insects' senses of smell, sight, and touch, reducing pest infestations. One study found that when cucumbers are planted in "monocultures" (without any diversity), they attract ten to thirty times more disease-carrying striped cucumber beetles than cucumber plots interplanted with good companions such as dill. Dill can be a good companion for cucumbers from the seedling flat to the pickle jar because it repels aphids and spider mites directly and attracts beneficial insects such as parasitic wasps and lacewings that control pests like the cucumber beetle. The herb also seems to stimulate a better flavor in cucumbers as the two crops mature.

Certainly, chemistry explains some of the mutual admiration among plant species. It's well documented that when certain plants are being attacked, they send out chemical "alerts" that stimulate other plants to increase the natural toxicity in their leaves. The fact is, garden plants have a vested interest in the health of their neighbors. They're all in it together, literally. Sometimes, just normal concentrations of toxins serve as pest deterrents. Solanine, a compound found in the leaves of tomato plants, helps keep cabbage loopers off neighboring broccoli and other cole crops, making tomatoes and broccoli good companions. In turn, the sulfur compounds in onions seem to prevent certain pests from attacking tomatoes, and the volatile compounds in mint seem to provide some protection for both tomatoes and cabbage. In addition to repelling the bad bugs, mint attracts and harbors many of the beneficial insects, because the good bugs like to eat mint-blossom nectar and pollen for dessert, after a hearty entrée of the vegetarian bugs.

Nasturtium is a good addition to a diverse garden for many reasons. It performs well as a "trap crop," attracting aphids that would otherwise prey on innocent garden crops. It also provides brightly colored blossoms (especially in nutrient-poor soil) that attract beneficial insects as well as beneficial gardeners, who would rather work in a colorful garden. (Keep the gardener at work and you increase the chances that he or she will finally do something right.)

There are other reasons why plants have preferred neighbors. Crops that get along well don't compete for nutrients and water. Deep-rooted squash, for example, is a good companion for shallow-rooted corn, and appreciates the late-summer shade the corn provides. Squash also likes to grow next to onions, which help keep squash bugs' appetites under control. In general, heavy feeders like cabbage crops grow well with light feeders like garlic and beans. In fact, many garden crops like to grow with beans and peas, because industrious colonies of bacteria that live on their roots pull nitrogen right out of the air (magic!) and share it with neighbors.

When you think about it, many beneficial plant relationships continue after harvest: Dill and cucumbers, basil and tomatoes, lettuce and radishes, and beans and savory often appear together in the skillet, salad bowl, or dinner plate. However, even if you force cabbage and strawberries to grow together, they throw taste tantrums if combined in a recipe. Tomatoes and corn may find common ground in succotash, but would rather not share common ground in the garden. Dill and carrots are openly antagonistic, and onions and beans are not great friends, either.

For the upcoming garden season, I'm on the lookout for potato allies to help me discourage the Colorado potato beetle. I have an established patch of horseradish, and I intend to test its reputation, as well as that of marigolds and possibly tansy, although the latter can spread quickly. I may try planting tansy in a bottomless nursery container, to contain it. This year, I'll also start several herbs from seed in pots and disburse them throughout the garden. Mint, fennel, catnip, southernwood, and borage can all find useful niches, and I'll let the wild chamomile keep its usual place on the edges of pathways. I'll also plan to interplant fragrant annuals such as nicotiana and petunias, and nitrogen-fixers like lupines and volunteer clover. I think of it as diversity by design that supplies pest control, fertility, and beauty all at the same time.

Overall, these strategies may help me achieve a primary goal: guiltless gardening. Rather than letting the crops be sitting ducks for bugs and hungry mammals, I'll feel like a better companion myself if I provide some protection. Here are a few more ideas for where to plant what:

Plant	Good Companions	Bad Companions
carrots	bush beans, pole beans, lettuce, onion, peas, radish, tomato, sage	dill
summer squash	beans, corn, mint, nasturtium, radish	potato
peas	carrot, corn, cucumber, eggplant, lettuce, radish, spinach, tomato	onions, garlic
peppers	basil, carrot, lovage, marjoram, onion, oregano	fennel, kohlrabi

GARDEN PESTS I HAVE KNOWN
· BRONTOSAURUSES IN THE GARDEN ·

NOBODY SAYS YOU HAVE TO be a gardener. If you decide *not* to be, as quickly as possible, you may still avoid gruesome encounters with leaf-sucking, orange-egged aliens that are out there right now, as you read—devouring crops you carefully nurtured from seed. These guerrilla encounters can be hard-fought, vengeful battles, and as you may already know, the aliens are well equipped. They leave behind half-eaten strawberries, wilted potato vines, and salads that never were, just to let you *know* they're winning. Sure, insects and other garden pests have to make a living, but why don't they do it on some other planet?

One of the most voracious pests I have known is the tomato hornworm, who eats more foliage, proportionally, than a brontosaurus. The hornworm is 3 to 4 inches long, with a black horn projecting from one of the last abdominal segments. Handpicking works if you watch every day for sheared leaves, greenish-yellow eggs on the underside of leaves, and greenish-black droppings about the size the tomatoes would have been. (Actually more like radish seeds, but still, that's a lot of chlorophyll.) Hornworms can also be controlled by beneficial insects like ladybugs, green lacewings, and *Trichogramma* wasps, and by a biological spray called *Bacillus thuringiensis* (*Bt*), variety Berliner if possible. Bt causes radical, lethal stomachaches in caterpillars. The good thing about Bt is it kills the caterpillars but does not kill other insects, allowing the beneficial bugs to survive and support your cause. (Many pesticides kill both the pests and the beneficials, sometimes resulting in more pests than you had before.)

The *Tyrannosaurus rex* of the garden, the ladybug, is there to help. Bless her heart, somebody's takin' care of business. Like other carnivores, she loves meat and "potatoes"—the nectar of small blossoms that typically surround a garden. So don't get too antiseptic about weed control, or you may lose a great ally to greener pastures. You can mail order ladybugs or get them at your local nursery, but don't set them loose in the heat of the day, or they may go aphid hunting on someone else's property. Water your garden in the early evening and set them loose then, while you play Mozart or Nat King Cole. (Okay, you can skip the music.) The bottom line is, each carnivorous ladybug can put away fifty aphids a day, as well as pests such as the larvae of the Colorado potato beetle.

Colorado potato beetles look like they're wearing gaudy, striped sports jackets, a fashion statement that doesn't work for me. Just because they dress up doesn't mean they can have my potato leaves.

They are controllable in a small garden by handpicking, but in a large garden, you'll want to use *Bt*—variety 'San Diego' tenebrionis if possible. Spray at first sign of infestation to control young larvae. Two early applications are recommended to provide adequate coverage.

Now, what about the slugs? How can a person forget fond memories like crouching in the garden in a raincoat, with a flashlight in one hand while the other hand picked slugs off defoliated leaves? The best part is tossing the slimy, green-blooded blobs into a jarful of gasoline as you mutter, "Fifty fewer aliens." However, that satisfaction is short-lived, because the next morning you discover that reinforcements continued the assault after you went to bed. Two whole rows of pea seedlings, clear-cut. State of the art slug control has advanced in the last ten years to include nontoxic approaches like copper barrier tape that carries a minute electrical charge that slugs hate. A band of this tape on raised bed structures or boards might prevent the unlawful entry of these marauding, nocturnal thieves. There are other good products out there for slug control, such as Sluggo, Slug Saloon, and Slug Stop. You either zap them with iron phosphate, get them fatally drunk, or gross them out with a barrier of coconut oil soap. Diatomaceous earth, the sharp-shelled remains of tiny sea creatures, can also be a great barrier, piercing slugs' skin so they can slither no more.

Many pests attack weak plants, but slugs don't seem to follow that etiquette. Your garden soil can be rich and full of organic matter and your crops radiantly healthy, but slugs will slither up the stems to howl at the moon while they feast. Try laying small boards near infestations. You'll find a coven of slugs under the boards in the middle of the day, cowering from the sun. Good luck—you may need it.

Mega-pests like deer may be closer to humans genetically than bugs are, but the catastrophic damage they can do to a fruit tree or row of greens has cast them as lead villains in the nightmares of many a victimized gardener. While neighbors are remarking how cute Bambi is, grazing so sweetly as she tiptoes toward the community garden, you're reaching for a slingshot. After deer have eradicated ten hours of work in three and a half minutes, they're not that cute anymore, and a few sharp stings in the flank may help define exactly where the buck stops, so to speak. Certain odor-carrying products like Deer Off, Not Tonight Deer! and dangling Irish Spring soap bars are fairly effective in spoiling their gourmet appetites, at least for awhile.

"I love the deer as well as the roses," writes Diane Ackerman, "so I decided to use smell as a weapon, and sprinkled a mixture of tobacco and naptha around the rosebushes. It worked, but it made the air raunchy and caustic. Unless you crave the smell of baseball players at winter camp, their mouths full of chewing mess, their pockets full of mothballs. This year I have another plan: lavender. Deer hate its strong nose-scrubbing smell."

Used CDs and strips of reflective metal—wider than tinsel—hung from a fruit tree or garden fence will also keep deer away for a few nights, but really, the only sure preventative is a heavy-duty game fence, seven feet tall. According to certain tall tales I've been told, even that strategy is futile. "I've seen deer jump a fence 10 feet tall," one visitor to my garden told me, shaking his head.

But back to the bugs, for one last suggestion. Let's say you've tried all the tricks mentioned above and many more, and the pests are still winning. Maybe it's time to pick up David Gordon's *Eat-A-Bug Cookbook*, because if you can't beat 'em, eat 'em. Fried Green Tomato Hornworms are one of his favorite recipes: "In a large skillet or wok, lightly fry the hornworms, about 4 minutes, and remove with a slotted spoon.... Garnish the paired hornworms with a single basil leaf...." That is, if the aliens haven't devoured your basil.

HOW (AND WHY) TO GROW GOURMET SALAD
· COLORFUL WEEDS AND OTHER DELIGHTS ·

AT FIRST IT LOOKS LIKE the waitress has brought you a colorful bowlful of weeds, but after she grates some pepper onto the salad and you sample it, your taste buds stand up and cheer. "This isn't the Pizza Hut salad bar anymore, Toto," they exclaim. Of course, salads that feature endive, escarole, baby lettuce, arugula, radicchio, watercress, and other slightly unfamiliar species have been on French and Italian tables for hundreds of years, but in America, they've only recently become "gourmet."

The bottom line is, when your grocery or health food store offers this salad mix fresh, it'll cost you at least six dollars a pound. What you're paying for is the extra care that goes into growing, picking, and distributing the diverse crop. Instead of just one or two varieties, the gourmet salad grower has to manage a cross-section of greens all at once. And instead of harvesting mature heads of lettuce and loose-leaf crops, he has to pick and wash tender, 2- to 3-inch leaves to bring them to market. If your grocery bills, appetite, and checking account are constantly at odds like mine, why not experiment with growing these greens yourself? You can start right now, by looking through a few well-chosen catalogs, and by exploring the Internet with keywords like "salad" and "garden seed companies."

Although I've grown most of these greens individually, this spring I'm going to orchestrate the planting so I can serve Provençal salad in May or June at the latest. And I suppose I'll have to acquire one of those pepper mills that look like huge chess pieces, a droopy chef's hat, and a few key French phrases like "bon appetit!" Maybe I'll skip the hat.

The goal is a variety of flavors, colors, and textures, and a lot of the art is in seed selection. You want colors that range from the pale green of inner Bibb leaves to the dark green of sorrel, from the reddish green of red leaf lettuce to the dark purple of radicchio. And you want round leaves, serrated leaves, and feathery leaves. Rather than buying so-called mesclun seed mixes, I'm going to customize my selection to include greens that grow well in Colorado's soils and climate. And I'm going to audition various heirloom seeds because of their many advantages. For example, they've been preserved through the years because of superior taste and hardiness; and, because they are not hybridized, they will produce the same characteristics in next year's garden if you decide to save them yourself.

Here's the cast:

Main Characters	Supporting Cast
'Mignonette' (butterhead) (a variety of Bibb lettuce)	arugula, chervil, endive, radicchio, purslane
'Red Salad Bowl' (bolt-resistant, red oakleaf lettuce)	mustard, sorrel, mizuna
'Paris White Cos' (romaine lettuce)	watercress

I may also include early spring dandelion leaves, colorful Johnny jump-up flower petals, thinly sliced carrots and Daikon radishes planted last fall and mulched under a blanket of leaves, and piñon nuts harvested in the nearby foothills. Hopefully, the overall result will produce adjectives like "crispy, tender, nutty, crunchy, tangy, and peppery" around the table. But if all I get is unsolicited comments like "just fancy weeds," I won't hang up my garden tools.

It's the *variety* of these greens that makes both the growing and the eating fun. The good news is that despite the exotic-sounding names, shapes, and colors, these greens are really very easy to grow. The ideal soil is well drained with a lot of organic matter—compost and well-rotted manure are perfect fertilizers in a bed that's been loosened to a depth of two shovel blades. The bed is ready for planting when the soil temperature is between 32 and 40 degrees, with no frost or frozen clumps left in it. Look around your garden for the emergence of early weeds in unprotected areas, then sow your first round of seeds. Remember to keep planting every few weeks to assure a continuous supply.

In general, planting two or three weeks before the last average frost date will get the greens going for salad by late May. Last year, I planted greens and radishes under a 1½-foot-tall clear polyethylene tent on my birthday in late February. I used a frame made out of PVC pipe bent into arches, inserted into slightly larger receiving pipe. The seeds germinated and grew slowly, but the tent (the French call them *cloches*) kept getting battered and buried under spring snows. This spring I'll wait until the third week in March to sow the seeds outside, but I'll start some Bibb and romaine plants about a month earlier, indoors.

Greens like to be kept cool and moist, a challenge in many areas of Colorado. Temperatures fluctuate wildly here, and rain is often a distant memory. If the greens get hot and dry, they'll "bolt," or go to seed. Fortunately, a spongy, organic soil can hold moisture for days, and hot summer sun can be tempered with an overhead lattice or shade cloth in midsummer. Try planting by the bed rather than the row, so the plants can shade each other and keep the soil and roots cool. Just scatter the seed on a moist bed and rake lightly, making sure your seeds are well mixed so your crop ends up looking "tossed" like it will in the salad bowl. The crop diversity will help keep leaf eaters and diseases like the virus "yellows" at bay. (Now, what about the deer?)

Young greens appreciate a soil rich in phosphorus for root growth, while more mature plants want nitrogen for leaf growth. I use a liquid fertilizer made from kelp for extra phosphorus for the seedlings, and composted poultry manure, composted kitchen scraps, or fish emulsion for extra nitrogen as the plants mature.

When you harvest your first greens with a pair of garden scissors, cut the plants an inch or so above the crowns, but pull up overcrowded plants so each plant is at least two inches from the next. The best time to harvest greens is early in the morning when the sugar content is highest and before the plants wilt in western, radiant sun. But a late afternoon watering will rejuvenate them for picking, washing, and chilling, right before dinner!

PLANTING THE WINTER GARDEN
· ARE WE CRAFTY OR CRAZY? ·

ONE OF THE GARDENER'S primary rules of thumb—preferably green, of course—is that next year's garden will be the best ever. This doesn't mean your garden always does get better year after year, but just that most gardeners tend to put their money on miracles. Surely next year's garden will be blessed with an abundance of beneficial insects that have heard about your garden and have come from miles around to protect it. Blessed with steady spring rains and mild summer days, with polite weeds that would never think of intruding where your crops are growing, and with hailstones that turn into butterflies before shredding your Swiss chard.

You don't see it happening? Okay, so let's move to a more down-to-earth rule of thumb: Keep Planting. Bury the evidence of the failed crops and plant new ones—with a little luck and a few polite weeds, surely they'll do better. This second rule applies throughout the gardening season, even in September, when most gardeners in the neighborhood are beginning to glean the last tomatoes from tired, discolored vines. When these short-timers have drifted away to watch a preseason football game, you'll still be out in golden fall sun, planting your winter/spring crops.

Of course, you've always picked up a few spring-blooming bulbs to plant in the fall—daffodils, crocuses, and tulips. But this year, you're planting a cross-section of greens, root crops, and seeds that will lie dormant until just the right moment in the spring. There are definite advantages in off-season growing. For one thing, there are fewer insect and weed pests after a frost. As fall comes in, the sun is less like a blast furnace and the winds less like a blow dryer, so the crops that prefer cooler weather can get back to business.

September is when I plant garlic seed, cold-hardy cover crops like winter rye, and a palette of crops that are proven winter winners. These "green light" crops can sometimes grow all winter, unlike warm-weather crops for which frost is a definite "red light." The green light palette includes green onions, mache, spinach, radish, kale, mustard, carrots, parsley, and a few hardy varieties of lettuce. These are crops I can harvest in the early winter months and sometimes even into spring. Last winter, for example, twenty spinach plants hung in there through below-zero temperatures without any mulch, just to prove to me how tough they were. After hugging the ground for any available heat for six months, the spinach took off in March and became a healthy, abundant crop that supplied salad for a gathering of forty.

A cluster of parsley plants also survived the winter, remaining bright green under a mulch of straw. A sweet-tasting, small-leafed salad green called mache (also known as corn salad) remained harvestable all winter in its niche next to (but not *in*) the cold frame. 'Buttercrunch' and 'Black-seeded Simpson' lettuce plants looked pitiful through the winter but took off in spring, like the spinach.

The idea for many of these crops, really, is to plant some of your spring garden half a year early. But you can also harvest a little in the winter, too, especially if you get warm spells. Planted early enough, crops like parsley and carrots will establish deep enough roots before a freeze, and they'll be extra-early crops in April and May.

To bring seedlings along quickly enough to withstand cold weather, you may want to give them some shelter as nights become cooler. Late September is when my garden sometimes starts to look like a garage sale, with used window sashes, inverted dresser drawers, and old suitcases performing their last functions. Look closely in any dumpster or recycling container and you'll begin to see little green-houses everywhere—one-gallon jugs you can cut the bottoms out of, cracked but not broken skylights, whatever.

I like to choose an out-of-the-way chunk of garden, mix carrot and radish seeds together, and sprinkle them on the soil surface. ('Thumbelina', a small, round carrot has proven hardiness, and Daikon, 'Spring Song', and 'Rebel' are even more vigorous than the average radish.) Then I rake very lightly, cover with a thin layer of dried grass clippings or straw (make sure there are no weed seeds in it, though), and water the seeds in. The thin mulch helps the seedbed stay moist while seeds are germinating.

The radishes may well become an edible crop by the end of October, and their germination and growth will stimulate the comparatively slow progress of the carrots. By the time cold weather sets in, the carrots will have made some good growth and be ready to be mulched for the winter. The ground is a perfect root cellar for the carrots if you provide a deep enough cover of straw, evergreen boughs, or other mulch that's easily scraped aside even in snow. But the blanket needs to be deep enough to prevent freezing and thawing, or you'll go out to harvest carrots and…Voilà! Carrot custard!

Another crop to plant in the fall is snow peas, which got their name because they sometimes pop up in early spring, right through the snow. Varieties like 'Extra Early Alaska' and 'Dwarf Grey Sugar' peas are good bets for an early start, but make sure the soil you plant them in is loose and well drained so the seeds don't get too soggy in the spring.

As Yogi Berra phrases it, "You can observe a lot just by watching." Next spring, take a look at which plants reseed themselves from last season, and you'll have a better idea what to intentionally plant in September. This year, I'm encouraging parsley, arugula, sorrel, and Chinese radish seeds to find soft soil around the parent plant. In the spring, I'll transplant some of them into new beds. I'm also finding places for a short row of leftover potatoes, because I noticed that some "undugs" volunteered this spring and made a good yield.

The important rule of thumb, Keep Planting, becomes a challenge when cold weather sets in, but it's worth a try. If you buy seeds in bulk quantities, you haven't lost much if your experiment fails. Just bury the evidence, and try again next fall!

MAKING YOUR GARDEN "INTERNATIONAL SOIL"
· NUTRIENTS FROM ALL OVER THE WORLD ·

THINK ABOUT IT—you could turn your vegetable and flower gardens into celebrations of world culture, simply by composting coffee grounds from Colombia, nutshells from the Middle East, molding egg roll skins from China, phyllo dough from Greece, banana peels from Costa Rica, and so on. You'll create a cross-section of minerals that can make your plants hardy and resistant to disease. (Maybe you'll earn the right to fly little international flags on the garden fence.) Of course, you'll give your soil a Colorado signature by using lots of leaves, grass clippings, seedless weeds, and local sources of manure in your compost pile, too. Overall, your crops are what they eat. Your plots will reflect what's gone into your soil, so make sure the "junk food" you feed it is healthy junk food.

Maybe look at composting as a sort of scavenger hunt. Picture this: You're cruising the alleyways and curbsides of old Denver on your way home from work, looking for free bags of leaves that will form the foundation of a new compost pile. Cottonwood and aspen leaves are waxy and slow to decompose, as well as being alkaline, so you don't get that excited when you see their trunks in the yards. But suddenly, in one mountain of bagged rakings from a large yard in Washington Park, you inherit ten light, fluffy bags of silver maple leaves. You feel like taping a thank-you note on the raker's dumpster.

Closer to home, you stop at the neighborhood barbershop, and then the produce section of the supermarket, to load containers of hair clippings and vegetable scraps into your truck. Garden manure is on sale at the supermarket, so you decide to spend a few bucks to add some good decomposers to the mix, compliments of the steer and chickens. All these ingredients will form the layers of a 4 x 4-foot compost pile you'll construct in the shade of a big cottonwood tree in your backyard. Mixed in with weeds pulled before they went to seed, grass clippings from a nearby park, shredded paper from work (white, not colored because of the chemicals in colored paper), and your own stockpiled kitchen wastes, the ingredients will ultimately result in compost that smells like a forest floor and looks almost good enough to eat.

There are many, many recipes for perfect compost, because really just about anything will work if you give it time. When it comes to compost, THERE'S NO WAY TO BLOW IT! You don't even have to turn the pile if you don't want to, although it will speed up the process and help prevent odors from oxygen-starved clumps. You also don't have to mix in the precisely correct ratio of "browns" (carbon) to "greens" (nitrogen), but if you do, the pile will just about cook itself.

Sure, there are occasional population explosions of fruit flies, but you can dampen their enthusiasm by not adding citrus peels to the compost, by covering each addition of scraps with soil or carbonaceous materials like leaves or shredded paper, and by keeping the pile turned so high temperatures cook the flies' eggs. Making sure the pile is about as moist as a damp sponge is always a good strategy, too, but that consistency will probably occur naturally, after rain. To make sure, give it a soaking every now and again when you water the volunteer squash and tomato plants that sprang up at the edges of last summer's pile.

If you're big on neatness, you can construct a compost container that enables you to physically move the pile through the decomposition process. Some people build holding units out of used shipping pallets, snow fence, chicken wire, or concrete blocks on their sides—so air can circulate into the pile. They shovel the contents of a month-old pile into an adjacent stall, then a few weeks later, they add additional air by moving that middle pile into a "finishing" pile. The compost is ready when it turns brownish-black, contains an earthworm or two, and no longer harbors recognizable bits of avocado skins or cabbage hearts.

A high population of "roll-up bugs" (actually tiny crustaceans) may indicate a slow pathway to decomposition. Roll-ups won't harm the process, but they may become hungry pests if they stow away in the compost and become incorporated into the soil. Ants and earwigs are also signals of a slower, colder compost pile, but they can be evicted by adding a nitrogen source like blood meal, manure, alfalfa meal, or shellfish shells to heat up the pile.

The bottom line is this: compost delivers. Legions of bacteria only one ten-millionth of an inch long glue soil particles together and make nutrients readily available. An incredible 400 to 800 feet of invisible, fibrous fungal threads in every teaspoon of fertile soil weave it together like a living tapestry, enabling it to hold water like a sponge. Compost aerates the soil, buffers the pH, supplies acids that dissolve minerals in the topsoil and subsoil, and even helps prevent disease and pest infestations. Because plants grown in compost-enhanced soil have a well-rounded, less pampered diet, they are more resistant to disease. And because compost contains organisms that secrete antibiotics, the plants are less likely to encounter disease to begin with.

Go international. Give your soil something good to eat.

THE SNACK FOOD GARDEN
· GUILT-FREE INDULGENCE ·

IF ANYONE DESERVES a higher intake of crunchy, delicious snacks, it's gardeners. (And please, please, tell someone to bring us lemonade!) It would be ideal to grow more snacks that can be eaten right in the garden, like the raspberries, asparagus spears, and snap peas that never make it to the kitchen.

And yes, in a perfect world, wouldn't it be great to be able to grow candy bars, right on the vine? But of course cocoa beans don't grow in Colorado, and neither do peanuts, really, although I've tried. After three years of hopeful field testing, I've decided to import my peanut supply from Texas, via the health food store—except for one experimental row, to amaze and confuse the neighborhood kids. Peanuts just don't like our rabbits, low humidity, cool nights, and alkaline soils.

Still, as I look out at a foot of wet March snow that blankets my garden, and begin to compile my wish list for this year, I keep drifting toward snacks. Snacks are a basic food group, in my mind—finger food, for people who use their hands.

Last summer at the CSU experimental fields where acres of globe artichokes were growing, I sampled the perfect candidate for a snack food garden: Sungold cherry tomatoes. Get some before the seed houses sell out, because this variety reaches back and rings your taste buds.

Then there's popcorn, of course—an old favorite, since about 3600 B.C. For starters, avoid any varieties that have the words "old maid" or "popless" in them. Experts tell us that popcorn defaults to old maidhood when it fails to reach full maturity in a given season. According to University of Nebraska horticulturists, when popcorn does reach full maturity, "heating the kernel converts the moisture inside to steam, and turns the kernel inside out...." Now you know the physics of it. A few varieties, like 'Tom Thumb', available from Johnny's Selected Seeds, mature in 85 days, but most varieties will need at least 110 days to mature.

The Nebraska fact sheet warns, "Any serious stress like water deficiency can greatly reduce yields and the quality of popcorn." I say, treat your snacks-to-be with respect. Don't let the corn dry down, and yet don't overwater either. Last summer I soaked a stand of sweet corn after it grew about a foot in a week, and then along came an unexpected afternoon windy downpour that blew the corn over. The next morning, I stood the stalks back up, packing muddy soil around the roots again. Despite that setback, I harvested my best corn ever, staying one step ahead of a raccoon family that had the first few ears.

Though popcorn and sweet corn are in the same family, they don't get along. The quality of sweet corn is reduced when it's cross-pollinated by popcorn, so keep them separate, like cousins that always argue.

If critters permit, allow popcorn kernels to dry in the field as long as possible. When harvested, the kernels should be hard and the husks completely dry. After harvest, remove the husks and place the ears in mesh bags and hang in a warm, dry, well-ventilated location. Then once or twice a week, shell a few kernels and try popping them. When the test kernels pop reliably and taste better than Orville's, shell and store the crop. If the popcorn is "chewy" or the popped kernels are jagged, it's too wet and needs to continue drying.

In the space where you'll grow corn next year, grow beans this year, because nitrogen-fixing bacteria on the roots of the beans improve soil fertility. The world's most treasured snack bean is edamame, or vegetable soybean. Edamame is a Japanese word for "beans on branches." Also called "sweet bean," this nutty, nutritious legume has been cultivated for over 2,000 years in China.

Plant edamame like bush beans, but expect a longer growing season. When the soil warms to 60 degrees F. (late May, usually), sow seeds 1 inch deep and 2 to 4 inches apart, in rows 2 feet apart. A 2- to 4-inch layer of hay or straw over some compost will retain soil moisture and keep weeds down.

Edamame is sensitive to coolness, so your choice of varieties is important. Sometimes western weather makes liars out of seed distributors. Varieties listed as maturing in 70 to 80 days may take more than 100 days. Among Asian varieties, 'Lucky Lion', 'Sapporo Midori', and 'White Lion' have proven to mature early and produce abundantly, while two American varieties, 'Butterbean' (not to be confused with lima beans) and 'Envy', are also proven winners.

Harvesting edamame at the right time is also critical. Beans reach their maximum sweetness about a month after flowering. When beans fill 85 percent of the bright green pods (similar to snow peas in color), it's time to pick. You can harvest individual beans off the plants or pull the whole plant out of the ground when most of the beans are mature, and then pick the beans later. This method preserves freshness a little longer. One 2-foot-tall plant may yield up to thirty pods, about the right amount to munch on as an appetizer or even the backbone of a meal on the run.

Unlike bush beans, edamame pods are not edible. You just bring a pot of salted water to a boil and boil the beans uncovered for five or six minutes, sprinkle the pods with a coarse salt (Japanese style), and squeeze the beans out of the pods into your mouth. The fuzzy pods make great compost.

Go ahead, venture into the world of snack food gardening. You deserve a break—today, tomorrow, and every day.

THE PEA, AN EARLY AMERICAN TRADITION
· IF PEAS COULD TALK ·

IF PEAS COULD TALK, wouldn't they have some secrets to tell us about the early days of America! Dried peas were onboard when colonial Europeans first crossed the Atlantic, because they were packed with nutrition, easy to store, and had a long shelf life. When these pilgrims landed, some of the cargo became seed. A 1635 list of the supplies a colonist needed for one year included "one bushell of Pease."

The nursery rhyme about "Pease porridge in the pot, nine days old" gives a glimpse of a kettle hanging over an open hearth, with dried peas as the main ingredient, *again*. But Thomas Jefferson liked to eat them fresh, in the new European style. Jefferson grew fifteen different varieties of the English or shelling pea, staggering the plantings so he'd have them fresh from the middle of May to the middle of July.

His *Garden Book* documents the dates each pea variety "came to table," a detail of particular interest since his neighborhood had a yearly competition. The first gardener to get ripe peas hosted a dinner for the contestants, and although Jefferson's Monticello garden had great soil and southern exposure, it was usually his solitary neighbor George Divers who won the contest.

Jefferson's grandson recalled a year his grandfather did have the earliest peas but told his family to "say nothing about it, it will be more agreeable to our friend to think he never fails." What a guy.

The 1796 book, *American Cookery*, has recipes for seven varieties of peas, but Americans can't really take much credit for a crop that archeologists have found in tombs and ruins of Mediterranean villages from 10,000 years ago.

According to Chinese history, the pea passed emperor Shu Nung's distinctive "laugh test" for edible and medicinal plants, some 5,000 years ago. This Father of Chinese Agriculture wandered the countryside with an unwilling legion of dogs and servants, experimentally feeding plants first to a dog, then a servant. If both survived, the Emperor himself would eat the new food. (It makes you pause to wonder how many dogs, servants, and suicide eaters have gone down over the years so you and I can plant our seeds and stir-fry our produce.)

Colonial traditions are still alive in New England, where many gardeners still plant peas on April 19, the anniversary of the battle of Lexington, hoping to have their first peas by the Fourth of July. In Seattle, the traditional date is Washington's birthday, February 22.

Packaged in designer pods like well-behaved quintuplets with matching outfits, peas don't ask much. They don't need much compost or other fertilizer, for example, since their roots host nitrogen-fixing bacteria that pull fertilizer right out of the air. They're tolerant of cooler weather in spring and fall—the very times we like to linger in the garden. And, more than crops like beans or potatoes, peas prefer slightly sweet soil like we have in the West, with a pH of 6.5 or higher.

Peas can be sown directly into the garden as soon as the soil can be worked, or about five weeks before the last expected frost. But they grow best in soil that has warmed to at least 50 degrees F. Experiments have shown that peas may take up to 36 days to germinate in soil below 40 degrees F., 9 days at 50 degrees F., and 7 days at 68 degrees F.

Drainage is the single most important requirement for peas. They respond to liberal applications of compost and a light, fluffy seedbed. Thomas Jefferson and his cronies may well have grown peas in elongated raised beds to ensure good drainage.

To give peas an early boost, soak them in water the day before you'll plant. When the peas are slightly green, they're ready. Sprinkle bonemeal or rock phosphate in shallow furrows, spacing seeds about an inch apart in double rows 6 inches apart. Then space the double rows 18 inches apart. This arrangement offers both mutual support of the vines and adequate root space.

Try sowing a line of carrots between the wider rows when the pea vines are about a foot tall. Peas and carrots are good companions because the peas stimulate carrot germination, help fertilize the root crop, and provide shady relief from the radiant sun of early summer.

After harvesting the peas, the vines can be clipped with shears so the peas' nitrogen-rich roots remain in place to slowly decompose.

Take inventory of the used materials you have around the garage or in back of the house, and see if they lend themselves to the construction of a permanent pea trellis. Standing in the gardens of master growers, you'll find lots of evidence that sooner or later a grower moves beyond the twine, stakes, and chicken wire phase of her gardening career, and into the realm of art. A lot can be done with 2 x 2s lashed into an A-frame, for example. Or try bunny-proof garden fencing about 4 feet tall, nailed to a spare 2 x 4 frame. The classic gardens of half-century gardeners Helen and Scott Nearing used neatly shaped branches for pea supports, but every time I've tried that technique it looks like kindling for a bonfire or miniature barricades in a battlefield (look out for the land mines!).

I've had good luck broadcasting bush-style peas into a bed, fencing the perimeter, and letting the peas support each other. But your soil has to be excellent to provide vigorous vines, and you have to hope the wind leaves your garden alone, or you'll spend a lot of time propping the whole intertwined mass back up.

Now for the important question: What kind of peas will you grow? In today's fast-forward world, edible pod peas have become a favorite. Chinese peas, or snow peas, are the flat-podded peas used in stir-fry. The pod is the important part, since you harvest this crop before the pea even develops. 'Dwarf Grey Sugar' is the most popular variety, but 'Oregon Giant' and 'Oregon Sugar Pod' are good bets, too.

The classic pea, grown at Monticello, is the English pea, or shelling pea. This type of pea is available in many varieties, from the dwarfs that grow less than a foot and a half high—and can sometimes produce a successful crop without support—to the tall varieties like 'Alderman' ('Tall Telephone') and 'Thomas Laxton' that grow from 3 to 5 feet tall. Varieties that are especially well adapted to western conditions are 'Wando' and 'Knight', which produce heavy crops in the heat of early summer or mid-fall.

The third kind of garden pea is the sugar snap, which blends the best qualities of English and snow peas. Like the snow pea, sugar snaps have low-fiber, edible pods, but like the English pea, you also harvest when the peas inside are reaching full maturity. Some varieties like 'Sugar Daddy' and 'Sugar Pop' have soft strings on the pods that eliminate the need for "stringing" the pods before cooking. However, popular varieties like 'Cascadia' and 'Sugar Snap' offer especially high yield, wilt resistance, and sweetness.

If good drainage and soil tilth are provided, disease and insect damage is usually minimal. The yellowing that sometimes occurs is *enation mosaic virus,* spread by aphids. Once contaminated, the vine will slowly weaken, turn yellow, make distorted pods, and die. This virus can be prevented by planting peas early enough to have vigorous growth before warm weather arrives and aphids hatch.

Powdery mildew, recognized by a whitish covering on the leaves, is also most destructive in warm weather, so again, planting early and using short-season varieties are the best defenses.

The trick in harvesting any of the three types of pea is to get them at their peak. This is where faithful on-site sampling comes in handy. Tough pods and overly crunchy peas are a bitter conclusion to the pea season, so be vigilant. The pods on the lower portion of the plant mature earliest—typically about three weeks after the flowers blossom. Pulling the entire plant for the last harvest makes picking easier.

Peas are best eaten, canned, or frozen when fresh, but edible pod peas can be stored for up to two weeks in a refrigerator at 40 degrees F., and shell peas remain prime in the vegetable drawer of a refrigerator for two or three days. Snow peas can be served raw in salads, but blanching them in boiling water for one minute brings out their vivid green color and heightens their crispness. The flavor of fresh garden peas is heightened by spearmint, marjoram, rosemary, and thyme.

Many gardeners forget to sow a heat-tolerant variety of peas in the fall. The trick there is timing. Allow more days to the first killing frost than the listed number of days to maturity because maturity is slow in cool fall days.

Freezing peas is easy, and the payoffs are great—they taste almost as good coming out of the freezer as they do coming out of the garden. Start with fresh green pods, avoiding the tough pods that will get even tougher during freezing. Blanch shell peas for two minutes and pod peas for five minutes in boiling water with a little salt, drain the peas, and store them in airtight, dated resealable plastic freezer bags. The peas will keep for at least a year and can be defrosted and cooked in the same way as fresh peas. Remember, freezing your peas will put them on your table well before the freezerless Thomas Jefferson ever had them!

LEARNING THE LANGUAGE OF POTATOES
· SSHHH–THE POTATOES ARE SLEEPING ·

IN THE COOL DARKNESS of millions of pantries and cellars worldwide, sacks of potatoes are patiently waiting for something to happen. Living, breathing organisms, they remain nutritionally and reproductively viable for three or four months. The potato is the world's fourth-largest crop after wheat, rice, and corn, and is familiar on all continents and native to South America. So familiar and endearing that our kids sometimes put glasses and noses on them before they are diced up and thrown in the skillet.

It wasn't always this way. Brought to Europe by Pizarro around 1570, the white-fleshed potato (*papa*) was an outcast at first. The French believed potatoes caused leprosy, and devout Scottish Presbyterians refused to eat them because they weren't mentioned in the Bible. By the late eighteenth century, though, the potato's assets outweighed its alleged shortcomings, and it was planted all over Europe and, eventually, Asia.

A paragon of adaptability both on the plate and in the field, the spud (named after a digging tool used in medieval days) grows in the high-altitude terraces of Peru—where beds are so steep that farmers sometimes fall out of their fields—as well as the crisp, short seasons of Idaho, Canada, and Russia. British gardeners seem to have a flair for this crop, holding the records for largest spud (over 7 pounds) and highest yield for an individual plant (370 pounds!).

In our western states, they're sometimes grown in beds of straw, making the harvesting of new and mature potatoes very simple. "Even a couch potato can grow a good crop with very little effort," says Colorado Master Gardener Steve Healey. "By using straw and a little soil preparation up front, it's easy to grow an admirable crop in a limited space." Healey digs a trench, plants his potatoes very shallow, then he covers them with clean, weed-free straw. Every few weeks, he carefully packs more straw around each plant, allowing plenty of space for potatoes to grow *above* the seed potato. Then he just lifts up the straw to harvest potatoes. (What if he pulled the straw back and Mrs. Potato Head screamed?)

Other growers get good results surrounding potato plants with old tires lying on their sides. As the plants grow, straw or soil is packed into a second tier of tire. These techniques are variations of "hilling," a practice used worldwide to increase potato yield. Dig a trench 8 to 10 inches deep, and pile the soil above the trenches (typically 30 inches apart). Add a cup or two of finished compost to feed the seed potato in its first, critical weeks of growth. Space the seed tubers about 9 to 12 inches apart in the row, then cover each seed potato with 3 or 4 inches of soil.

When the potato sprouts reach about 6 inches tall, mound soil around them, covering up half the plant. Do this again when the stems grow another 6 inches, being careful not to step near the all-important root zone of each plant. Potatoes need lots of air and drainage to avoid getting fungal and viral diseases. Don't water the newly planted potatoes for a week or so, instead planting the tubers in premoistened but not soggy soil.

I've adapted the hilling technique to include about a 50-50 blend of rich soil and acidic leaves like maple and oak, scavenged in the fall. I plant seeds in this blend and then mulch each plant heavily with leaves. The leaves drop the pH a little and hold moisture. I make sure the soil is rich enough in nitrogen, because the leaves are largely carbon and can rob the soil of nutrients. Potatoes need about three-fourths of their nitrogen in the first month, during the initial burst of growth but before tubers begin to develop. Fish emulsion, available at most garden centers, is a good source of nitrogen in a readily available form.

A general rule of thumb is to plant three or four weeks before the last expected frost date, or when the soil has warmed to 55 degrees F. In many western gardens, this means plant when native trees have come into leaf. If you get a freeze at the end of May like I did last year, the potatoes need to be covered, but even if their early growth gets nipped, other shoots will usually follow in a week or so.

Good varieties to try are 'Yellow Finn', an heirloom potato with great taste, 'Sangre', a red-skinned potato with good storage capabilities, and 'Norgold Russet', a great baking potato. For early-season spuds, try these varieties, field-tested by Colorado State University (see table on p. 105).

After plants come up, water fairly deeply every three to five days. Walk the fine line between too much and too little water by aiming for a soil that holds its shape in your hand but doesn't contain "wringable" water. Don't let potato plants dry out, because this will lower yields and increase chances of disease. You can spot water stress by wilting, a dark gray-green hue to the foliage, and leaves that roll up slightly.

Always buy certified, disease-free seeds. (Usually, supermarket potatoes won't work as well because they have sprout inhibitors on them.) Cut your seeds into egg-sized pieces, each with a few eyes (immature sprouts) on them. Use a sharp, clean knife to cut whole tubers into seed. A 10-percent solution of regular household bleach (1 ounce bleach to 9 ounces of water) makes an excellent dip for sterilizing the knife between cuts.

To give seeds a jump-start in the race against the elements and pests, try "chitting" seed potatoes before planting: Lay egg-sized seed tubers on cookie trays or shelf board in the darkness. When sprouts

Early-Producing Potatoes

Name	Type of Potato	Harvest	Uses	Characteristics
'Yukon Gold'	Oblong tuber shape with buff skin and yellow flesh. High yielding.	Very early	Baking, mashing	
Roasting	Attractive appearance and good flavor. Suitable for many culinary uses.			
'Russet Norkotah'	Long tuber type with golden russet skin. Medium yielding.	Very early	Baking	Very attractive appearance. Well suited to production in the San Luis Valley.
'Dark Red Norland'	Round tuber type with bright red skin. Medium yielding.	Very early	Boiling, roasting	
'All Red'	Oblong tuber type with light red flesh and skin color. Medium yielding.	Medium	Microwaving, salad, baking	
'Sangre'	Round tuber type with dark red skin. High yielding.	Medium	Baking, boiling	
Salad	Developed in Colorado. May emerge erratically. Develops a slight net in some soils. Stores well and has excellent cooking quality.			

Maturity in days from emergence (DAE): Early 65–85 DAE, Medium 85–100 DAE, Late more than 100 DAE.
(Source: Colorado State University Cooperative Extension Service, "Potatoes for the Home Garden.")

appear, bring the trays into medium light to prevent long, creepy shoots from forming. This widely used technique can significantly increase yields, especially in locations with a short growing season.

Depending on the variety, potatoes take between 90 and 120 days to reach maturity. New potatoes, or "earlies" as the Irish call them, begin to be ready about the tenth week—usually about the time flowers appear. Unless you get aphids, psyllids, Colorado potato beetle, or leafhoppers, all of which can munch leaves and spread blight to potato foliage. In that case expect a harvest of mini-spuds, always a heartbreaker. In alkaline soils like we have in the high West, the bacterial disease scab is also a distinct possibility, especially if the soil dries out and/or horse manure was used too liberally.

"To avoid pests and diseases," says potato grower Bill Lamont, "Don't grow potatoes in the same location year after year. A three-year rotation is much better, preferably including some legumes like beans or alfalfa to recharge the soil."

Another strategy is to provide habitat and food sources for the pests' natural enemies. A wide variety of plant types including sunflowers, yarrow, feverfew, carrots, dill, and fennel support beneficial insects and promote biological control of pests. Horseradish is a good companion for potatoes, too—said to stimulate better yield.

Handpick striped potato beetle adults, and wipe orange eggs off the underside of leaves. Try *Bacillus thuringiensis* (*Bt*) if the beetles seem to be winning. Wash aphids off leaves, and in a pinch, spray organic insecticidal soap for the psyllids and leafhoppers. You can do it—fight for those spuds!

You'll know they are mature when the plant foliage has naturally died, although some potato varieties should be peeked at before then. 'Yukon Gold', for example, produces large potatoes, and spuds may be ready before dieback. In that case, whack the vines down and wait a few weeks to harvest potatoes you plan to store. Cover them with light mulch so they don't bake prematurely. This reduces skin peeling, bruising, and rot in storage. Dry the potatoes for three or four days in a warm shady spot before storing. Then tuck them away in paper bags, unwashed, and let them get some sleep.

FORT COLLINS, COLORADO: ARTICHOKE CAPITAL OF THE ROCKIES?
· AND THEY SAID IT COULDN'T BE DONE ·

WE THINK OF OCTOBER as a time to harvest pumpkins—that is, if the squirrels, raccoons, and deer haven't already had their fill. It's true there's something very satisfying about the emergence of jack-o'-lanterns—those visionary veterans of the pumpkin patch who lead us reassuringly through the portals of another winter. But if Dana Christensen's field tests continue to be successful, we may also be harvesting globe artichokes in October, in autumns when Jack Frost remains agreeable.

It's true that artichoke hearts for Halloween treats or "choke o'lanterns" with scaly, green grins may never become American traditions, but there are many western gardeners who like to experiment (I'm one of them), and artichokes are a worthy challenge. Christensen, a horticulturist with CSU for the past twenty-one years, makes a living experimenting. In the last three years, he's been field-testing artichokes on an organic farm east of Fort Collins, with exciting results.

When I pulled into the parking lot at CSU's Experimental Station, Dana and his crew of four had just harvested and packed 1,700 pounds—about 3,500 artichokes. Their pickup was loaded with forty crates of half-pound chokes, sold to an organic grower and distributor in Wellington. "The artichokes we harvest are about half the size of the California standards, but they are locally grown, and they'll be a few days fresher," he says.

As we walk over to the three and a half–acre field of artichokes, Dana explains that the vegetable whose heart we lay bare for an appetizer is really a flower bud. The purple tinge of the heart is the first stage of a composite bloom that looks like a purple sunflower or a giant thistle. "If you don't get all the buds picked before they go to flower, you've still got a pretty nice ornamental," he says. Still, the truth is the globe artichoke is a member of the thistle family, and if it weren't for the bounty it bears, Dana's field might look to some folks like a field of scraggly weeds. For reasons he can't fully explain, the crop this year reached a height of less than a foot, but still produced very well. "Last year," he tells me, "we had plants that were 3 or 4 feet tall, and in California, they get 6 feet tall and about as wide."

The arid West's frozen winters reduce the possibilities of growing artichokes as perennials, but soils here are more alkaline, which chokes prefer, and summer temperatures are a little cooler overall than midstate California because nighttime temperatures drop a little lower. "Like lettuce or broccoli, chokes make their best growth in cool weather," Dana says. "They're like broccoli in another way—they produce a large, primary bud, followed by many secondary buds. And like broccoli, you want to harvest each bud when it's firm and tight. When either plant's buds begin to open, you're past the prime harvest."

In the past, artichokes have been thought of as a California or southern European crop. They originated in the Mediterranean region, where they were once the vegetable of the aristocracy in the ancient Roman Empire. Until recently, they were only grown in these mild, slightly humid conditions, but new seed varieties like 'Imperial Star' and 'Emerald' are more adaptable for growing in arid western states.

Dana's CSU colleague, entomologist Whitney Cranshaw, already has ten years of experience growing chokes in his backyard. He especially likes to make artichoke dip, and his wife makes wreaths out of dried artichoke flowers. "They're really pretty easy to grow, if you don't try to overwinter them," says Cranshaw. "In Colorado and surrounding states, they're annuals, to be started indoors no later than March 1, and harvested in August, September, and even into October, depending on the season." As a hobby grower, Cranshaw is less rigorous than Christensen about growing conditions. For example, he pays little attention to research that calls for at least ten days of below 50-degree temperatures, after seedling transplant. "I just put the transplants out after danger of frost is past, and let nature take its course. Over the years, I'd say 90 percent of my plants have yielded artichokes."

The long but fruitful growing season begins when Cranshaw germinates 'Imperial Star' or 'Green Globe Improved' seeds in moist paper towels in the dark, in mid- to late February. "Some seed companies will try to sell you cuttings, or 'stumps,' but I think you're better off with the seeds, which look like small sunflower seeds." He plants the sprouts in 4-inch pots, in a soil mixture designed for seedlings—heavy on the peat moss. Throughout March and early April, he tries to get the choke seedlings outside as often as possible on warmer days to harden them off. When the plants have six true leaves and frost danger is past, he transplants them into deeply dug beds—their home for the next 90 or 100 days. "After transplanting, they'll just sit there for a month, without much aboveground growth. Then in July they'll take off, and get to be 3 feet tall or so before beginning to bud out."

Extended periods of hot weather that heat soil temperatures above 85 degrees F. will make artichokes go into dormancy and refuse to produce buds. Four inches of leaf or hay mulch will help keep the soil temperatures down, as will afternoon irrigation.

Cranshaw has observed that from the first bud to the final bud is a period of about five to six weeks. He emphasizes the need to space the plants widely—at least two and a half feet apart. "Every time I tried closer spacing, my yield fell dramatically."

Looking for another challenge in the garden (as if there aren't enough of those already)? Amaze your friends, amuse your family as you perform another minor miracle out there, in the shape of a globe artichoke.

WINTER GARDENING WITH COLD FRAMES AND SOLAR PODS
· LIKE SAILBOATS, THEY'RE POWERED BY NATURE ·

MY NEIGHBORS NOW HAVE definitive proof that I'm loopy, if they're watching me slip-slide out to the garden through four inches of snow, with a watering can in one hand, an empty Tupperware container in the other, and thinning scissors in my pocket. But if they are watching, they'll see me come back with a container full of salad: white icicle radishes, bunching onions, arugula, cilantro, sorrel, spinach, and three kinds of lettuce. So I guess I'll have the last crunch today, won't I?

Last winter, we harvested about three bushels of greens and herbs from the 21-foot-long cold frame my neighbor Bob and I built out of scrap lumber in late October. We dug a trench 2 feet deep and backfilled soil around the bottom of the walls, which are essentially "particleboard sandwiches," with 2 inches of Styrofoam board in the middle. We tacked asphalt sheeting over the particleboard before backfilling, and painted the aboveground sections of wall to weatherproof them. We salvaged used sliding doors from a window and door installer, and scrap lumber from a construction pile, so the cost of the cold frame was no more than twenty dollars. The best part of the construction process was when we hinged and tested the doors. There was a solid thunk as they fell into place on the frame near the ground.

We transplanted salad greens left over in garden beds, before they froze, and also started seeds on our living room windowsills as we finished building. Now we're getting ready for Round Two in the wrestling match between Winter Gardener (that's me) and Jack Frost (Zone 5—windy, dry, and cold).

There's nothing complicated about building or operating a cold frame. It's really just a plant bed with a protective cover over it. Used for hundreds of years by Dutch and French commercial growers, cold frames require fewer cubic feet of heat than greenhouses, because they have just enough volume for the crop. The sun is their only source of heat, other than warmth stored in the ground itself. When we built our frame, we lined the back wall with one-gallon jugs filled with water, which serve as a solar heat "battery." They store solar energy in the daytime and release it slowly at night. The difference between inside and outside temperatures in cold frames is generally not more than 5 to 10 degrees, but that's enough. We're not trying to grow bananas—or even tomatoes—we're just trying to make the cold-hardy crops think it's spring or fall.

I borrowed a high-low thermometer from a friend last year, but because I had to put it in a sheltered, shaded area so it wouldn't record false highs, I didn't usually bother to look at it. (Plus, if the plants are staying healthy, who cares how cold it got last night?) I do know that nighttime temperatures below 20 degrees sometimes frosted the inside of the glazing, but at ground level there was no sign of frost. The water in the jugs never showed signs of freezing, either.

For the past few nights, it's been dropping below freezing, and I draped a few blankets over the glass to increase the temperature a few degrees. Spinach and lettuce still growing outside in the garden are surviving the nights, but the plants inside the cold frame are doing much better than that. I think my greatest satisfaction is in the viewing: bright green, exuberant plants even in the dead of winter, cozy in a mulch of dark, moist compost.

Unless you install solar devices that automatically open and close the doors (or "lights") of the cold frame, count on making quick morning and evening visits, because with the high West's radiant sun, your crops can bake quickly in a closed-up unit. I open the cold frame when outside temperatures reach about 40 degrees F., propping the doors open with broomstick-sized poles until late afternoon, when I close the doors to store up heat for the night. Since I work at home, this routine works for me, but variations in the schedule will work, too. Just watch the weather report, and vent before you go to work on a day that will be warm, even if it's 30 degrees when you leave. Or get one of the solar vents that can do your work for you if the lights are light enough. The venting arms can lift up to twenty pounds, far less than our sliding doors weigh.

Eliot Coleman, author of *Four-Season Harvest,* uses the cold frame as a workhorse in his garden on the coast of Maine, harvesting more than eighteen kinds of fresh vegetables throughout the winter. But he explains that for completely freeze-proof operation of the cold frames, he builds a movable plastic greenhouse over them, tall enough to walk in. Comments Leandre Poisson, a grower in nearby New Hampshire and author of *Solar Gardening,* "Isn't that kind of a complicated way of getting double glazing? Why not double glaze on the growing box itself?" The two growers are good friends, enabling Poisson to jokingly call Coleman "the most successful 19th-century gardener I know."

Poisson adds high-tech refinements to the traditional cold frame design with materials called Sunlite and Angel Hair. Sunlite is an advanced plastic material often used in greenhouses. The Solar Pod's design calls for two layers of Sunlite as the unit's "light," with a few inches of Angel Hair, a glass-fiber mat, sandwiched in between. Poisson originally came across Angel Hair at the county dump. He traced the material back to its manufacturer and began experimenting with it as a translucent insulator. "Plants prefer diffuse light to direct sun because it doesn't scorch the crops. The Solar Pod design works well in Colorado," he told me, "because the sun there is so radiant." I'm anxious to try it out, but for the moment, I'm going to see what my more traditional cold frame can do—like a sailboat, gliding through winter with only Nature as an ally. (Or else crashing and burning in a week-long arctic freeze in January.)

INVITE HERBS INDOORS FOR THE WINTER
· BUT DON'T INVITE THE WHITEFLIES ·

I'LL BE HONEST WITH YOU. The last herb I potted up and invited inside—a cilantro—died unceremoniously a week or so later, the victim of aphids who must have stowed away. The plump, juicy little devils are back outside now, their fate still linked with the cilantro that lies wilted on top of the compost pile. Have you noticed that aphids like to eat human food whenever possible? They had little interest in my ficus tree, split-leaf philodendron, or Swedish ivy plants; but when the cilantro came inside, all of a sudden they were crazy for salsa ingredients and salsa music.

Like the whiteflies that appeared last winter as soon as the heirloom tomatoes were coming into blossom in the living room window. Where do they come from? I took the same action with the tomato as I did with the cilantro—it became fuel for the compost pile.

I intend to try another annual herb this winter, basil, because fresh basil in the supermarkets is roughly in the same price echelon as pine nuts. And faced with a choice between pine nuts and basil or soap and light bulbs, I'll take the good food, thanks. So what if it's too dark to see it?

In general, however, I think perennial herbs may be a better bet to handle the hardships of the great indoors—things like overwatering, underwatering, peering at the plants too much, and reading cookbooks right in front of them. One thing the plants have going for them is south and southwestern exposures on extra-wide windowsills, built specifically to replicate a Mediterranean climate right here in Colorado.

Oregano, said to be a creation of Aphrodite, the goddess of love and beauty, will be an aromatic addition to my windowsills, because it likes lots of sun and because I like to eat it. Planted in very well-drained, lightly alkaline soil, a variety such as 'Compactum' will grow no taller than about a foot but will produce an abundance of fragrant little leaves for Italian and Mexican recipes. Out in the garden, I usually divide oregano clumps every three years to keep them vigorous, side-dressing the plants with compost mulch. Indoors, I'll let it get pot-bound and encourage it to produce lots of leaves, with an occasional pitcher of seaweed tea. Although oregano is cold hardy to -20 degrees F., I suspect it would rather spend the winter at 69 degrees, with a little music and a sense of being part of the household.

Another contender for windowsill space is sage, long renowned for its health-giving properties. The botanical genus name for sage, Salvia, means "to be in good health." Ancient Chinese merchants traded three pounds of tea leaves for one pound of sage, because it was in demand. A hardy biennial, sage is not as persistent as oregano. It tends to thin out in a pot over time and should be replanted from seed or cuttings taken from the outside shoots of the plant.

Chives are easy to bring indoors, and the bugs will leave them alone. I've seen chives survive in one location for fifteen years, adding purple blossoms to the vegetable garden early in the season. This mild-tasting relative of garlic has historical longevity as well—it's mentioned in 4,000-year-old Chinese literature. Having a winter crop of chives is as simple as putting a few clumps in a pot in early fall and leaving them outside through the first few frosts to let them re-root. Once inside, the chives will grow in 6-inch diameters to 9 inches tall, providing a fresh, tasty touch to omelets and potato dishes throughout the winter.

The genus *Thymus* includes about 100 species, most of which are tiny leafed and low growing. Thyme is one of the essential ingredients in Italian herb seasoning and is also a great addition to green salads. It needs well-drained soil, moderate watering, and moderate exposure to sunlight. Indoors, it might prefer a southeast, rather than due south exposure.

Here are a few specific varieties for trying indoors:

- Arogulan chives (*Allium schoenoprasum*): Strong flavor and thick, dark leaves. Developed for forcing, 8 to 12 inches tall. Seeds germinate in 10 to 14 days at 60 degrees F.

- 'Spicy Globe' basil (*Ocimum basilicum minimum*): Dense, compact form of basil, 8 to 10 inches tall. Good flavor, easy to germinate from seed in 6 to 12 days at 68 to 77 degrees F.

- Greek oregano (*Origanum vulgare hirtum*): The true oregano for Mediterranean cooking, with excellent flavor and white blossoms. Watch out for the imposter (called wild marjoram), with pink flowers and no flavor. Greek oregano grows well in pots, reaching 8 to 12 inches. Germinates easily in 7 to 21 days at room temperature.

- Broadleaf thyme (*Plectranthus amboinicus* or *Coleus amboinicus*): Also known as Spanish thyme and Cuban oregano, this plant has broad, fleshy leaves unlike those of ordinary thyme. Its pungent, spicy thyme-oregano flavor is useful in many of the same recipes as ordinary thyme. Never goes dormant, grows from cuttings only, and reaches 10 to 12 inches tall. Cuttings sprout at room temperature.

Herbs can be dried or frozen, of course, but my advice is plan your meals around what you have fresh. Clip the herbs with a pair of scissors, and have them in the frying pan or marinating dish within two minutes of harvesting. That's livin'!

ORNAMENTALS FOR THE WEST
· FLOWERS, TREES, AND SHRUBS
THAT TAKE A LICKING AND KEEP ON TICKING ·

CREATING A LIVING LANDSCAPE AT HARMONY VILLAGE COMMUNITY
· A PLANT LIST FOR HIGH AND DRY PLACES ·

CREATING A LANDSCAPE PLAN for our Harmony Village neighborhood was like choosing favorite paintings in an art museum exhibit. Technically, we weren't landscape architects who knew all the Latin names and had already planted dozens of landscapes. But we knew what we liked, and we made every effort to see each tree, shrub, and flower on our list in its preferred location—whether at the Botanic Gardens or in a neighbor's yard.

Our neighborhood is surrounded by prominent features on all sides—Lookout Mountain to the west, Table Mesa with its jutting butte to the east, a newly constructed golf course to the south, and Boulder's Flatirons way in the distance on the north. When the six-acre neighborhood was developed six years ago, twenty or thirty cottonwood trees were preserved, along with river birches on the creek and lots of native shrubs like rabbitbrush, chokecherry, and yucca. The land slopes down from a fairly inactive residential street, and the highway is about half a mile away. We're within city limits (10 blocks from downtown Golden, Colorado), but the property feels rural and secluded. So the landscape framework was already in place when our homeowners' association began to select plants for the property.

By acting as our own landscape team, we saved $6,000 that was budgeted for professional landscape design. We began by listing the qualities we wanted to include in the landscape, things like a sense of welcome, a sense of enclosure, a sense of entry, a sense of flow, and a sense of place. We knew we wanted a landscape that also:

- **Looks great,** with a variety of appropriate colors throughout seasons; visual and fragrant "surprises," including optimum use of niches as well as vistas; water features to help keep traffic noise in the background; artistic features such as sculpture or ornamental paving to accentuate spaces.

- **Integrates/unifies physical and social aspects of the community,** complementing our Southwestern style of architecture; defining private/public spaces with plantings and features; welcoming both residents and visitors to a place that feels cool in summer and warm in winter.
- **Provides interface with the natural environment,** retaining natural (or naturalized) species such as cottonwoods, river birches, and hawthorns as a link with nature; provides shade, wind protection, noise suppression, optimum solar income.
- **Is affordable,** optimizing existing features and species; using volunteer and student expertise and sweat equity for designing and planting.
- **Minimizes maintenance,** using plants that are appropriate for their space and don't require pampering; using native species and other adapted species with proven hardiness.
- **Is environmentally conscious,** using a minimum of pesticides; capturing rooftop water for use in the landscape; using all compostable materials from the community as soil amendment; using landscaping materials (paving, tools, pots, etc.) that are from recycled materials.

We decided to complete our landscape in phases, first putting in trees, shrubs, and water-conservative turf, then gradually infilling with perennial flowers and ground covers to replace the grass. Rather than the conventional lawn grass, Kentucky bluegrass, we chose Tall Fescue, a turf with greater tolerance for shade and drought as well as being more resistant to pests and diseases. Fescue doesn't "fill in" as readily as bluegrass, so on several occasions, we've scattered a little seed in well-worn areas, but after six years of use, we're pleased with the way the grass performs.

Harmony Village Plant List (5,700 Feet Elevation)

Trees

Acer ginnala	Ginnala maple
Acer glabrum	Rocky Mountain maple
Crataegus crus-galli inermis	Thornless cockspur hawthorn
Crataegus mollis	Downy hawthorn
Fraxinus americana 'Autumn Purple'	'Autumn Purple' white ash
Juniperus scopulorum	Rocky Mountain juniper
Malus 'Thunderchild'	Crabapple
Pinus cembroides edulis	Piñon pine
Pinus nigra	Austrian pine
Prunus americana	American plum
Prunus cerasus 'Montmorency'	Montmorency cherry
Quercus macrocarpa	Burr oak
Quercus rubra	Red oak
Tilia cordata	Little-leaf linden

Shrubs

Amelanchier alnifolia	Shadblow or serviceberry
Amorpha canescens	Lead plant
Arctostaphylos x *colorado*	Manzanita
Artemisia tridentata	Tall western sagebrush
Caryopteris x *clandonensis* 'Blue Mist'	'Blue Mist' spiraea
Cercocarpus montanus	Mountain mahogany
Chrysothamnus nauseosus	Rabbitbrush
Cotoneaster multiflorus	Many-flowered cotoneaster
Fallugia paradoxa	Apache plume
Perovskia atriplicifolia	Russian sage
Philadelphus lewisii	Cheyenne mock orange
Philadelphus microphyllus	Little-leaf mock orange
Prunus x *cistena* 'Cheyenne'	'Pawnee Buttes' sand cherry
Rhus trilobata	Three-leaf sumac/skunkbush
Ribes aureum	Golden currant
Robinia neomexicana	Desert locust
Rosa foetida 'Bicolor'	Austrian copper rose
Rubus deliciosus	Boulder raspberry
Syringa vulgaris	Common lilac

We ran into a little trouble with trees being planted with their root balls still contained by the "cages" they came in. Four or five trees have failed, and invariably, this was the problem. We don't make that mistake anymore.

PERSISTENT PETALS
· PERENNIAL FLOWERS THAT BLOOM MORE THAN A MONTH ·

WESTERN GROWING SEASONS often seem like video games or adventure movies. You're the action hero, doling out emergency rations of water during a drought, or flinging an old shower curtain over your berries as hailstones pelt the top of your head. You're the hero, that is, if the plants survive. But if they don't make it, what exactly were you *doing* out there on all those hot afternoons? You may as well have been watching professional bowling on TV.

Heroism springs from informed planting. Let's face it, if you grow flowers and vegetables that need pampering, there's a better than even chance they'll keel over in gusty winds or fickle frosts before they mature. After all your efforts, you'll end up being the "goat in the garden," rather than the hero. To eliminate or at least reduce your goatliness, why not choose plants with proven track records?

Three of my favorite perennial flowers for drought tolerance, long blooming periods in hot temperatures, and overall dependability are bee balm (especially *Monarda didyma* 'Cambridge Scarlet'), purple coneflower (*Echinacea purpurea*), and Russian sage (*Perovskia atriplicifolia*). The overlapping flowering seasons for these three provide a solid three months of lavender/pink/purple/red blooms. I've watched each of them add bright color to landscapes that otherwise look pretty beat up by the heat.

Here are a few of the adjectives in Simon & Schuster's *Garden Flowers* to describe *Monarda*: "abundant floriferousness; tomentose, sub-cordate, sinuate-dentate, labiate, and compact verticils...." There, does that make growing *Monarda* less of a mystery? Probably not. But what you do need to know is that *Monarda* can thrive in full sun as well as partial shade. That the species has lots of common names, including bee balm, wild bergamot, Oswego tea, and horsemint. That it originated in the Blue Ridge Mountains of North Carolina and likes to root in moist soil.

Last summer, walking home from the grocery, I admired a stand of bright red *Monarda didyma* 'Cambridge Scarlet' across the street—the centerpiece of an oval perennial garden in a well-kept front lawn. The bee balm was still in flower almost two months later, in the middle of a brutal heat wave. I stopped to ask my neighbors which variety it was and how they'd started it. They told me they'd bought a starter plant at the local native nursery, and invited me to help myself to a cutting. The next time I walked to the store, I put a trowel and a baggy filled with compost in my backpack, so I could dig up a clump and then replace the divot.

Monarda is hardy in Zones 4 through 9 (Colorado varies from Zones 3 to 5, depending on elevation), expressing itself in shades of red, rose, pink, violet, and white. It attracts butterflies, hummingbirds, and bees to your vegetable garden and orchard, which all help in pollination. Ranging from two to four feet in height, it can be started by digging clumps, by cuttings, or from seed. Search on the Internet with key words "perennial flowers nursery" or just "bee balm" if you can't find seeds or cuttings locally. Smell the leaves of *Monarda* and you'll know why it's sometimes used as a tea—it smells like wild oregano, which it is, botanically.

The second species in our long-blooming garden is *Echinacea purpurea*, the purple coneflower that has literally taken root in health food stores as an immune system booster. In fact, there is such a demand for echinacea that sadly, the northern prairies are becoming pockmarked by scavengers of the marketable flower. "I dug echinacea for a summer job," admitted one South Dakota student, with embarrassment.

The purple coneflower is not only valuable as medicine but also as a cut flower and a purplish-pink backdrop in the perennial bed. (In fact, the three long bloomers spotlighted here would collectively make a great backdrop for shorter perennials such as white oxeye daisies or musk mallows, multicolored lupines, and bright red penstemons or

Other Perennials that Bloom More than a Month

Achillea millefolium	Common yarrow
Alcea rosea	Hollyhock
Agastache	Giant hyssop
Alyssum montanum	Basket-of-gold
Anaphalis margaritacea	Pearly everlasting
Anemone japonica	Japanese anemone
Argemone	Prickly poppy
Aster x frikartii	
Callirhoe involucrata	Prairie winecup
Campanula poscharskyana	Creeping bellflower
Campanula rotundifolia	Harebell
Centaurea dealbata	Pink knapweed
Chrysopsis	Golden aster
Coreopsis	
Delosperma cooperi	Purple iceplant
Dicentra eximia	Fringed bleeding heart
Digitalis	Foxglove
Geranium pratense	Meadow cranesbill
Heuchera sanguinea	Coral bells
Iberis sempervirens	Evergreen candytuft
Lavandula angustifolia	English lavender
Leucanthemum x superbum	Shasta daisy
Malva	Mallow
Nepeta x faassenii	Catmint
Oenothera caespitosa	Tufted evening primrose
Origanum laevigatum 'Herenhausen'	Showy oregano
Penstemon centranthifolius	Scarlet bugler
Penstemon barbatus	'Prairie Fire' penstemon
Phlox divaricata	Sweet William phlox
Platycodon grandiflorus	Balloon flower
Ratibida pinnata	Prairie coneflower
Rudbeckia hirta	Black-eyed Susan
Salvia azurea grandiflora	Azure sage
Saponaria officinalis	Soapwort
Scabiosa	Pincushion flower
Tanacetum parthenium	Feverfew
Veronica spicata 'Red Fox'	
Veronica x 'Sunny Border Blue'	

Oriental poppies.) Echinacea reaches heights of 2 to 3 feet, with flower heads on the end of rough-hairy stems that bloom from June to July. It will self-seed if the bloom stalks are not cut off, and does best in well-drained soil. With its long, thirsty taproot, it can withstand both wind and drought and still be there in the morning.

The third long bloomer is Russian sage, which looks like lavender and smells like sage. *Perovskia atriplicifolia* is a shrublike, somewhat gangly perennial that also tolerates heat and drought, making it a star performer in the low-water (Xeriscape) garden. Its 12-inch spikes of light-blue-to-lavender flowers become a fixture from July through September. The plant's preferences for slightly alkaline soil and dry climate make Colorado a perfect home away from home. (Home was originally Afghanistan and Tibet.) If you don't like its straggly stems in the winter, cut them back to next year's buds near the base of the stems, and quit griping. Any plant whose long-blooming flowers appear cool and airy in the dry heat of late summer deserves a place in your garden.

Remember this, though: Just because you've chosen flowers that stand up to Colorado weather doesn't mean you're a hero. Not yet. You can still be the goat if your plants survive but then are overrun by 3-foot-tall weeds while you're on vacation. There are simply no guarantees in this ramble-gamble game of gardening.

WINTERGREEN
· DECIDUOUS GREEN SHRUBS FOR THE COLD MONTHS ·

WHEN YOU COME ACROSS a deciduous shrub or ground cover that still has green or bronze leaves in the middle of a Colorado winter, it probably means one of two things. Either you've been drinking, or else you've found a protected little spot that considers itself part of New Mexico or high-elevation California. Much of the arid West is in Zones 5 (low elevation) or 4 (higher elevation), and with very few exceptions, broadleaf species lose their leaves in the winter here.

Let's look at some of those exceptional plants, because when they're planted in the right places, they can make winter feel a little like spring on a warm day. Why did holly become a Christmas tradition? Because even in the High Plains and mountains, semihardy varieties such as 'Blue Boy' and 'Blue Girl' are often still in leaf. And so are the curl-leaf mountain mahogany, purple-leaf winter creeper, boxwood, Oregon grape, and English ivy. I've even seen exotic rhododendrons in leaf at that time of year, if their niches provide snow cover for extra humidity and there are evergreens nearby to acidify the soil. The very delicate, sweet-smelling daphne can brave the winter if planted in a protected spot. The 'Carol Mackie' variety of daphne is brightly variegated and deserves a spot in any garden, either in shade or dappled sun.

One of my favorite activities is to discover plant-sheltering niches—such as little pockets between fallen trees where I'll find Jacob's ladder in the summer, spotlighted by a single shaft of sunlight. Or northeast exposures in the L of a brick house (or English castle) that enable English ivy to remain a wall of green all winter. Sometimes, though, those niches fall on bad times. Keith Williamson, an employee at the Little Valley Nursery, a wholesaler south of Brighton, Colorado, remembers the English ivy that grew on a neighbor's house in Sterling, Colorado, where he grew up. "The ivy clung to the side of a brick chimney, and it looked beautiful until new owners moved in who actually used the fireplace. That was too much stress for the plants, with the alternating heat and cold. The green chimney had turned brown by the end of winter."

Like me, Williamson likes to nose around in the high country to see what's hardy enough to survive winter conditions. He remembers the first time he saw the miniature version of the curl-leaf mountain mahogany (*Cercocarpus ledifolius* var. *intricatus*) at the Colorado National Monument. "Deer like to browse on the mountain mahogany, and they had pruned this particular plant into a beautiful globe shape, about two feet tall," he recalled. The *intricatus*, like its taller cousin, likes to grow in rocky soil, in a warm location. It has long, narrow, gray-green leaves that curl under slightly and whitish-gray bark. The plant's seed-heads, fuzzy corkscrews that appear in late summer, add unique autumn interest. They have adapted a strategy for burrowing into the soil to germinate by flattening out when dry and curling up when moist. We have three of these plants growing in a western exposure against the house. In each of the last three years, they've retained winter foliage, growing about a foot per year. The taller variety can reach heights of 10 feet or more, but *intricatus* stays compact—about 2 to 3 feet tall.

Another compact wintergreen is the boxwood. If you tour Denver Botanic Gardens in the winter, you'll see several clumps of this species, still glossy green under a dusting of snow. Boxwood does not get straggly or rangy, and is a good accent plant for a corner of the house or next to a stone wall. It likes good humidity and well-drained soil, and can take a southwest exposure with afternoon shade, but prefers northern and eastern exposures, away from the wind. "Boxwood has been used in Europe for ages, as a parterre, or miniature hedge," said Williamson. "We've found the 'Winter Gem' variety (*Buxus microphylla insularis* 'Winter Gem') to be a good bet for Colorado. We recommend that growers plant boxwood like they would evergreens, amending the soil to create good drainage."

Another good winter performer is winter creeper vine (*Euonymus fortunei*), which clings to walls and trellises with tiny rootlets, and also makes a reliable ground cover for moist, well-drained shady areas. The winter creeper has a wide range of seasonal colors: glossy green leaves in summer, purplish-red leaves in fall and winter, and small greenish-white flowers that develop pink fruits with orange seeds. "The fall and winter color reminds me of 'Autumn Purple' ash leaves," said Williamson. The plant can be put in the ground as soon as the soil can be worked in early spring, through early fall. Like other vines, it will take a few years to become established. A cedar bark or pine needle mulch will help maintain moisture around the roots. "The winter creeper tolerates drought better than boxwood," commented Williamson, "but it won't form free-standing plants as a ground cover—just a thick mat."

English ivy (*Hedera helix*) can grow in the same garden as the winter creeper. Its glossy green leaves have three to five lobes with whitish veins. As a background mat of green, this ivy makes a good addition to a shady perennial garden. It can also climb the trunks of trees and leap tall buildings with a single bound, or at least it sometimes seems like it. English ivy, the kudzu vine of the West, can reach heights of thirty feet or more, sometimes providing nests for songbirds that can either drive you crazy or make you feel like you live in the country—depending on your attitude and where your bedroom window is.

The Oregon grape (*Mahonia aquifolium*) looks like a holly but is not. It's actually a member of the barberry family that is an excellent foundation plant in a north or east exposure. An aggressive grower that spreads by underground stems to form irregular colonies, it also has fragrant yellow flowers in May, followed by clusters of blue berries that resemble miniature Concord grapes. In contrast to the poisonous berries of the English ivy, the Oregon grape's berries are edible. The native variety, *Mahonia repens,* is very drought-resistant and grows well under evergreens.

Put some wintergreen in your landscape. It may take a few years for these broadleaf species to become established, but they're worth the wait.

FIRECRACKERS IN YOUR FLOWERBED
· PETUNIAS, A CELEBRATION OF SUMMER ·

WHEN IT COMES TO FLOWERS, annuals and perennials are like your cousin Ned and Aunt Betty—they have completely different approaches to life. The evolved strategy of annuals is to cover disturbed areas quickly, dispersing seeds by the thousands. It's a somewhat blind approach, because the plant has no information about where a given seed will end up. Snapdragons, California poppies, or cosmos are essentially seed factories, casting their fate to the wind, water, gravity, and various other furry and feathery carriers. In a sense, these annuals are gypsies—home is anywhere seed meets receptive ground.

Perennials, on the other hand, are place-based. Their primary energy goes into becoming integrated with a given landscape—literally becoming rooted. In plant years, they're as long-lived as Aunt Betty, developing the ability to withstand drought, frigid winters, and even fire, to re-emerge when times are better. Their flowers are often less prolific and enduring than annuals, and their colors and fragrances often less dramatic, but perennials do know how to sustain themselves, year after year.

I admit I'm somewhat partial to the persistent quality of perennials, but some annuals also have traits that can't be overlooked. For example, petunias have a range of colors, a long bloom time, an almost infinite capacity for spreading, and a sweet fragrance that have made them an American tradition. Look around you on the Fourth of July—in flowerbeds, hanging baskets, and window boxes throughout America—and you'll see a spectrum of petunias in bloom—from purple and yellow through red, white, and blue.

A garden catalog I leafed through this spring gave me a chuckle. Because of a typo, the petunias were offered in "all tones of rose and oink." But the petunias I've encountered neither look nor smell like pigs. I remember working in a greenhouse one summer and having vividly colorful dreams about the sparkle of petunias, whose fragrance reminded me of hard candies I ate as a kid. (For some reason, white and lavender varieties seem especially fragrant.)

It's true that supermarkets and garden shops hawk petunias by the truckload in the spring, at very tempting prices. But you'll get a wider choice of colors and varieties if you start your own seeds. Petunias come in a few basic types. The *multiflora* cultivars have smaller flowers, but more of them than *grandiflora* cultivars. *Grandiflora* varieties are often bred to cascade from hanging baskets. When botanists first discovered wild petunias in South America in the 1700s, they were interesting but fairly lackluster compared to today's showy varieties, like 'Flaming Velvet', 'Cream Star', and 'Salmon Beauty'.

Other Good Annuals and Biennials for High/Dry Western Gardens

Snapdragon	*Antirrhinum majus*
African daisy	*Arctotis*
Borage	*Borago officinalis*
Rock purslane	*Calandrinia umbellata*
Pot marigold	*Calendula officinalis*
Bachelor's button	*Centaurea cyanus*
Larkspur	*Consolida ambigua*
Calliopsis	*Coreopsis tinctoria*
Cosmos	*Cosmos bipinnatus*
Annual pinks	*Dianthus chinensis*
California poppy	*Eschscholzia californica*
Snow-on-the-mountain	*Euphorbia marginata*
Annual Indian blanket	*Gaillardia pulchella*
Treasure flower	*Gazania rigens*
Annual baby's breath	*Gypsophila elegans*
Mexican tulip poppy	*Hunnemannia fumariifolia*
Rose mallow	*Lavatera trimestris*
Four o'clock	*Mirabilis jalapa*
Annual evening primrose	*Oenothera*
Desert bluebells	*Phacelia campanularia*
Moss rose	*Portulaca grandiflora*
Black-eyed Susan	*Rudbeckia hirta*
Salvia	*Salvia* vars.
Sweet William catchfly	*Silene armeria*
Nasturtium	*Tropaeolum majus*
Verbena	*Verbena*
Zinnia	*Zinnia angustifolia*

If you start seeds five to six weeks before the last expected frost and keep the seedlings in bright enough light to avoid "legginess," you'll be ready to establish a bed of blooms that will last for several months. But there's a trick to starting the tiny seeds—they need light to germinate. Sow the seed in moist, well-drained potting soil with lots of peat or compost in it. Don't cover the seeds, but keep them moist by covering the seed flat with clear plastic or a pan of glass. During germination try to avoid conditions that favor damping-off disease, such as seedlings being too thick, excessive soil moisture, and cool soil temperatures.

As the seedlings start to grow, move them outside on warm days to slowly acclimate them. Direct sunlight prevents the seedlings from becoming elongated. After the last frost, plant on a cloudy day if possible. Petunias can be spaced about 12 inches apart in the garden, and will do best in full sun, with up to a few hours of light shade a day. Generally, the more sun they get, the more they'll flower. They've typically been bred to be fertilized, but too much nitrogen causes excessive vegetative growth and sparse flowers. Slow-release compost that also provides good drainage is the best way to go. In high pH soils like we have in the West, iron uptake may be a problem, causing yellowing of the foliage, but lots of organic material should solve that one, too.

Like many other annual flowers, petunias generally require 1 to 1½ inches of water each week, but they are drought tolerant if you get busy and forget them. Petunias benefit from "pinching" a planting, which increases the number of flowering and spreading stems and discourages excessive vegetative growth. Remove old flowers (deadheads) when they start to fade to encourage repeat blooming. (There's that annual flower compulsion, again: to disperse seeds at any cost.) Petunias often reseed in the garden, but will not always return true to type. They usually revert to a mix of small white, lavender, and rose flowers.

Petunias make excellent cut flowers, but keep in mind if you bring them indoors that they're toxic. Look at them, smell them, but don't try eating them!

A new development in the world of petunias is ground cover or spreading varieties. They're only about six inches tall, but spread so rapidly that they can cover a large area in a single growing season. This makes them a good choice for covering the slope of a hillside garden, or even replacing a little chunk of grass in the backyard. When grown in full sunlight, they are so covered by flowers that you hardly see any foliage.

'Purple Wave' is a 1995 All-America Selection of the ground cover variety. Plants grow only 4 to 6 inches high, but can spread 2 to 4 feet. The burgundy-purple flowers measure 2 inches across. 'Purple Wave' is also an excellent choice for hanging baskets.

If you want firecracker colors in your flowerbed, check out the wide range of possibilities of petunias.

INVASION OF THE LAND SNATCHERS
· PUBLIC ENEMIES TO WEED OUT OF YOUR GARDEN ·

"BEAUTY ISN'T EVERYTHING," says Eric Lane. The Colorado State Weed Coordinator agrees that non-native, invasive flowers like butter-and-eggs (toadflax) and the moisture-loving oxeye daisy are nice to look at in small areas, but he's seen them take over people's entire properties. "When that happens," says Lane, "Your pasture or meadow—or your town's open space—becomes a monoculture. You lose species diversity—both animal life and plant life—and the invading weeds become so well established that you may never get them under control." Lane's job has taken on a sense of urgency in recent years, since 500 native plant species out of 3,000 have already been displaced by non-native vegetation.

For example, half a million Colorado acres have now been swallowed up by the Canada thistle, a perennial that can outcompete just about all our natives, in both plains and mountain habitats. Lane explained that the roots of a Canada thistle—the plant's "anchor"—can radiate out as much as 16 feet horizontally and from 2 to 22 feet in depth. "That's why it won't kill the weed if you dig up just part of it, because there's a lot more ready to come up next spring." He advises homeowners, gardeners, and ranchers to mow thistles down two or three times during a growing season, to weaken them. By mowing, you make the plant deplete the energy in its root system as it tries to produce seeds.

This is a very successful, very well-armored plant he was talking about—a plant I've battled like Zorro with a weed whacker for thirty years. Originally imported into Canada in grain shipments from southeast Europe, the Canada thistle has moved southward and expanded its Colorado domain from the eastern plains up into Rocky Mountain National Park and over onto the Western Slope. Everywhere it goes it has devastating impacts on native plant communities, backyard environments, and rangeland. "Besides its habit of establishing root-connected colonies, it also spreads prolifically by seed, so even if you mow only once and don't spray, you've got to at least get them before they go to seed," he urged.

Lane was more optimistic about controlling the musk thistle, a biennial with larger flower heads than the Canada thistle. Musk thistle overwinters its first year as a ground-hugging rosette, goes to seed in the second year, and then dies. "Sometimes in a mild winter it survives into its third year, and becomes a monster with the stalk of a young tree. But overall it's easier to manage than the Canada thistle, because it doesn't have the massive perennial root system. You dig into the musk thistle with a sharp spade, right below its crown, and it won't have the strength to regenerate."

I asked him if the Canada thistle was Colorado's "Public Enemy Number One." After a little thought he answered, "Certainly, plants like Canada thistle, field bindweed, and leafy spurge are near the top of the dirty dozen list, but I'm always careful to point out that relative newcomers like the 'Yellow Star' thistle and the 'Yellow' toadflax and 'Dalmatian' toadflax can sneak up on us while we battle the others. The 'Yellow Star' thistle has already devoured 10 million acres in California, and when Californians see pockets of the weed here, they shake their heads knowingly." The 'Yellow Star' thistle, like Russian knapweed, can cause irreversible brain disease in horses that graze on infested pasture. "Both weeds can cause degeneration of brain tissue that controls chewing, so the disease is called 'chewing disease,'" Lane said. "Unfortunately it often goes undiagnosed, and the horse dies of hunger or dehydration."

Flowers to Avoid in Western Gardening	
Purple loosestrife	Escapes gardens, displacing native vegetation like cattail marshes
Dame's rocket	Displaces native vegetation in wet meadows
Mediterranean sage	Forms monocultures that outcompete natives in grasslands and pastures
Chicory	Competes with natives in roadsides and open areas
Creeping bellflower	Escapes in foothills, especially shady areas
Scentless chamomile	Competes with natives on montane roadsides
Wild carrot, Queen Anne's lace	Compete with natives in plains and foothills

His comments about weed toxicity reminded me of an incident a few weeks earlier, when a few kids in my neighborhood were playing house. The leaves of a poison hemlock looked like parsley to them, and they made the potentially fatal mistake of putting some in their mouths. A worried parent rang my doorbell and asked me to confirm that the plant she was holding was hemlock. We looked for purple veins on the stem, and then quickly called 911. The kids were OK, but the ten hours they spent under observation at the hospital will most likely prevent further "wild meals."

Another weed that's trying to colonize my neighborhood is bindweed, a tenacious member of the morning glory family. Its small, white or pink bell-shaped flowers aren't that bad looking, especially when mottled with red patterns inside the bells. But the question is, do I want to see little white bells wringing the vitality out of my tomatoes, perennial flowers, and fruit bushes? This weed embodies the term "persistent" with seeds that can remain viable for more than half a century and an extensive root system that stores three years of surplus food reserves. When you pull out bindweed foliage, you don't get that feeling of satisfaction, because typically you leave behind a monstrous mass of roots. "In the garden, bindweed requires persistence," said Lane. "But gardeners are by nature pretty persistent. Just keep pulling it up, and you'll eventually get it under control."

The more serious risk statewide from bindweed is in the eastern plains, where it can smother whole fields of wheat. "It wreaks havoc on farm equipment," Lane commented, "because the vines gum up the works like pieces of string."

I asked him about research with biological controls for Colorado's non-native invaders.

"When our natural areas began to be threatened by invasive weeds, we started searching for insects that control specific plants," he replied. "We've had quite a bit of success with St.-John's-wort, a weed of particular concern to sheep producers. Scientists found the right bug—that *only* likes the target weed—and brought it through the rigorous licensing process. When they released large numbers of the beetle, you could clearly see the battlefront advancing and the weeds disappearing." He joked, "Since St.-John's-wort is used by humans as an herbal antidepressant, you have to wonder how content those busy little beetles must be."

LANDSCAPING FOR DOLLARS AND SENSE
· CONSERVING ENERGY WITH YOUR GREEN THUMB ·

THE WAY WE LANDSCAPE our yards plays a major role in how much energy our houses use. If we plant the right trees, shrubs, vines, and grasses in the right places, we can keep our houses cool in summer and warm in winter, by design. We can also reduce winter heating bills by as much as 25 percent and summer cooling bills by as much as 50 percent. At the same time, we'll reduce air pollution and noise, provide habitat for wildlife, and increase the resale value of our houses.

Computer models from the U.S. Department of Energy show that just three trees, strategically placed around the house, can save an average household between $100 and $250 in heating and cooling energy costs annually. The National Academy of Sciences (NAS) estimates that America has 100 million potential tree spaces in urban areas alone, and probably many times more in rural areas.

Buying a shade tree when it's an 8-foot sapling costs about as much as an awning for one large window. It will begin shading windows the first year and, depending on the species and the home, will shade the roof in five to ten years.

Energy-conserving landscaping isn't rocket science (it's more like rock science), but it requires site-specific analysis and a little research. Call your extension agent for local data, or do some searching on the Internet for keywords like "shade trees" and "windbreaks." Fortunately, the goals are very easy to understand:

1. During winter, keep heat in and cold out by blocking wind with a windbreak and letting in as much sunlight as possible.
2. In summer months, it's roughly the opposite: To give your air conditioner a rest, let cool breezes flow through but keep out the sun.

A good first step is simple, no-brainer observation. Track the sun's path on your property and house throughout both summer and winter days to pinpoint strategic places for deciduous (leaf-bearing) trees and shrubs. Notice how sunlight heats up pavements, walls, and roofs, and how it penetrates windows in all seasons. Make special note of how the sun strikes the house between 9 A.M. and 3 P.M. in the winter—your only opportunity to warm up your living room with passive solar energy.

Also, notice which directions the winds blow in from, so you can position wind-deflecting shrubs and trees in the right places. Remember, if the outside temperature is 10 degrees F. and the wind speed is 20 miles per hour, the wind chill is a very uncomfortable (and expensive) -24 degrees F.! A study in South Dakota found that windbreaks to the north, west, and east of houses cut fuel consumption by an average of 40 percent.

After recording your observations, set up shop on the dining room table. A Department of Energy fact sheet advises:

Use paper and different colored pencils to begin designing your landscape. First, sketch a simple, scaled drawing of your yard. Locate its buildings, walks, driveways, and utilities (e.g., sewer, electric, and telephone lines). Note the location of all paved surfaces—streets, driveways, patios, or sidewalks—near your home. Then identify potential uses for different areas of your yard: vegetable gardens, flower beds, patios, and play areas.

The components of your plan could include deciduous trees and plants, coniferous trees and plants, earth berms, walls, fences, sheds, and garages. Draw arrows to show sun angles and prevailing winds for both summer and winter. As you sketch, circle the areas of your yard needing shade or wind protection.

The most effective way to keep your home cool is to prevent heat buildup in the first place, so keeping hard surfaces cool is important. Trees and vines create cool microclimates around walls, pavements, and other hard surfaces that reduce ambient temperatures dramatically. Planting shrubs, bushes, and vines next to your house creates dead air spaces that insulate your home in both winter and summer. Leave at least a foot of space between full-grown plants and your home's wall.

Steve Cramer, a Colorado extension agent, suggests Rocky Mountain juniper and Eastern red cedar as sturdy, durable evergreens for windbreaks. His favorite low-maintenance shade tree is hackberry. "It's a medium-speed grower, so it doesn't get brittle, breakable branches. That's a great quality for a tree planted near your house," he explains. "It's also very drought-tolerant with deep roots, and it doesn't get diseases." He recommends Virginia creeper as a dependable vine to enhance energy conservation. Other good bets for shady areas are winter creeper and English ivy, which usually hang onto their foliage in winter. For sunny locations, Cramer's favorite is the brightly colored clematis vine.

"Use a large bush or row of shrubs to shade your patio or driveway," Cramer suggests. "Plant a hedge to shade a sidewalk, or a trellis for climbing vines to shade a patio area." He also suggests using fences, windbreak plantings, and shade trees to provide a "sun pocket" on the south side of your home where outside activities can take place during sunny and cool but still comfortable winter days.

Low-maintenance turf and ground covers also prevent heat buildup. There are many good choices for ground covers and grasses like buffalo grass that cover bare spots but require very little water or maintenance. Studies conducted by the Lawrence Berkeley National Laboratory documented summer daytime air temperatures to be 3 to 6 degrees F. cooler in tree-shaded neighborhoods than in treeless areas.

As a general rule, provide shade by planting deciduous trees in an arc around the east, south, southwest, and west sides of your home. This blocks sun in the summer, but lets it come through in the winter, when leaves have fallen.

Locate windbreaks—often consisting of evergreen trees and shrubs—on the north and west sides of the home, where sunlight is sparse in the winter and winds are usually strongest. The best windbreaks block wind close to the ground by using trees and shrubs that have low crowns (leaves and branches). Research has shown that a windbreak will reduce wind speed for a distance of as much as thirty times the windbreak's height. But planting your windbreak away from your house a distance of two to five times the mature height of the trees will keep your home even cozier.

Using shade effectively requires you to know the size, shape, and location of the moving shadow that a tree casts. For example, if you want to plant a shade tree for your yard but don't want it to block sun into your house, a 50-foot tall tree planted 100 feet from the house will work. Location of shade trees also depends upon the shape of the tree crown, the height of the roof or walls, and avoiding overhead wires and underground pipes.

Deciduous trees with high, spreading crowns can be planted to the south of your home to provide maximum summertime roof shading. Trees with crowns lower to the ground are more appropriate to the west, where shade is needed from lower afternoon sun angles.

Shading and windbreaking may be the most evident methods of conserving energy in a landscape, but certain other approaches can help save energy in a larger sense. For example, if you replace bluegrass turf with low-maintenance shrubs, grasses, and trees, you may reduce the energy connected with mowing the lawn with a gasoline-powered mower. There's energy "embodied" in fertilizer, pesticides, and water, too. These materials require petroleum feedstocks, manufacturing energy, transportation energy, and pumping energy long before they arrive at our houses. And concrete, one of the materials that heats up the quickest in your landscape, requires a lot of energy in its manufacture. By substituting skill, knowledge, and good landscaping design for these energy-intensive materials, we can reduce the heat load on the planet itself.

NOTES FROM A COLORADO RAIN FOREST
· LONG-LIVED HOUSE PLANTS FOR YOUR LIVING ROOM ·

THE FAMILY OF PLANTS that lives in my house is collectively more than 150 years old. The jade tree, aloe, Swedish ivy, and spider plants have all been with me twenty-five years or more, and four or five others are now ten years old. I like living in an "ancient rain forest" in the middle of the arid West. In fact, since I work at home, I'm considering growing a tropical vine in my living room so I can swing to work.

Over the years, the plants and I have bonded. How can I forget the aloe's clutch performance that helped prevent my daughter from having a burn-scarred face? When she was six or so, she was dancing around the living room, tripped over a Lego town, and fell into our red-hot, cast-iron wood stove. One whole side of her face melted into a first-degree burn, but within seconds that wound was treated with fresh gel from a handful of aloe leaves. I remember the doctor commenting how quickly she healed up, and thirteen years later there's no trace of the accident. I keep the aloe completely organic— using no fertilizers or other chemicals—just a very rich, loamy soil like Fertilome, occasional compost "snacks," and very stingy watering.

The jade tree, now a perfectly symmetrical family member, was once chopped in half when I fell off a ladder while remodeling the living room. It also suffered near-fatal sunburn when put outside too abruptly one spring day. (It's too big to move around much now, but when it *does* go outside, it goes gradually—a few more minutes each day.)

The spider plant and her leggy daughters came from a handful of cuttings a friend gave me around 1973. Despite being left on front porches in heavy frosts and underwatered during a few vacations, the spiders continue to send out hopeful, flowery runners in search of soil or marshland. I've found that keeping their oversized plastic tray filled with water works fine for spiders. They don't seem to object to "wet foot" that can cause rot in other plants.

The Swedish ivy, the other elder of the jungle, has also weathered less than ideal light conditions and unintentional drydowns without too much complaining. Because I know what it looks like at its best— shiny-leafed and fully extended—I wait until it's off that mark just a little to give it a complete soaking, which lasts up to a week.

I've noticed that my family of plants is happier growing in a thicket than individually. A diversity of plants seems to keep insects and diseases from gaining a foothold. The plants share humidity and shelter each other from drafts. My living room jungle especially appreciates the tabletop fountain I bought from a Boulder artist a few years ago. I know the little waterfall transpires half a gallon of moisture into the air every day—especially during periods of low ambient humidity—because I routinely refill the little pond each morning while my breakfast is cooking. As I'm watering the plants themselves, I check for any problems they may have. The grove of avocados, for example, is susceptible to a leaf disease that spreads very quickly unless I cut off diseased portions of the leaves. As I remove the diseased pieces at the leaves' edges, I'm careful to wash the scissors in soapy water or a mild solution of rubbing alcohol in between cuts.

I don't consider it work to take care of my houseplants, but if I did, it would be work that pays off in tangible benefits like good indoor air quality. Lab tests have proven that plants like spider, golden pothos, and English ivy can remove up to 100 percent of dangerous indoor pollutants like carbon monoxide, formaldehyde, and benzene, converting the pollutants into harmless compounds like carbon dioxide. I don't seem to get persistent colds, and I give a lot of the credit to my family of plants.

Probably the biggest reward my living room garden conveys is a sense of vitality in my house. It feels comfortably *alive,* and there's always something new going on. My avocado plants that have grown eight feet in two years were the classic elementary school experiment in propagation. I tried the toothpick and water-filled glass technique, the damp soil technique, and the damp sand technique to sprout the pits. They all worked, but I had to wait up to two months before some of them germinated. After planting a few seedlings in a large pot, I began just pushing new pits into the pot and forgetting about them, because they got watered as I watered the plants.

Five years later, I'm beginning to watch for blossoms. I love avocados!

In general, I like to plant most species in groups of three or more because they're bushier and fuller looking that way. I try to give each plant a quarter turn when I think of it, to balance its exposure to sun. Garden stores have trays with wheels on them to turn the plants, but I've never tried them—I just grab hold of the tray and turn the pot inside it.

Much of the literature on houseplants cautions against keeping plants in "standing water," but in our dry climate, I've never had a problem using oversized trays, frequently filled with water. The plants can take up as much water as they need. Every few weeks, I soak each plant from the top down, to wash residual salts out of the soil. I've adapted hanging pots that are sold in garden stores to provide larger trays, by drilling holes in plastic pots and trays and wiring them together.

When it comes to fertilization, I'm a firm believer that less is better. The conventional fertilizers, with nutrient formulas like 20-15-20, may pump up the growth of your houseplants, but in an artificial way—sort of like a human diet of sugar and steroids. Fast, lush growth pushes a plant's health out of balance, making it more susceptible to insects and diseases. I like to rely on excellent potting soil with worm castings and other organic materials that releases nutrients *slowly*. I've had pretty good luck with Osmocote pellets for hungry, pot-bound plants like the jade, the ficus, and the profusely flowering kolanchoe—engineered to flower itself to death without nutritional boosts. But my favorite fertilizer is seaweed, which contains all the micronutrients plants need to be healthy and resilient. An occasional misting with liquid seaweed may temporarily make your living room smell like a harbor at low tide, but notice the difference in greenness and shininess of the leaves, and witness the new growth a few days later.

The fact is, it may be a "jungle" out there, but my jungle *in here* definitely helps me handle the craziness.

SOLVING THE CASE OF THE DISAPPEARING DWARF BULBS
· THE EVIDENCE MAY POINT BACK TO YOUR HOSE ·

WHEN SPRINGTIME BECOMES a long-awaited reality, you're wishing you'd planted more bulbs, aren't you? You wish you'd taken the time last October to plant some of the colorful little "dwarf" bulbs you've never tried before. No, you can't plant them now (with a few exceptions like anemone), but you can be on the lookout as they emerge in neighbors' yards, at the Botanic Gardens, and in other well-designed landscapes. You can figure out which bulbs you want to plant next fall, and then write down their names so you won't forget. You can even mail order them now for fall shipment.

But beware of the disappearing bulb. One fall, I bought hundreds of these cute little bulbs and corms, brought them home, and spent an afternoon digging them into strategic corners and niches in the rock garden. I dug in some composted leaf mold with supplementary bonemeal, carefully spaced clusters of the miniatures 3 or 4 inches apart under 3½ inches of soil, and...by spring, *most of the bulbs disappeared!*

I decided to learn more about these miniatures, so I could find out who/what was responsible for their disappearance. I discovered that spring-flowering bulbs sometimes get buried too deeply and eventually rot, or get eaten by mice, moles, and gophers. Crocuses are especially relished by critters. This problem can be solved by planting the bulbs in a bed "within a wire basket" or by using gravel barriers around the bulbs. In general, bulbs are relatively free from diseases and pests, and they are adaptable to various sun/shade conditions, but they are particular about moisture. *Leucojum, Scilla nutans,* and *Fritillaria* prefer moist conditions, but for most of the other small bulbs, a cold, waterlogged clay soil will cause their disappearance during the dormant months as readily as dry, desiccating soil will during the growing season.

Most of the small bulbs are native to the Mediterranean region, east to Turkey and the Russian steppe. They are commonly found growing wild in locations that dry out in the winter and then get a spring soaking. The master bulb growers of Holland, who grow nine billion bulbs a year, have learned to mimic the bulbs' natural growing conditions. Since 1593, when a handful of Turkish tulips were planted at the University of Leiden, the Dutch have also been constantly hybridizing spectacular colors and qualities such as variegation, the ability to naturalize in lawns and woodlands, and winter hardiness.

Another reason the little bulbs tend to disappear may be that they get tucked here and there as a sort of afterthought at the end of the gardening season. In among the perennial or annual flowers, their corms and offsets become victims of fanatic transplanting or weeding.

If given a loamy place of their own, they will multiply and naturalize without any assistance. When clumps become overcrowded, they can be lifted with a trowel or spade, divided, and immediately transplanted to another location. Or else they can be pulled up in clumps when foliage starts to yellow, separated into individual bulbs, and hung up in dry storage, like in garlic baskets.

The small bulbs that are least likely to disappear in western gardens are snowdrops (*Galanthus*), snowflakes (*Leucojum*), squills (*Scilla*), glory-of-the-snow (*Chionodoxa*), grape hyacinths (*Muscari*), and most varieties of crocus. Equally as attractive but less predictable are anemone or windflower (*Anemone*), miniature iris, spring starflower (*Brodiaea*), fritillaries (*Fritillaria*), and dogtooth violet (*Erythronium*).

By using different varieties, an early blooming period of six weeks or more can be achieved. A planting of snowdrops, *Puschkinia*, *Scilla siberica*, and *Chionodoxa*, for example, will overlap nicely with the flowering of the larger bulbs and early perennials.

It's important to buy good, certified bulbs that aren't spotty or spongy. If the foliage of a plant or clump appears misshapen or mottled, remove it immediately before the virus spreads. Be sure to control aphids, since this pest spreads viruses such as mosaic.

When selecting bulbs from bins at the hyper-hardware or garden center, make sure you don't get a mixture of bulbs by mistake, if adjacent bins have similar-looking products.

Here are a few more tips:

- Create grouped "bouquets" of color, rather than "here an iris, there an iris," because masses of color are more attractive from close up as well as from a distance.
- Try planting the early-flowering small bulbs directly in the lawn—they'll be ready for cut back before the mowing season begins. Crocus, snowdrops, *Chionodoxa*, and *Scilla* are good choices.
- Split snowdrops, anemone, and crocus after a few years to encourage growth and increase your bed.

- Remove flowers as soon as they wither to avoid energy-wasting seed production.

There you have it: Treat them right and they won't disappear. If they do, chances are good that the location is either too wet in the winter or too dry in the spring and summer, or that they became overcrowded. Maybe your protective snow cover melted just in time for the arrival of an unexpected arctic front. For insurance against freezing, try giving the beds some cover. Pine boughs work well and add green color to your winter garden. Some cities grind up Christmas trees and make the mulch available free, which also adds fragrance—especially in your car on the way home.

One more time—don't forget to buy bulbs this fall! Help stamp out starvation in Holland—they can't eat bulbs, can they? Buy more bulbs than you can afford. Skip a meal, sell your golf clubs, charge it.

POINSETTIA PERFECTION
· A SECOND YEAR'S BLOOM, IF YOU'RE LUCKY ·

MY FRIEND DENNIS CAME BACK from Copper Canyon in northern Mexico talking about poinsettias that are 8 to 10 feet tall. "Yeah right," I said. "Sorta like the 30-inch trout that you also forgot to take a picture of?" But since I'd seen familiar-looking ferns and other "houseplants" about the size of houses in the rain forests of Belize and Vietnam, I checked into my friend's report. It turns out I owe him a beer, because relatives of America's most popular potted plant (70 million poinsettias sold in a typical year) can indeed reach heights of up to 25 feet in their native habitat, southern Mexico and Guatemala.

Maybe I need to get even with Dennis by betting him that poinsettias are not poisonous. Like many people, he may believe there's a risk in having this "toxic" plant in the house. However, studies have repeatedly proven that poinsettias are no more poisonous than, say, your aunt's brick-like fruitcakes. If a child (for some unexplainable reason) somehow ended up eating five hundred poinsettia leaves, that binge would no doubt result in a stomachache, but would still be comparable to the experimental dose administered without consequence to laboratory animals. But don't get me wrong—I'm not advising that you eat your poinsettia—it has more value in your entry or living room, on a windowsill with bright light.

What is true about poinsettias is that they can be kept alive during the summer, and with special care in the months of October and November, they will rebloom. Some enterprising nursery should offer to recycle some of the millions of poinsettias that are routinely pitched in January, because if the plants are kept healthy over the summer, then given twelve to fourteen hours of darkness for eight weeks before the holiday season, they can be recycled into bloom in mid-December.

I suppose some people may not want a reminder of the dizzying holiday season (and all the money that was spent!) for much longer than the middle of January, but it's a fact that the new breeds of poinsettias often remain ornamental until late spring, if they are cared for properly. The first step is to choose a plant whose flowers have not yet opened, but whose bracts (the brightly colored part of the plant) are already vibrant. Choose the most vigorous plant—dark green leaves, completely free of disease and insect pests, and without the need for ties or stakes. Don't buy a plant that looks wilted when wet—this is a sign of root disease. Don't allow the plant to experience drafts of cold air less than 45 degrees on the way home. Instead, ask for a protective sleeve, to make sure your plant doesn't lose leaves.

At home, poke a hole in the bottom of the decorative foil that's often wrapped around the plant, to ensure good drainage. The secret to a healthy poinsettia is water control—they don't like standing water in their trays, and they like to dry out a bit between waterings. They also like occasional misting during flowering season. Keep your poinsettia in bright light but avoid strong, direct sun to preserve bract color, and don't allow house temperature to dip below 50 degrees. Also, don't let leaves touch cold windowpanes.

If you bond with your poinsettia and can't bear to throw it away, see if you can get it to rebloom in December. Here's how you do it. When the leaves have fallen in April or May, prune the plant back to 4-inch-tall stems. (You can try propagating those cut stems in damp soil to get some new plants.) Keep the plant fairly dry and shaded for a few weeks, then repot in fresh potting soil and increase watering. Some gardeners put the plants outside in a partially sunny spot, digging the plant into the soil, right in its pot. The challenge begins right after the fall equinox—September 21. You'll have to get in the habit of putting your poinsettia to bed every night, under a black polyethylene bag, in the closet, or in a kitchen cabinet. A co-worker puts her plant in a desk drawer every night and over the weekend, and says it's worked in the past. The key thing is to make the plant think it's in the tropics, with more than twelve hours of darkness every night. Is it worth it? Sure. With a little extra care, azaleas, kalanchoes, and Christmas cactuses can also be coaxed into natural holiday color.

Poinsettias have come a long way since the nineteenth century, when some botanists referred to them as weeds. In addition to "ratweed," they've also been called fire flower, flame leaf, and lobster flower. To Aztec kings near Taxco, poinsettias were *cuetlaxochitle*—symbols of purity, fever-fighters, and sources of reddish-purple dye. By the seventeenth century, when Franciscan monks in Mexico began using poinsettias in nativity processions, they were *flores de la noche buena* (flowers of the Holy Night).

The poinsettia got its current name when the first ambassador to Mexico, Joel Poinsett, found them growing on Mexican hillsides in 1828, and promptly sent cuttings back to his South Carolina plantation. In the twentieth century, the name Ecke became synonymous with poinsettia. That California family has been the dominant force in the poinsettia's brilliant evolution. From the original, leggy-stemmed red variety, the Eckes and their colleagues have genetically developed compact, long-lasting varieties that are white, pink, lemon drop, salmon, and even Monet—a cultivar that impressionistically blends pink and peach tones.

Winter Rose, with curly leaves that appear to be double, is now widely available during the holiday season, and the newest variety—a miniature two-inch-tall poinsettia, is also becoming available in many garden centers. Come to think of it, maybe I should bet my friend that there are now poinsettia varieties only two inches tall that self-water themselves with a wick. He'd never believe it.

THE ANCIENT ART OF FLOWER DRYING AND PRESSING
· ADVICE FROM TWO MASTERS ·

IF YOU'RE A PLANT PERSON, trees, flowers, and prized vegetable plots are often props or even main characters on the stage where your memory holds forth. Scripted into my own memory are sunflowers that were ten feet tall (I have pictures to prove it); the Year of the Columbines in the garden in front of our log house; and Sungold cherry tomatoes in the Harmony Garden that tasted as sweet as berries.

I recently pulled a vintage copy of *Rodale's Encyclopedia of Organic Gardening* off the shelf and found five or six wildflowers pressed in its pages. They triggered a few more scenes from the past—of hikes I'd taken years before in the foothills overlooking Denver, before picking wildflowers became politically incorrect. (With increasing numbers of hikers, some flowers like the brilliantly red wood lily have been picked out of existence.)

One hike was in late spring and the other early fall, evidenced by the pasqueflowers, bluebells, and sand lilies in one collection, and the asters and coreopsis in another part of the book. As I examined the flattened relics, I vaguely recalled walking and collecting the flowers at Mount Falcon Park on crisp, sunny days sometime in the early 1980s.

Wondering what the current state of the art was for an art that's been around since the pyramids were built, I searched a half-dozen websites. On the *Learn2* website, I did learn a thing or two: "Often, a flower's dried state depends on the length of the period between when it was picked and when the drying process began. Keep in mind that fully bloomed flowers are more likely to fall apart than ones just past the bud stage. Also, the time of day affects a flower's drying success, since many flowers go through changes throughout the day, such as opening and closing their petals according to light and moisture."

"For small flowers," the website continues, "Get out the old phone books. Open to a page toward the end and line both pages with paper towels, so the flowers will have top and bottom liners. Carefully spread your flowers around the page, making sure each has plenty of room to spread or move. Close the book and keep it under other heavy books in a safe, cool place. Leave them for a period of two to three weeks...."

On the *Reports from the Garden* website, P. Allen Smith reports, "I made a simple flower press from two ¼-inch plywood boards, measuring 14 inches square. On each corner I put a 3-inch-long threaded ¼-inch (diameter width) bolt with wing nuts and washers. To separate the layers of flowers, I used some recycled cardboard cut the same size as the plywood, then trimmed the corners to fit around the bolts." Smith urges the reader to mount each flower on a piece of cardboard in the press, label it, and describe what kind of growing conditions it came from.

I thought I'd caught up with the state of the art, more or less. That is, until I came across some beautiful, three-dimensional–looking cards at the Rocky Mountain Seed Company. I realized by their luster that there must be more to flower pressing than just beating the wilt. I made a point of talking with the cards' designers, curious how they got started, and what memories their cards are made of.

Cathie, the business's manufacturer and marketer, recalled how her deceased Mom loved to work with the geraniums, pansies, and tulips in the yard where the family has lived for forty-two years. "We'd go camping in the mountains," she said, "and the wildflowers we would see have always been a favorite memory." Her sister Jackie, the team's flower arranger, explained, "Cathie and I have been making cards for three or four years now, and after a lot of experimentation, we're getting our technique down, using hand-pressed flowers that come right from our garden." (She emphasized that they, too, now avoid picking wildflower blossoms.) What began as a hobby—making cards for family and friends—quickly blossomed into a successful business, CJ's Colorado Cards.

A few years ago, Jackie planted $200 worth of columbine seedlings, and the sisters began to find techniques to "put smiles on people's faces." They eventually discovered the value of both laser printer and microwave oven for their cottage industry. (Now *this* was state of the art.) Freshly picked blossoms from the backyard and the gardens of friends go immediately into a terra-cotta press, and then into the microwave. After being quick-dried, they are sorted on Jackie's "palettes" (cookie sheets or the large lids of plastic bins), where the real magic takes place. "My own favorite colors are the yellows and oranges," she told me, "because they maintain their brightness so well."

After the arrangements are created, they are rushed to the print shop while still at the peak of their vibrancy. Although most of the cards don't have the original blossoms on them, they *look* like they do. You pick up a card and run your fingers across it, just to be sure. This technique enables fewer blossoms to be harvested each year, and means that more quality can go into the design.

Their inventory of card designs is well over fifty now, as the business continues to grow. Following the tragedies of 9/11, one of their cards was sent to a New York woman who lost her husband. Another card—and memory—was recently created by a little neighbor girl whose mother works. The little girl learned about drying flowers from Cathie rather than spending the whole workday with her mother. "The girl learned the whole process," Cathie told me, "and created a beautiful card she gave to her Mom."

AND THE WINNERS ARE...
· BLUE-RIBBON CHOICES FROM THE PLANT SELECT PROGRAM ·

EVERY YEAR SINCE 1997, a sort of Academy Award of western flowers and shrubs is announced. It's called the Plant Select program, a cooperative effort among Denver Botanic Gardens, Colorado State University, and the nursery industry. "Oscars" are awarded to unique plants that have been proven to thrive in western soils, climate, and moisture conditions. The goal of the program directors, Jim Klett from CSU and Panayoti Kelaidis from the Botanic Gardens, is to seek out, identify, and distribute the best plants for gardens of the mountains and plains.

Explains Kelaidis, "Many of the plants that are standards in western gardens came to us from Western Europe, where the growing conditions are totally different. A few decades ago, it occurred to western master growers that we should go back to the wild and find plants that grow well in semiarid regions of the world that resemble Colorado." He emphasized that any such choices would be rigorously field-tested to prevent pest-plants from being introduced.

Kelaidis traveled in recent years to highland South Africa, the mountains of Spain, and Pakistan to find hardy species that will add brightness and reliability to Colorado gardens. The Plant Select team also explored wild local areas like Pawnee National Grassland, where researchers found the 'Pawnee Buttes' sand cherry. They explored Cheyenne Research station as well, where the Cheyenne mock orange caught their eyes. Says Jim Klett, "Since the research station has been closed since 1974, the plants that survived on their own were as hardy as they come. We were excited by the Cheyenne mock orange, and rigorous field tests have confirmed it's a winner."

In fact, according to Kelaidis, all thirty-five of the selections have proven successful. "Typically, the evaluation process takes between five and ten years, and it also takes awhile to build up inventories of the plants in nurseries and garden centers. In that period of time, we come to know if we've got a winner."

My own favorites from the Plant Select list include a few under-appreciated natives as well as exotic introductions from other continents and from southern reaches of this continent—as far south as the highlands of central Mexico. Each has a story behind it.

The 'Prairie Jewel' penstemon was developed from Great Plains stock in a Denver garden by Mary Ann Heacock. It has giant flowers that range from pure white through rose-pink to deep purple. A true Xeriscape champion, it likes dry soil and is hardy up to 8,000 feet.

Winecups are also Colorado natives that the Plant Select team wanted to tell the world about. The 5- to 8-inch plant's red wine blossoms last from April to frost without pampering. Last summer, a stand of winecups sprawled over a rocky bank in my neighbor's yard and remained in blossom for a month without any water while she was on vacation.

'Spanish Gold' broom is a subalpine shrub that Kelaidis found growing in the mountains of Spain. It grows 4 to 6 feet tall with a mound of yellow blossoms in mid-late spring. "So far, it hasn't shown any freeze damage," says Kelaidis, like a proud father. The Fort Collins Nursery has been responsible for increasing the plant's inventory, but the Big Kahuna is located at the Denver Botanic Gardens, where the shrub is now ten feet across.

'Coral Canyon' twinspur is a heat-tolerant perennial that Kelaidis found in the mountains of South Africa. "Growers here had tried it," he says, "and it was fabulous but too tall—it would always flop over. So I was looking for a genetically dwarfed race of the plant, and I finally found one small plant that I harvested seeds from." He describes the fifteen-inch-tall plant as "a cloud of soft pink, oval flowers."

'Coronado' hyssop and 'Sunset' hyssop bring a fragrant touch of the southwest to northern gardens. The Plant Select team describes 'Sunset' as "Yellow stained with orange helmets of fiery color from midsummer to autumn frost." A 1940s botanist exploring the area from central Mexico to northern New Mexico mentioned this perennial of the agastache family, but few growers had tried them until recently. Last summer I brought a few plants back from a greenhouse in Santa Fe, and smelled their outrageous root beer/mint fragrance all the way up to Denver.

'Remembrance' columbine, derived from the Colorado state flower, honors the memory of the students and teacher of the Columbine High School tragedy. The plant serves as a living memorial, and proceeds will benefit organizations that promote diversity and tolerance in schools.

'Carol Mackie' daphne is the last of my favorites from the Plant Select list. I've grown this variegated, almost-evergreen shrub for several years in my shady, protected front yard. Leaves often persist into January or February, and the fragrance of the pale pink flowers in spring and sometimes again in fall is outstanding.

Here's a complete list of the thirty-five winners, now widely available in nurseries, where they bear Plant Select tags:

Plant Select Varieties for Gardens of the Western Mountains and Plains

2002: 'Mesa Verde' ice plant, 'Table Mountain' ice plant, Alpine willowherb, Apache plume, Siberian spiraea, 'Smith' buckthorn.

2001: 'Coronado' hyssop, 'Remembrance' columbine, 'First Love' dianthus, 'Cheyenne' mock orange, 'Comanche' gooseberry, 'Orange Carpet' California fuchsia, 'Denver Gold' columbine.

2000: 'Spanish Gold' broom, 'Princess Kay' plum, 'Prairie Jewel' penstemon, 'Pawnee Buttes' sand cherry, 'Coral Canyon' twinspur.

1999: Winecups, 'Silver Blade' evening primrose, 'Red Rocks' and 'Pikes Peak' purple penstemon, 'Spanish Peaks' foxglove, 'Blue Velvet' honeysuckle, prairie cordgrass, silver dollar plant.

1998: 'Starburst' ice plant, 'Lavender Mist' sun daisy, silver butterfly bush, 'Pink Crystals' ruby grass, 'Colorado Gold' hardy gazania.

1997: 'Sunset' hyssop, silver sage, 'Carol Mackie' daphne, Allegheny viburnum, Turkish veronica.

TREES AND SHRUBS WE CAN COUNT ON
· CHAMPIONS OF THE HIGH AND ARID WEST ·

UNTIL RECENTLY, the tall silhouette of a hackberry tree on a hill in Arvada, Colorado, linked the era of the Great Plains bison with our SUV and mega-mall era. According to legend, the hackberry sprouted from a seed in the leather pouch of a dead Arapahoe Indian and survived late into the twentieth century, witnessing in its own way the radical transformation of the High Plains landscape. An hour's drive away, on Mount Goliath, bristlecone pines have survived 1,500 years of cold wind and telephone pole–deep snowdrifts.

Proven survivors—that's the kind of trees and shrubs we need to plant in western landscapes! Some of the best examples around are at the Hildreth–Howard Arboretum, an agricultural field station founded in the 1920s. After forty-six years of operation, during which hundreds of native tree and shrub species and other naturalized species from all over the world were planted, the field station was converted to grasslands research, and many of the experimental plantings were left high and dry. And that's exactly why they are now being studied—because they are proven winners. Like the Ginnala maple from Manchuria, the seeds of which were planted in 1933, or the Norwegian apple, planted in 1934. Because of the station's high, cold, and dry location (6,000 feet in elevation, only 14.4 inches of moisture a year), windiness (13 mph daily average), and poor soils (alkaline and poor moisture retention), if a plant makes it in Cheyenne, it can make it almost anywhere in the West.

Before the field station's mission changed, 1,300 varieties of woody ornamental plants were tested, including over 100 different types of hedge materials and 200 species of trees and shrubs, for dryland windbreaks. Some of the survivors have been chosen for the Plant Select program described in the chapter, "And the Winners Are…" Others are being studied by the Colorado State Forest Service, which operates a nursery outside of Fort Collins where hardy trees and shrubs are grown.

If you sometimes feel like you can't properly care for the hundreds of plants in your garden, try growing 2.8 million trees and shrubs every year, like forest biologist Randy Moench does. For the past sixteen years, he's overseen the production of species that can provide windbreaks, wildlife habitat, and land restoration for western residents. "We sell

Cheyenne Field Station Survivors, Observed in 1995

Acer tataricum spp.	Ginnala Tatarian maple
Aesculus glabra	Ohio buckeye
Amelanchier alnifolia	Serviceberry
Amorpha nana	Dwarf leadplant
Chaenomeles speciosa	Flowering quince
Cornus stolonifera	Redtwig dogwood
Crataegus ambigua	Russian hawthorn
Crataegus mollis	Downy hawthorn
Euonymus europaeus	Spindle tree
Fallugia paradoxa	Apache plume
Fraxinus pennsylvanica	Green ash
Kolkwitzia amabilis	Beauty bush
Lonicera tatarica	Tatarian honeysuckle
Lonicera tatarica 'Zabellii'	Zabel's honeysuckle
Philadelphus coronarius	Sweet mock orange
Philadelphus lewisii	Wild mock orange
Quercus rubra	Northern red oak
Quercus macrocarpa	Burr oak
Rhodotypos scandens	Jetbead
Rhus trilobata	Three-leaf sumac
Ribes aureum	Golden currant
Rosa x *harisonii*	Harison's yellow rose
Syringa reticulata	Japanese tree lilac
Syringa persica	Persian lilac
Syringa vulgaris	Common lilac
Tilia americana	Basswood
Tilia Americana 'Redmond'	Redmond linden
Tilia cordata	Little-leaf linden
Viburnum carlesii	Korean spice viburnum
Viburnum lentago	Nannyberry viburnum
Viburnum opulus	European cranberry bush
Rubus deliciosus	Rocky Mountain thimbleberry

mostly dormant, bare-root seedlings for conservation purposes," he says, as we tour the operation from seedlings to packaging and distribution. "Buyers have to certify they won't resell the seedlings, and that they have two acres or more of land. If they meet those conditions, they can get seedlings very inexpensively."

"One of our steadiest customers is Phillips County, out on the plains near Kansas. They plant up to 300,000 trees and shrubs every year, partly to enhance wildlife habitat and increase pheasant populations for hunting."

Over the years, I've planted many seedlings grown by the state nursery, and had great success with species like Common lilac, Peking cotoneaster, Siberian peashrub, and Nanking cherry. Although the process demands patience and intensive care at first (flag them so you won't forget where they are), I love it when the "twigs" my neighbors laugh at emerge three or four years later as a hedge or riparian thicket. Sometimes I find out what a particular plant needs by default. This spring, for example, I observed that the Siberian peashrub does very well without much irrigation. Last March, when I soaked the hedge—planted five years ago as a windbreak for the garden—I unwittingly made the shrubs vulnerable to a freeze in late May. This year I haven't watered the peashrubs at all, instead relying on moisture stored under a thick mulch of leaves. The hedge looks great and last week survived a record-setting freeze, partly because its leafy tissue wasn't swollen with water.

"Our quirky weather, especially in the spring and fall, presents a real challenge for woody plants," Randy comments. "For example, it takes about a month or more for a tree to go dormant, and if its cells are flush with water, a hard freeze in early fall can do a lot of damage, which we may not notice until the following spring." Moench recommends cutting back on watering in mid-August, to prepare a tree or shrub for that all-too-familiar cold snap in September or early October. "After the tree has successfully gone dormant," he advises, "then soak it down to get it through the driest part of the year in early winter."

Moench has seen many good intentions result in dead trees and shrubs—victims of overwatering. "A lot of people do their watering by schedule, even if the soil is already moist. They saturate the soil so the roots can't get enough oxygen. Instead, they could be a little more observant by digging a shovelful of soil near the tree to see if it's moist."

The most popular seedling the state nursery grows is Rocky Mountain Juniper, an all-star performer in most western conditions, including the low temperatures of the high country and the hot, dry, and windy conditions of the plains, canyons, and scrublands. To get this tree started, dig a hole two or three times wider than the containerized root system or root ball, keeping in mind that most of the root system will remain within 2 feet of the surface. If planting bareroot stock, make sure the hole is big enough to accommodate the roots without crowding, and that roots are not tangled, upturned, planted in an air pocket, or planted too shallow. After backfilling with soil and watering in the roots, mulch the tree with wood shavings, pine needles, or fabric mulch.

In the home landscape, the Rocky Mountain juniper can be vulnerable to spider mites that cause the juniper to look grayish or yellowish. But this barely visible pest can be controlled with routine sprays of high-pressure water.

Moench is a firm believer in native soils for native and adaptive species. "The species we grow are adapted to native soil conditions, so the soils don't need amendment," he says. "The most important rule of thumb is *balance* between 'root and shoot,'" he says. "If your soil is too rich, you may get vigorous growth on top but poor root development."

After many years of observation, he's a strong advocate for landscape fabrics as no-maintenance mulches to conserve water and reduce weed competition. The success rate of fabric-mulched trees and shrubs is many times higher than for unmulched plantings, largely because of improved water retention. While I acknowledge the potential of "plasticulture," I remain reluctant to leave plastic in the landscape, where it will ultimately degrade and leave plastic particles

Hardy Trees and Shrubs for Windbreaks and Habitat Restoration

Shrubs

Buffaloberry	10 feet high, hardy to 7,500 feet
Chokecherry	6 to 20 feet high, rapid growth, to 9,000 feet
Cotoneaster	Cold hardy to 9,500 feet, good for wildlife
European sage	Drought resistant, hardy to 6,000 feet
Four-wing saltbush	3 feet high, drought resistant to 8,500 feet
Golden currant	Moist soil, drought resistant to 8,500 feet
Honeysuckle	Drought resistant, cold hardy to 8,000 feet
Lilac	Alkalinity tolerant, 8 to 12 feet, to 8,000 feet
Mountain mahogany	Good wildlife, drought resistant to 9,000 feet
Native plum	Rapid growth, cold hardy to 8,000 feet
Nanking cherry	Cold hardy to 8,000 feet, good fruit
New Mexico privet	8 feet high, cold hardy to 11,000 feet
Red-osier dogwood	Cold hardy to 11,000 feet, wet sandy soil
Sand cherry	Sandy soils to 7,500 feet, short-lived
Serviceberry	6 feet high, cold hardy to 9,000 feet
Siberian peashrub	Drought resistant, hardy to 9,500 feet
Skunkbush sumac	Drought resistant, cold hardy to 8,000 feet
Snowberry	3 feet high, cold hardy to 9,500 feet
Wild rose	4 feet high, hardy to 10,000 feet

Trees

Aspen	35 to 50 feet high, cold hardy to 11,000 feet
Austrian pine	To 40 feet high, long life span, 7,000 feet
Bristlecone pine	Long life span, hardy to 11,000 feet
Burr oak	To 75 feet high, cold hardy to 7,000 feet
Colorado blue spruce	To 100 feet high, long life span, 9,500 feet
Douglas fir	To 100 feet, long life span, 9,000 feet
Engelmann spruce	Cold hardy to 11,000 feet, to 90 feet high
Eastern red cedar	Drought resistant, long life, 7,500 feet
Golden willow	To 35 feet high, moist soil, tolerates salt
Green ash	35 to 75 feet high, cold hardy to 9,500 feet
Hackberry	4 to 60 feet high, cold hardy to 7,000 feet
Honey locust	35 to 75 feet high, long life span, 7,500 feet
Hybrid cottonwood (poplar)	75 to 100 feet high, hardy to 8,500 feet
Limber pine	To 35 feet, cold hardy to 11,000 feet
Lodgepole pine	35 to 70 feet, cold hardy to 11,000 feet
Narrowleaf cottonwood	To 50 feet, cold hardy to 9,500
Native willow mix	Moist soil, cold hardy to 9,500 feet
Piñon pine	Drought resistant, good wildlife, 15 to 30 feet
Ponderosa pine	To 100 feet high, hardy to 9,000 feet
Rocky Mountain juniper	Drought resistant, cold hardy to 9,000 feet
Scotch pine	To 65 feet high, good Christmas tree
Siberian elm	To 40 feet high, cold hardy to 8,000 feet
White fir	To 100 feet, cold hardy to 9,000 feet

behind. I'd rather scrounge the classifieds and neighborhoods for truckloads of gravel or wood chips to use as mulch.

Another of Moench's observations is that the rate of growth of a certain tree or shrub can be deceiving. "People want to know, 'How fast will it grow?' but I've seen even the slow-growing species catch up after ten years or so, after their roots are well-established." He recalls planting Eastern red cedar and Austrian pine on the same property. "At first, the cedars grew much faster, but years later, the slow-growing Austrian pines are taller."

"The critical element is planting in the right place. For example, the Colorado blue spruce loves sun, but the Engelmann spruce hates it. Aspen and bristlecone pine do well in high country but don't thrive at lower elevations. The redtwig dogwood is a great wetland species but doesn't do well in a dry landscape."

Moench recommends the skunkbush sumac for wildlife habitat enhancement. This shrub has great red-orange fall color, good resistance to cold and drought, and doesn't smell a bit like a skunk. "If you want to attract the birds, plant fruiting shrubs like Nanking cherry, golden currant, and chokecherry," Moench suggests. "And for wet areas, we've found the coyote willow, peach-leaved willow, and wild rose to be good choices."

Throughout the arid West, the champions of the landscape are demonstrating what evolution has taught them: Stick with conditions that are familiar. Sometimes those conditions may be found on the other side of the planet, but similar climate, soil pH, and moisture make the plant feel at home. And even for a plant, there's no place like home.

A Winter Tour of the Denver Botanic Gardens
· The Exotic (inside) and the Hardy (outside) ·

IT WAS PUSHING 60 DEGREES on a February day, and I was going to be in Denver. So I called to see if someone at the Botanic Gardens could give me a short tour of the grounds and conservatory—a huge greenhouse that looks like a spacecraft that swallowed a rain forest. Harriett McMillan, who has been involved with the Denver Botanic Gardens since the 1970s, took time out of her schedule to show me some of her favorite plants and locations.

First we walked through the Tropical Botanica in the conservatory, where the humidity was over 75 percent and the scent of tropical blossoms thickened the air. I felt like I was back in my favorite vacation spot, Belize. I commented that the banana plants looked much less beat-up than those I'd seen in the wild. "They don't have to deal with the wind and rain, so they don't get as tattered," she explained. Clusters of ripening bananas hung over our heads, ten or twelve feet in the air—enough fruit for breakfast cereal at the Broncos training camp. As we walked toward the chocolate tree (*Cacao theobroma*), I noticed jaguar footprints and fern imprints on the path under my feet, courtesy of volunteers from the Denver Museum of Nature and Science who participated in the renovation of the greenhouse.

"Kids love the pathway imprints, because they get their imaginations going. They also love our 'Children's Guide to Tropical Botanica,' about how a person could survive in a habitat like this," she said. In the colorful brochure, cartoon kids drink water from moisture-capturing bromeliad plants, make rafts from bamboo stalks, and harvest cocoa beans and sugarcane to make chocolate. I felt like asking if I could try a week or so in the wilds of the conservatory. But then she showed me the *Cacao* tree's yellow fruits that looked like elongated acorn squash, and told me the cocoa beans had to be fermented. It started sounding like too much work even for a chocoholic like myself.

We walked past many species familiar to lovers of indoor houseplants, except in these ideal conditions they seemed like silly dream versions of themselves. The 'Moonlight' philodendrons were glossy green and vigorous shrubs. The purple-leaved Ti plants and sculpture-like fan palms were Disneyesque characters that might start talking any minute. Victoria water lilies floated in the small lagoon, and blossoming powder puffs and *Euphorbias* seemed convinced that if this was

Colorado, it must be 65 million B.C. As we walked out of the conservatory, I could swear the bamboo had grown half a foot, to tickle the roof of the greenhouse.

Outside, the plants seemed a little less ecstatic, but as my tour guide pointed out, Colorado's winter landscape shouldn't be overlooked, because it's filled with understated shapes and colors. "For a lot of people, fall is when you cut everything in the landscape back, but it doesn't have to be that way," she said. She pointed out the subtle beauty of ornamental seed heads still on their stalks, winter berries still clinging to the bush, tree trunk textures you might not notice when the trees are in leaf, and the ground-hugging greenness of perennials like *Penstemon mexicali,* candytuft (*Iberis sempervirens*), and woolly veronica (*Veronica pectinata*).

"This is a dormant landscape, but not a dead one," she emphasized. We examined the cold-hardy blossoms in the gazania and pansy beds, and noted the green shoots of irises that liked the mild winter weather.

We stopped and observed the distinctive, mottled gray and green bark of the lace-bark pine—an exotic import from China—and the pussy willow–like buds of a magnolia shrub. The foliage of creeping Oregon grape and yellow-flowering ice plants were various shades of violet and burgundy, and the abundant, bright red berries on a compact variety of barberry made the small shrub look like an oversized Christmas ornament.

"Coloradans seem to be looking for more compact varieties of evergreen that don't take over an area," Harriett observed, "and we have a lot of them here—like the Mugho pine and the dwarf spruces. There also seems to be a trend toward the blue and bluish-gray tints of the 'Blue Star' juniper, the Colorado blue spruce, and the various sages."

Her enthusiasm was apparent throughout our hour-long exploration, but her favorite place of all seemed to be the Japanese garden at the west end of the property. "This garden, called *Shofu-en,* or Garden of the Pine Wind, really transcends the seasons. It's a Japanese garden with a Rocky Mountain twist, because the dominant species here is

Ponderosa pine collected from Lyons, maintained in bonsai-like shapes," she said. "I think the garden's strength is in the subdued colors and shapes of the pines, willows, birches, and barberries."

We met Bert, who has maintained the Japanese garden for several years. From up in the branches of a tree, where he was taking down strings of ornamental lights, he commented that the Japanese garden was the perfect place to meditate, in summer or winter. "Don't meditate too hard up there," Harriett said, "or we may have to scrape you up." A little farther down the pathway, Julie was working in the Monet garden. "This is the first year we've kept water in the pond in the winter," she told me. "We're hoping the bubblers keep the water circulating so it doesn't freeze over." Beneath the surface, we could see the shapes of aquatic plants that would be bright green in a few months.

No doubt the mild winter weather had something to do with the smiles on Harriett's, Bert's, and Julie's faces, but there was also a definite sense of connection to the diverse landscapes they tended. They seemed keenly aware of micro-events that take place throughout the seasons at the Gardens, one of the finest plant exhibitions in the high and arid West.

ZEN MASTERS OF THE WEST
· HARVESTING 500 YEARS OF WESTERN GARDENING EXPERIENCE ·

SOLAR GREENHOUSES THAT GROW PEOPLE
· SHANE SMITH'S CHEYENNE BOTANIC GARDEN ·

WYOMING HORTICULTURIST Shane Smith has a recipe for community growth. You build a 6,800-square-foot solar greenhouse with donations and federal and city assistance, then you invite senior, handicapped, and at-risk youth volunteers to work in it. Stir in a healthy dose of horticultural expertise and passion, and what emerges is a place that grows people.

The Cheyenne Botanic Garden, a line item in the city's annual budget, has since 1977 become a vital community center where hundreds of weddings, garden club meetings, and educational tours take place every year. In 2001, 28,000 people from fifty states and thirty countries visited the Botanic Garden. They come to examine the technology of a solar greenhouse that provides 100 percent of its own heat and 50 percent of its own solar electricity in the harsh climate of Cheyenne (No. 4 in the nation for wind, 6,000-foot elevation, No. 1 in the nation for hail). They also come to see firsthand how horticulture can be used for social rehabilitation. Every year, senior, youth, and handicapped volunteers put in more than 5,000 hours, taking care of the plants, themselves, and each other at the same time.

Shane believes it's the only municipal greenhouse whose primary mission is to provide social services. With degrees in both horticulture and horticultural therapy, he exemplifies Japanese horticulturist Masanobu Fukuoka's belief, "Gardening is not just the cultivation of plants, but also the cultivation of human beings." Shane explains, "The most important crops are the pride and self-esteem of the many individuals who work here."

As we stand in the tropical part of the conservatory amid hibiscus, bird-of-paradise, bananas, oranges, and figs, he explains, "We work with 100 different volunteers every year, who accomplish 90 percent of the work. They plant 50,000 bedding plants every year for city gardens, they water and fertilize the perennials and trees, they regulate greenhouse vents—and they know that without their help the greenhouse wouldn't function."

One of the volunteers is ninety-eight-year-old Pauline McCabe, who's been coming in for ten years. Like many senior citizens, she considers the greenhouse a second home. "She'll sit at the table, and people bring her plants that need repotting," he says. "She feels useful, and she feels like part of the community."

"Kids working off court fines are another critical component of our staff. They'll come in for a few months and work twenty-five hours, and then they're gone, but they'll take more than free food and plants with them," he says. "They take away a sense of pride and self-esteem, and they also take away respect for other people." In a world where family members are often distant from each other and handicapped people become isolated, the Botanic Garden is a tossed salad of personalities. Volunteers are exposed to cultures and belief systems they've never experienced before, which helps the city at large become more tolerant and trusting.

Horticultural therapy isn't a new practice. In the 1600s, when poor people worked in gardens to pay for their hospitalization, English doctors noticed quicker recovery rates than for other patients. Similar results were seen in the mental and physical rehabilitation of American veterans of World War II. In fact, many colleges now offer degrees in horticultural therapy, including Kansas State and Texas A&M. Horticultural therapy (HT) is widely used in hospitals, prisons, day care centers, and homeless shelters. According to practitioner Jan Doherty, HT is "medicine that doesn't need a prescription, and that has no limit on dosage."

Shane Smith knows it works, by the smiles on the faces of volunteers. A few years back, staff and volunteers together tried to measure its effectiveness by monitoring the blood pressure of volunteers both before and after working in the greenhouse. The results weren't conclusive, but Shane insists that "if you interviewed our senior volunteers, every one of them would tell you they feel better after being here. 'Meaningful' is a key word for all of us. Our volunteers know their work is valuable. They know they're keeping our building open on the weekend, planning a bed for community beautification, or watering a plant that would die without their attention."

Shane's interest in the social aspects of horticulture takes physical shape in the south-facing greenhouse that converts a tiny chunk of windy Wyoming into a rain forest. Twenty-five years ago professors at Colorado State University urged him to abandon his fascination with solar greenhouses, because they thought that they could never work. It was far more practical, they told him, to focus his studies on landscaping, golf course design, and turf—that's where the money was. But it was the mid-seventies, and the energy crisis had lots of people thinking about alternatives. Solar pioneers like Jim DeKorne, Steve Baer, and Bill Yanda captured Shane's imagination far more than the sugar content of potatoes—a subject he was advised to do a master's thesis on.

Shane was fascinated by ancient Anasazi cliff architecture that took advantage of the natural angles of the sun. "They had solar energy figured out a thousand years ago," he says, pointing to photos of cliff dwelling ruins. "In the winter, when the sun is lower in the sky, its rays shine right into the dwellings. In the summertime when the sun is higher, the homes are comfortably shaded."

The Botanic Garden he helped design uses principles like these to maintain tropical conditions even when temperatures slide to -20 degrees F. The north face of the building is not glazed, but rather looks like a large, gabled house. The south side is glazed with triple-walled polycarbonate that holds heat in. Black fifty-five-gallon drums and floor-to-ceiling glass cylinders are filled with water, which captures the sun's heat and then slowly releases it at night when temperatures drop.

"Gardening in a solar greenhouse is a whole new agricultural climate, like an island surrounded by cold on all sides in winter," he says. "We have to adapt the crops to the climate rather than just turning up the heat—because we don't have a heater to turn up." Out of necessity, Shane and his staff have pioneered biological pest control in greenhouses, learning the ecology of both pests and predators. I asked him about natural controls for whitefly, a pest that always seems to come on strong toward the end of winter in my large cold frames. His favorite control is a small parasitic wasp, *Encarsia formosa,* but he's also worked with a small black ladybird beetle, *Delphastus pusillus,* beneficial spider mites, beneficial sprays like insecticidal soap, horticultural oils, botanical-based sprays such as neem oil and a spray made from a natural fungus (*Beauvaria*), and even physical controls like vacuuming them up with plug-in vacuums and Dust Busters.

"We sneak up on the whiteflies by turning over leaves and exposing their hiding places. Then we suck 'em up and make sure to throw away the vacuum bag." Shane and crew have developed control hierarchies for all the other greenhouse pests, too, and he has compiled his many years of pest control and greenhouse gardening experience in the book, *Greenhouse Gardener's Companion,* written for the home greenhouse gardener.

Shane warns with tongue in cheek, "Sometimes the worst pest is you, because gardeners are so prone to overwatering, overfertilizing, or other ways of loving their plants to death."

A sign in the greenhouse asks visitors, "Please do not wander, tread, mosey, saunter, hop, run, creep, trudge, trot, meander, romp, stumble, skip, stomp, ramble, waddle, plod, march, gallop, traipse, tiptoe, prance, jump, roam, or walk on the plants." But another sign, down the pathway toward the fountain, requests, "Please touch the herbs."

Shane's advocacy of solar greenhouses reflects his belief that our food system is becoming class-based. "People of means are buying the premium food—organic locally grown food that has higher nutritional value and fewer unhealthy residues. Meanwhile, those of lesser means are stuck with the fast food and factory-farmed food that has likely been genetically modified, heavily sprayed with pesticides, and grown on the other side of the world. The typical factory burger might contain meat raised in Brazil fed with grain grown in Argentina and sprayed with pesticides made in Germany."

"But gardening is classless," he continues. "It doesn't matter if you're a millionaire or a blue-collar worker, if you have a 10-by-10 chunk of ground, you can grow some food with a great quality of nutrition that also tastes great and is fun to grow."

He tells a story about a friend of his, Isador Lopez, who caught the solar greenhouse bug and built a sunspace onto his house for about fifty dollars. "His wife was delighted to see him take a truckload of junk to the landfill, but very surprised to see him return with a truckload of *different junk*—two by fours, fifty-five-gallon drums, sheets of corrugated plastic— just about everything he needed to build a greenhouse. He pretty much made it up as he went along, because building a solar greenhouse is not like building a computer—you just need to catch the sun's heat and store it."

Shane believes it's not a question of whether to put a greenhouse on one's house, but whether we can afford *not* to. Attached solar greenhouses can actually heat your home—for every 1 square foot of greenhouse, you can heat 1 to 3 square feet of your home, depending upon the design of the structure and your local climate. Given the quality of our food, and what it's doing to our health and the health of the environment, he believes, "Every neighborhood should have a community garden with a greenhouse on it. Every Junior High School should combine education with food production. Think of all the benefits that would come out of that.…"

IMAGES OF AN HEIRLOOM GARDEN
· BILL SIMPSON'S GOLDEN BACKYARD ·

BILL SIMPSON AND Barbara Goodrich's vegetable garden in Golden, Colorado, is much more than just a garden—it's a way of life. Spend a few hours in their yard and kitchen and you'll get a philosophy lesson; a fruit-, vegetable-, and wine-tasting party; an oral history of the region; and a notebook full of new ideas about what grows best in the shadow of the foothills.

As we stand in the backyard crunching sweet, just-picked 'Royal Gala' apples, Bill points out the advantages of the long, narrow lots laid out more than a century ago by civil engineer Edward Berthoud. "Berthoud, who was a founder of the Colorado School of Mines, lived right down the street," he explains.

"And my great-grandfather on my father's side had a garden right where we're standing. He was the first marshal of Golden, after coming west during the gold rush of 1859." Walking to the back corner of the lot, where black currants now grow, he points out where the garden, chicken house, and outhouse were, more than a century ago.

The fact is, gardening is in Simpson's blood. His maternal grandmother came to Colorado from Slovenia in 1913, settling on seven acres in Fairmont with an apple orchard and a large garden. "The area's first grange meeting was held at that farmhouse," Bill says with a smile. "My grandmother picked wild asparagus on the perimeters of the farm, and my father would take two weeks of vacation every year to pick forty trees' worth of apples and take them down to Denargo Market in Denver. I still have a photograph of his '55 Chevy pickup, loaded down with crates of apples."

He admits he has a soft spot for apples. He and Barbara make two kinds of cider—sweet cider and hard—using Gala, Jonathan, and Wealthy apples from their own yard, as well as the harvest from abandoned trees throughout the Golden area. "I won't tell people where the trees are, but I will let them sample the cider," he says, laughing. Barbara, a harpist at the Brown Palace in Denver, brings home champagne bottles to brew the cider in. Like other aspects of gardening, cider making is a tradition in Bill's family. His parents still have the cider press they used on his grandmother's farm, and once a year he "presses" it back into service.

"Apple trees are a historic, living relic of this area," he says with conviction. "If we could get the local microbreweries to make hard cider along with beer, we could preserve that tradition." He recalls harvesting the apples from a farm across from his grandmother's, before the farm became a subdivision. "I also got permission to cut some of the older trees for firewood, and I have a vivid memory of sitting in front of an apple wood fire that year, drinking hot cider."

Bill is what I call a "strategic gardener," because he knows at the time of planting what he'll do with the harvest. Seven-foot-tall raspberry bushes provide snacks as he gardens, as well as freezer bags full of berries. Celery, carrots, and onions are frozen together as *mirepoix,* for a traditional French soup stock. 'Yamato Extra-Long' cucumbers and especially lemon cucumbers are good enough to eat right off the vine, but they also become pickles for the winter. Cascade hops growing in the front yard become gallons of home-brewed beer—right within a stone's throw of Coors Brewery.

"Pioneers used to stuff pillows with hops for sweet dreams," he says, as I sniff the blossoms. I ask him about the grapes growing on the fence spanning the length of his backyard. "They're one of my most prolific crops, great for table grapes, jams, and wine. I'd like to be able to grow cabernets and zinfandels, like they do on Colorado's West Slope, but they're a little warmer out there—mostly Zone 6, while the Front Range is Zone 5. So I grow varieties that are a bit hardier, like 'Concord', 'Canadice', and 'Leon Millet'."

He observes that grapes thrive on neglect, with deep root systems that forage for nutrients and water on their own. Every other year, he trims the vines, so he gets heavy crops one year and light crops the next. Although his vines have been in the ground only five years, he's already harvesting gallons of grapes every year. "The 'Concord' grapes are very dependable, but you really can't make good wine out of them—you get something that tastes too much like Welch's grape juice," he comments.

One of the courses Simpson teaches at Metro State College in Denver is Environmental Ethics, and clearly, he likes to practice what he teaches. "In many of our jobs," he says, "we don't get to see full cycles—of nature or human effort. In the garden, we do. For example, the fruit skins left over from making wine or cider are recycled in the chicken coop into compost, which then goes back into the garden. What could be more elegant than that?"

Another guiding principle is to grow things he can't usually get in the store, such as the 'Chojuro' Asian pear. He picks one from a tree heavy with fruit and hands it to me. Once I get past the expectation of soft "pearness," realizing the fruit is really more like a crisp apple, it's a treat.

"I try to grow different varieties of the same crop, to hedge my bets," he says. "For example, in a rainy season, 'Brandywine', or 'potato-leafed,' tomatoes will do well, but they don't thrive in a hot and dry season. I'd want an old-fashioned beefsteak variety in the ground in a hot summer."

He sums up his philosophy of gardening with the observation that "the crops will tell you what they need, if you learn how to look. I just try to figure it out as I go."

A MASTERFUL FOCUS
• MARY ELLEN KESKIMAKI'S PRECISION TIPS AND TECHNIQUES •

MARY ELLEN KESKIMAKI'S gardening genius shows up best in her precision, focus, and orderliness. She wants to get it right and keep it that way. She showed me garden logs from years past that included photos of each year's peak garden, soil tests, and carefully drawn schematics of each bed. She's carefully logged each variety, dates planted, and results observed. "Why make the same mistakes twice?" she reasons. "I have a finite number of gardening seasons in my life, and I want to make the most of each."

Her garden reflects a synergy between mind and nature. What's born on the master clipboard matures in her many ornamental and vegetable gardens, tucked flawlessly into nearly every inch of the lot that surrounds her large house in Golden, Colorado, where she and her husband live.

A patch of grass is reserved for the dogs (who also merit an arbor of climbing roses over the doghouse), but otherwise the property is a botanical potpourri of rock gardens, espaliered fruit trees, grape vines, and thickets of native turf, shrubs, and trees.

I visited her garden in mid-April, when hardy species like crocus, rhubarb, and garlic were in charge and fruit tree buds had not yet burst open. "There are three ways to grow in a climate like ours," she says, standing in front of a west-facing bed of perennials. "You can go native—and there are lots of interesting species that do well in our mineral-rich native soils. You can choose Xeriscape species from areas like the Mediterranean and South Africa, which have similar conditions to ours. And with a little extra care, you can grow the exotics, which come from bioregions unlike ours. When you think about it, many of the fruits and vegetables we grow here are exotics, except for things like currants and serviceberries. By knowing where a certain species comes from, you also know a lot about what it needs to grow."

Mary Ellen orchestrates all three approaches, dividing her lot into irrigation zones; each receives appropriate amounts of water, and no more. But her favorite gardening activity by far is fruits and vegetables. She first got the "grow bug" when she was a little girl, growing up in a neighborhood with half-acre lots. "My neighbors had huge vegetable gardens in their backyards, and you could munch from early spring to late fall on strawberries, carrots, apples, you name it."

She and her engineer husband used a variety of durable materials to create multilevel garden spaces on all sides of a house that's perched on a sloping hillside. Pressure-treated wood beams were used to create retaining walls that form the backbone of her vegetable plots. Large boulders dug into the hillside are the groundwork for her full-spectrum rock garden. And sturdy 1-inch steel plumbing conduits are used for a variety of purposes, including several handsome, arched arbors for climbing roses, a few solidly cemented trellises for espaliered fruit trees and grapevines, and the framework for a few trellises for tomatoes, cucumbers, and squash.

She refers to the seedless grape varieties she grows as "hardy as iron," a phrase that describes her gardens as well as her Zen-like philosophy of growing. "We like to grow table grapes and eat them fresh," she explains. "Microclimates like our protected backyard are ideal for them. I grew 'Concord' grapes in my old garden, but we didn't like the fact they had seeds, and I still have jars of jam from them, years later." She grows 'Reliance' (purple), 'Himrod' (green), and 'Canadice' (red) grapes on supports that run along one of the wood beam retaining walls.

Two plum trees, 'Stanley' prune–plum and 'Earliblue', produce about eighty pounds of fruit almost every year. They were supposed to bear fruit a month apart, but because the 'Stanley' was in a sunnier, warmer location, they tend to bear about the same time. "I like to prune fruit trees to have a strong central leader, even though that's not what you're 'supposed' to do to get good production. But I want my fruit trees to have a good shape because they're ornamentals, too."

A classic work of art she began sculpting in 1988, her espaliered trees inspired me to try the Old World technique that saves space and can benefit from the warmth of walls. Over the years, she's trained a few 'Golden Delicious' and a few 'Early Blaze' apple trees into shapes that resemble grape vines, on both western and eastern exposures. "You start by topping a young fruit tree, and then working with the three shoots that grow back. You let the leader become a trunk, and train the two side shoots into a Y that later becomes a T," she explains, as if the process were easy or happened overnight. She does a lot of pruning to keep new shoots under control, and prefers to prune in the summer. "Whenever I mow the lawn, I also prune the fruit trees." One of the domesticated trees is a comparatively young-looking replacement for a fatality that occurred a few years ago during a deep freeze.

Zen Master that she is, she readily points out the failures that inevitably occur in her beds. "You have to be adaptable, and willing to listen to your plants, and move them to better locations. You have to try new varieties of ornamentals as well as the edibles, to see what works best in your garden," she comments. For example, she's not a fan of the 'Heritage' raspberry, which bears in fall and then again in the spring on the same canes. The problem, characteristically, is unruliness. "The canes got so gangly I always wanted to prune them back, so I would lose next year's harvest. My next-door neighbor has anonymous transplants from the eastern plains of Colorado, which bear heavily on first-year canes and then can be pruned back. He's invited me to dig up some starters, and I may give them a try."

Aspen trees didn't work well in her native garden, either. She suspects it was because her elevation of 5,900 feet is not quite high enough. She planted western wheatgrass, which does very well in that garden but makes it difficult for anything else to thrive. "I've watched the *Penstemon strictus* migrate down the native garden slope, to be closer to the lawn, which gets watered more frequently."

Another unsatisfactory experiment was a 'Madison' peach tree. "There was no problem with the productivity," she told me, "but the fruit wasn't edible! I must have gotten a runt or something."

She's constantly on guard against powdery mildew, a leaf disease she believes gets started when crops like zucchini and cucumbers are allowed to dry out and become stressed.

Among the many experiments she considers successes are 'Derby' green beans, a variety she's seen consistently outproduce and outlast more popular types. And she's had great success planting spinach in August or September, protecting it with used window sashes, and eating it all winter long. Similarly, she insulates her fall carrot bed (she likes 'Nantes' and 'Bolero') with bags of leaves so she can pull and crunch them until spring.

Her face lights up when she talks about materials she scavenges for compost and mulch. She made a deal with employees at a local restaurant to drop off pine needles when they're raked up in the fall. Her commitment to the garden is evident when she goes through the needles to remove candy wrappers and cigarette butts. "Those pine needles are worth the effort," she says. "They make a great mulch that stays in place even in heavy winds, lets the soil breathe a little and

Mary Ellen Keskimaki's Ten Favorite Plants

Catmint (*Nepeta* x *faassenii*). Fragrant purple flowers in early summer; gray-green foliage; 8–12 inches tall.

Desert beard tongue (*Penstemon pseudospectabilis*). Bright pink flowers all summer; bluish green leaves; 3–4 feet.

English lavender (*Lavandula angustifolia* 'Munstead'). Fragrant lavender blue flowers in midsummer; gray-green foliage.

Greek windflower (*Anemone blanda* 'Blue Star'). Blue daisylike flowers in early spring; 10–12 inches.

Greek yarrow (*Achillea ageratifolia*). Dainty white flowers in spring; gray-green foliage; 4–10 inches.

Ice plant (*Delosperma nubigenum*). Bright yellow daisylike flowers in spring; succulent lime green foliage turns maroon in winter; 1 inch.

Soapwort (*Saponaria ocymoides*). Pink flowers in spring; glossy green foliage; 6 inches.

Sunrose (*Helianthemum nummularium* 'Wisley Pink'). Coral pink flowers in spring; gray-green foliage; 6–8 inches.

Sunset penstemon (*Penstemon clutei*). Showy pink flowers June through August; bluish evergreen foliage; 3 feet; short-lived perennial.

Turkish speedwell (*Veronica liwanensis*). Blue flowers in spring; tiny deep-green leaves; 1–2 inches.

Adapted from *Sunset* magazine article, April 2002.

get some sunlight." She acquires her favorite compost material from a landscaper she met at the gas station.

"There's a narrow window of opportunity to get the last lawn clippings of the year mixed together with the first fallen leaves that are all ground up by the lawn mowers. It's great stuff!" she says excitedly. She uses some of that mixture, along with a little horse manure, to plant squash in—a variety called 'Tetsukabuto', or Japanese black pumpkin, which she cooks like acorn squash, adding butter, ginger, and maple syrup.

If you ask Mary Ellen what the central theme of her garden is, she might just respond, "minestrone." Just about all the warm-season vegetables, from carrots to canellini beans, go into her favorite, flexible recipe throughout the summer. "I start to make soup when the zucchini is ready," she says. "And I freeze containers of it for cold winter nights, too."

An early reader of Mel Bartholomew's square-foot gardening methods, Mary Ellen makes each plant count. Spacing widely, she gets good yields from nine canellini bean plants, for instance, or eighteen edamame bean plants. If a person needed to find those eighteen plants, she'd only have to consult Mary Ellen's clipboard, where each year's garden begins.

FARMS THE SIZE OF TENNIS COURTS?
· JOHN JEAVONS' VISION OF BIOINTENSIVE GROWING ·

SOMETIMES THE CHALLENGES we face seem too big to deal with. Feeding the world's hungry people, for example, does not seem like something we can accomplish from our recliners or as we commute to and from work. North Koreans may be eating bark off trees, and the Chinese may be plowing under their cemeteries for additional farmland, but what does this mean to us? Even when we consider that millions of homeless and underemployed Americans do not have enough to eat, we think of hunger as a mega-problem, too big for individuals to solve.

But if John Jeavons has his way, the problem of world hunger can be reduced using operable units of land the size of tennis courts—mini-farms that deliver not only food but fulfillment. Jeavons is a gardening activist whose demonstration plots are tucked into the foothills of Willits, California, at an elevation of 2,000 feet. I visited him near the end of the conventional growing season, but his beautiful mini-farm was still abundant and productive.

Jeavons is author of *How to Grow More Vegetables: And Fruits, Nuts, Berries, Grains, and Other Crops Than You Ever Thought Possible on Less Land Than You Can Imagine*. Despite its playfully laborious title, this book is now in its fifth edition, with more than 350,000 copies sold to date. The book and the methods it presents have launched mini-farming centers in Kenya, Mexico, India, the Philippines, and other countries, where people whose annual incomes have never exceeded $500 are now able to make that much on farms smaller than the candy and pop aisles in a U.S. supermarket.

Mini-farms are also appearing in many American backyards and vacant lots, with impressive results. Ask Michael Norton, a northern Californian who successfully uses "biointensive" practices in his market garden—in fact, "successfully" is an understatement. Jeavons commented, "Before Michael grossed $238,000 in one season growing vegetables on a quarter of an acre, some people thought our economic projections were a bit exaggerated." Jeavons explained that a more typical mini-farm might yield closer to what the average American farmer makes—$12,500 a year—but instead of 500 acres, the mini-farmer may manually work a tennis-court–sized farm, and avoid the purchase and handling of hazardous chemicals.

"What's the smallest area in which I can grow all of my food and make an income?" is the basic question posed by John Jeavons' work. He believes the goal is not simply to grow crops but to grow soil. When we grow crops but don't regenerate the soil, it's like "milking a cow but not feeding it." His techniques for growing crops specifically to make compost result in a buildup of soil up to sixty times faster than nature does it.

Instead of tractors, the biointensive farmer uses spading forks, trowels, and "U-bars" (multitined devices to loosen soil). The methods are not high tech but rather "high touch"—full of intuition, information, and operating experience. Third millennium science enables a more thorough understanding of what happens above and below the soil than when the Chinese first practiced intensive agriculture 4,000 years ago. The "raised bed" that was a standard method in Greece 2,000 years ago is now understood to be an integrated ecological system. And French growers whose "French intensive" methods treat soil like cake now take advantage of space-age soil testing that tells them if they have precisely the right ingredients.

But you don't have to be a farmer or scientist to use the principles of biointensive growing. You can simply make best use of the area you plant in ornamental or edible crops. The techniques have been proven to reduce water consumption by as much as 88 percent, fertilizer consumption by 50 percent, and energy consumption by up to 99 percent, efficiencies that boost a household's general fund. What's responsible for all these savings? A lot of the credit goes to the microbes that thrive in premium, loamy soil.

"In each handful of cured compost, there are more living organisms than there are humans on Earth," Jeavons explained, holding up a fistful of his own well-composted soil. "These legions of busy workers aerate the soil, supply minerals and nutrients directly to the roots of plants, and create a carbon-rich structure that holds water like a sponge. In the process, plants become healthy and less vulnerable to disease and pests," he said. I had brought a few bagsful of wood ashes as a contribution to his compost, but Jeavons politely turned it down, explaining that the pH was already in balance, and the ashes would make it alkaline.

"Many farmers and gardeners think the goal is simply to grow plants, but a more successful and satisfying approach is to grow the soil. And when the system is really working, *people* are the ultimate product."

The operable unit of biointensive mini-farming is the 100-square-foot bed—typically 5 feet by 20 feet. Paths on either side of the bed enable easy access for transplanting seedlings, weeding, and harvesting. In twenty-nine years of field trials, Jeavons has documented precisely how close to space different varieties of vegetables and fruits, and at what stage to transplant each seedling into the bed. He's learned which crops like to grow next to each other, and how deeply the roots of each crop penetrate. He has conclusive data proving that in most cases, transplanted seedlings out-yield directly sown seeds.

It might be said that biointensive practices stress the vertical plane rather than the horizontal, because at the heart of the method is a practice called "double digging," which enables a closer spacing of crops. Double digging—two shovel blades deep—provides a loose, aerated root zone. By loosening the beds to a depth of 24 inches and using up to 12 buckets annually of compost per 100-square-foot bed, Jeavons creates a soil structure that boosts yields dramatically. (Many vegetable roots and root hairs go 5 to 10 feet deep.) Double digging also makes weeding easier, because the entire weed root usually comes out intact.

"The goal is to create a soil with 4 to 6 percent organic matter that nurtures seedlings like a womb," said Jeavons. To create that soil, he devotes more growing space to the compost pile than to the dinner plate. Crops such as alfalfa, sorghum, and Japanese forty-five-day millet become layers in his compost piles, along with food wastes and already composted soil. In effect, the compost pile is the "kitchen" where a continuous banquet of vegetables and grains is prepared. Jeavons' pile is intentionally "cool," or slow to decompose, because a high-temperature pile that's frequently turned releases much of its carbon and nutrients into the air.

"One recipe for good compost is (by weight) one-third rehydrated dry vegetation, one-third green vegetation (including kitchen wastes), and one-third soil," he explained. "The materials should be added in 1- or 2-inch layers with the dry vegetation on the bottom, the green vegetation and kitchen wastes second, and the soil third. Add the soil layer immediately after the kitchen waste. It contains microorganisms that speed decomposition, keep the smell down to a minor level, and prevent flies from laying eggs in the garbage."

Biointensive growing is about taking care and being focused. Respect and even ritual are at the heart of it. For example, walking across one of Jeavons' raised beds would be like walking on an Oriental carpet with muddy boots. Because the whole idea is to keep the soil loose and the microbes happy, you *never* walk on a bed. You double-dig the bed from each side of the 5-foot-wide plot with paths on either side. When planting seedlings or seeds, Jeavons sits cross-legged on a 4-foot by 2-foot piece of plywood. And as he demonstrates the best way to double-dig beds, to preserve knees and backs, his movements resemble those of an aikido master.

As we watched his spade slide effortlessly into the soil, he repeated a question he had posed a few minutes earlier: "Why *wouldn't* we want to re-create the Garden of Eden?"

100 SHORT YEARS OF AGRICULTURAL HISTORY
· BOULDER'S BASIL KING AND AGRICULTURAL GEOGRAPHER ·

WE TEND TO OVERLOOK the history connected to the food on our plates. What part of the world did this sweet potato come from, and how is it grown? Think of all the joyful trials and fatal errors involved in finding out what was safe to eat, and what could kill you! (How many died eating the parsley look-alike, poison hemlock?)

For Nick Helburn, who lives eight or ten miles north of Boulder, the history of cultivated species became a career. He was a professor of agricultural geography for many years before retiring to his rural home and garden. As we walk on his well-used garden paths, he comments, "Most of the crops we plant early in the season, like lettuce, carrots, and cabbage, are from Europe and other temperate zones." He bends over (vigorously for an eighty-two-year-old) to examine a row of germinating romaine lettuce, and then continues, "It makes sense that the crops we plant later in the year—like corn, tomatoes, and many types of squash, for example—originated in tropical areas."

Several of Nick's favorite crops come directly from the dinner tables of European friends. "My wife, Susan, and I were served a yellow and green squash in France that we loved the taste of, and we dried a few seeds and brought them home. We still grow that squash every year, and we also love the small, tender variety of French green bean—the *haricot vert*."

Nick's gardening buddy Lou Tenenbaum also brought a taste of European culture into his backyard. An interpreter for Italian prisoners of war in World War II, he traveled extensively in Italy at mid-century. The color, fragrance, and freshness of Italian fruit and vegetable markets made such an impression on him that he quickly learned the fundamentals of gardening and began to plant Italian heirloom seeds.

"I grow many different kinds of vegetables, but without a doubt, my favorite is basil," says Lou. "It has the smell of paradise." Tenenbaum's eyes light up when he explains that the best basil in the world is grown in Genoa. "The mountains come down close to the coast there, but there's a green zone in between the mountains and the sea that provides the perfect conditions for basil. I can't re-create the sea breezes here in Colorado, but I do have the mountains."

The retired seventy-eight-year-old professor enjoyed growing basil so much that he began taking bushels of it to the Boulder Farmers Market every week. "They began to call me the Basil King," he says with pride. [Interestingly, the plant's name comes from the Greek *basileus* meaning "king."] "I'd crush open a few leaves in a bunch of basil and throw it to people at the market, and when they smelled its fragrance, they were hooked. Every week they'd be back for more."

For nine years, he'd get up at 5 A.M. on Saturday mornings and pick basil for the market, so it would be as fresh as possible. (His daughter Thea, a professional potter, remembers many a chilly morning spent helping him harvest basil as the sun was coming up.) He sold bags of the herb for a dollar apiece, and at the end of the summer, sales usually totaled a few thousand dollars. "The real payoff was seeing my friends every week, and enjoying a lively community based on great food," he says.

As we stand next to his unplanted basil plot, about 20 feet by 80 feet in size, he explains a few of the techniques that resulted in his herbal royalty. "I never plant before June 1, because basil is very cold-sensitive," he said. "But on the other hand, it's a great germinator, and it stands up to summer heat waves as well as any other crop. It really is one of the easiest crops to grow in Colorado." He grows mostly sweet basil (large green and lettuce-leafed varieties) but sometimes adds lemon basil to his inventory. "I plant a little more each week, so it comes in all summer long." His favorite way to use the herb is in fresh pesto, but he also dries it on screens with cheesecloth stretched over to keep it from blowing away. "If you freeze fresh leaves in ice cube trays, with olive oil dribbled over it, you'll have just the quantities you need to prepare meals."

Basil likes a soil pH of 5.5 to 6.5, and Lou's annual applications of sheep and goat manure do bring his soil pH down a bit from

Colorado's usual alkalinity. But he's careful not to overfertilize, because the herb is more fragrant in soils that are only moderately rich. To get bushier plants, he pinches off new growth, especially before flowers emerge, and throws it directly into the skillet. "For the freshest taste, don't add the basil until the last few minutes of cooking," he counsels.

Like tomatoes, basil can be grown in the same bed for many years without developing soil-borne disease. However, Lou's plots might finally be reaching their limits on that one, because last year some of his plants developed *Fusarium* wilt—a botanical "heart attack" in which crops suddenly keel over. He's anxiously waiting for a shipment of Genovese seeds that are *Fusarium* wilt-resistant, so he can get the basil bed back into service.

"Basil has been cultivated for 5,000 years in India and Asia," he tells me. "In those warmer climates, it can be grown as a perennial, but it doesn't do so well when you try to extend the season here by bringing it indoors. It transplants easily, but after a few weeks indoors, the whiteflies and aphids somehow find it. I guess you can't blame them for wanting a little taste of paradise, too."

PARADISE BY THE RAILROAD TRACKS
· GARDENING AS A WAY OF LIFE FOR BUTCHER RAY OLETSKI ·

SOME PEOPLE THINK OF gardening as recreation for the idle rich. A place to putz around and while away the hours. But for Raymond Oletski, who worked for years as a butcher at a meatpacking plant, it's much more than that. The son of a Polish immigrant, Oletski has lived seventy-two years in the house where he was born, gardening the same third of an acre ever since he was a kid. The two most important things in his life have always been his large, extended family and his large, extended garden.

He, his son Ray, and daughter Shirley are busy planting flowers when I arrive. "Is the garden big enough for you?" he asks, smiling. It's late spring, and I see more soil than plants, at this point. A heavy rain the day before has left the beds and paths slippery, and various equipment and garden gadgets give the impression the space does double duty as a storage area. But then I begin to see the rows of asparagus, rhubarb, and baby tomatoes, growing in protective mini-hothouses made from bottomless three-gallon Deep Rock bottles. I see ten or twelve fruit trees scattered in the landscape, and a lush boundary of Jerusalem artichokes, raspberries, and native shrubs around the periphery. On the far side of the garden, a railroad track, elevated three or four feet above the level of the garden, is the visual boundary. A train chugs by while we talk, but the Oletski family doesn't seem to notice it.

"This whole area used to be truck farms," Oletski tells me. "All the way up to Thornton, and all the way over to Brighton." Across the tracks, instead of a truck farm, there's now a trucking company, where a hundred semis are lined up in front of a warehouse like a huge litter of nursing pups.

"The Marabino family used to have hothouses over there and grow every kind of vegetable and flower you can imagine. But there's been lots of changes since then." As he talks, it's easy to imagine what Globeville, Colorado, near the intersection of I-25 and I-70, must have looked like half a century ago—before the Asarco smelter was found liable for $28 million in damages and forced to remove thousands of tons of soil proven to be laced with toxic cadmium and arsenic.

"Lots of things have changed," repeats the father. "The Argo Ditch used to bring water from the Platte River to hundreds of growers, but now the only users of that water are Xcel Energy and us." Acres of vacant land surround the Oletski property, retained by Xcel Energy for access to high-voltage power lines that run through the neighborhood. There are dozens of trees planted in mini-groves on that vacant land, compliments of Raymond Oletski. "In dry summers, we load barrels of water in the pickup and make the rounds," says Shirley. "One way or another, we're going to keep those trees alive."

Shirley refers to her Dad as "her hero." She remembers how, forty years ago, he would dig a shallow pond in the garden in the fall, so his seven kids could ice-skate in the winter. She remembers how a cousin would always catch crawdads in the ditch, and bring them home to boil, like low-rent lobster tails. She remembers her grandmother slaughtering chickens with a practiced sling of the neck.

As a little girl, she'd watch the animals that lived in and around the Oletski garden. "One year a coyote or fox killed a mother duck, and one of our hens took responsibility for the duckling. It was the sweetest thing," she recalls with a smile. "One day I watched the hen push the duckling into an irrigation furrow. She wouldn't go near the water herself, but somehow she knew the duck should."

"This whole area was DPs," she tells me. "Deported people from Poland, the Ukraine, Lithuania, after the War. Their small cottages were like little dollhouses, and each one of them had a garden. The German houses were all starch and lace, like music boxes. But now the yards are unkempt, and the neighborhood is contaminated with crack houses."

Although Shirley lives five or ten miles away, she comes by the house just about every day to work in the garden. Recently, she took a week's vacation from her job as a nurse to rototill the soil and help plant the crops. She shows me a few long rows of corn she planted across the fence, in the black soil of the railroad right-of-way. "You see how good that soil is?" she asked. "That's how our soil used to be, before the remediation."

After the court settlement with Asarco, bulldozers invaded the Oletski garden and scraped away a foot of soil. "Compared to the soil my Dad had built up over the years, the soil they brought in was like concrete," she said. "We've improved it since then by growing winter rye, adding tons of manure and compost, and continuing to work the soil. But it's nothing like it was."

Over the years, the family built a life around the garden. "One of my earliest memories," recalls Oletski's son Ray, "was walking down the rows with a salt shaker in my hand, just grazing on all the produce."

The family experimented with many unusual remedies and devices in the garden. "We shaved off the inside of flares to get the sulfur," Oletski explains with a smile, "and we even strung tin wires across the garden because we heard it would break up molecules of air after a thunderstorm, and put nitrogen into the garden." The latest experiment is a large, rusty horse-exercising unit in the shape of a merry-go-round. "We're going to grow vines on it," he explains, with the air of an artist.

Even though Asarco has contributed much more than its fair share of toxic chemicals, Oletski refuses to spray pesticides in his garden. "I don't want to kill the birds," he says. One of the concoctions he's tried on weeds is a mixture of gin and vinegar, which "works a little bit." To battle the bugs, he boils garlic and sprays the tea on plants.

A place of refuge and joy for generations of grandkids, aunts, and uncles, the Oletski garden has provided Polish sausages, horseradish, and pickled beets for many family holidays, as well as fortunate neighbors. Like a sailboat in choppy waters, the garden has weathered toxic waste clean-ups and industrial development, and in the process, it's helped bind a family together.

"Come back and see us again," calls Shirley as I get in my car. "You know where you can find us."

Choose and Cut
· KEEPING A CHRISTMAS TRADITION ALIVE ·

THE THOUGHT HAS OCCURRED to me before, too—put a few hundred evergreen trees in the backyard or vacant lot, protect them from dogs and kids, and then sell them as Christmas trees six or eight years later. John and Janice Windsor, of Windsor, Colorado, actually did it. Over the years, they've overcome fluke winter freezes and salty soil to realize a dream they've had since college days.

After settling near the college they both attended thirty years earlier as "aggies"—then Colorado A & M, now Colorado State University—

they bought a wedge-shaped piece of land with water rights in the adjoining agricultural ditch, and began to plant Scotch pine on it, row by row. They planted the first tree seedlings, purchased from the State Forest Service, in 1982, and right before Christmas 1988, they sold their first tree. That year, an article in the *Windsor Beacon* announced the opening of a "choose and cut your own" operation.

"When our family—the two of us and four kids—lived in South Dakota, one of our family traditions was to go out and cut our own tree," Janice explains. "But in today's metropolitan world, a lot of people don't have that opportunity. Our farm and a few others in Colorado, like our son's in Palisade, continue the tradition."

Both Janice and John like to work with the trees—things like planting seedlings in May, pruning and shearing the larger trees in June, and keeping more than 2,500 trees well watered in the hot months with an automated sprinkler system. They also like the busy season— November and December, when they get to see the familiar faces of steady customers, who come to choose and cut trees and tour the farm by hayrack ride (this year, Clydesdale horses will pull a carriage). "We've had some repeat customers for eleven years. When we see people around town in the fall, they'll ask us how the trees are looking this year."

Three acres of land provide up to 300 Scotch pine, blue spruce, and white fir trees every year for Front Range living rooms. At an average of $32 a tree, the tree operation will gross close to $10,000 this year. The Windsors also collect boughs in the wild in late October to make customized wreaths. "If our wreaths are displayed on the north side of a house, they may last up to four months," says Janice. One regular holiday-season employee works for wreaths rather than money. The trees are usually selected and tagged in November, so a person has to plan to go out to the farm on one of the pre-selection days.

One of the most valuable assets of the Windsor farm is John's interest in tinkering with equipment and inventing devices like a tree shaker, to shake dead needles off the trees before customers take them home. He also modified an old corn chopper into a mulcher to feed his huge compost piles tree trimmings from local businesses and recycled Christmas trees. Nutrients that leave the farm in the trees are replenished at planting time by compost that also includes truckloads of leaves, spoiled alfalfa hay from neighboring farmers, and grass clippings from lawn-mowing operations.

John also built "shade houses" to protect seedlings from sun and wind during their first year, and planted windbreaks to shelter the mature trees. "Winter winds desiccate the trees, making them more susceptible to winter freezes. A deep freeze in April one year wiped out our whole inventory of seedlings, and we had to replant."

The pair also problem-solved their way around existing soil deficiencies. "Our soil tested high in salt, and we had a drainage problem as well," explains John. "So I came in with a posthole digger and filled dozens of 3-foot-deep holes with sand. Drainage improved and the salt problem did too, as salt leached out of the root zone.

The trees are planted 6 feet apart, with 4 feet between each tree in a row. In the spring, John pulls the stumps of harvested trees out with a device he rigged up, fills the hole with compost, and puts seedlings in each hole. Six or seven years later, customers choose from among the mature trees.

Janice and John have noticed that the market seems to be moving away from Scotch pine, their main crop, and toward various fir and spruce trees, so they're slowly adjusting by mixing in some of the other species. "We feel like we're growing a good environmental crop— each tree puts enough oxygen in the air for nineteen people to breathe. We don't clear-cut the trees—we only harvest about 10 percent every year. And quite a few of the trees are recycled into mulch after Christmas—either here at the farm or by the town of Windsor." (His comment reminded me of the Christmas mulch I collect every year from the City of Golden's free mulch piles. I leave a few buckets of the fragrant, ground-up mulch in the back seat of my car, and even in a traffic jam, it smells like I'm in the middle of an evergreen forest.)

Says John, "People ask me why we want to grow such a slow-maturing crop. By the time the trees we've just planted are ready for harvesting, I'll be seventy-six. But it's good exercise, it's really not very demanding time-wise, and it keeps us out of trouble."

Bringing the Farm to the Community, and the Community to the Farm
· LIFE AT THE CRESSET FARM ·

DID YOU EVER ASK a talkative two-year-old where a potato comes from? Chances are, he'll look puzzled and explain in toddler language that they grow on tables, at the supermarket. This kind of response is cute enough coming from a child, but alarmingly, many adults are not much more aware than their children. Traditional links between Americans and the soil, seeds, and sun that sustain us have been dramatically severed in a single generation. While our attention is diverted by agribusiness foods, farms are quickly disappearing from both metropolitan and rural areas. In Colorado, with a $4 billion/year agricultural industry, we lose ten acres of farmland every hour to housing, shopping malls, roads, and other development.

As I drove up I-25 to visit the Cresset Community Farm last summer, I saw FOR SALE signs on miles of farmland—from just north of Denver all the way up to Loveland, where I turned off. It's not hard to guess why: It's simply more lucrative to grow subdivisions and shopping malls than it is to grow organic produce, as Larry and Ursula Holmes do at the Cresset Farm. Larry spent twenty-eight years in Germany, where he learned how to farm organically. As we eat a supper of rice and fresh vegetables and the freshly baked bread Ursula markets, he explains, "Instead of using heavy amounts of fertilizer, pesticide, hybridized seed, and other conventional inputs, we work with nature to build up the soil and diversify the farm."

He wants his farm to deliver health—for him, Ursula, and on-site interns, for consumers of the farm's produce, and for regional communities. The Cresset philosophy is to bring the farm to the community, and the community to the farm. It's one of more than 600 farms in the U.S. and Canada in the Community Supported Agriculture (CSA) movement, in which shareholders or subscribers get weekly allotments of produce—typically five to ten pounds of what's currently in season. Once a week, Larry, Ursula, and volunteers load up their truck with produce bound for Denver, Boulder, and Longmont CSA members.

Sometimes the support is more than monetary. One subscriber is an electrician who's interested in farming. He rewired the barn in exchange for a box of produce. Other members volunteer to drive the produce to drop-off locations, contribute to the newsletter, and perform other outreach activities. In the spirit of creating community, the farm has field days at which visitors can tour the farm, folk dances with music provided by the Oat Bran Band, and last year, a harvest festival that happened to fall on a very cold day. But twenty-five or more people toured the farm, ate stick bread and pumpkin pie, and heard stories around the bonfire.

Similar activities take place at Hedgerow Farm, another Front Range CSA farm. Farmer and high-school science teacher Jim Barausky believes that our society needs to reconnect to its roots, literally. The farm is a living classroom for students enrolled in Naropa University's sustainable agriculture program, as well as elementary and high-school students who visit the farm year after year to observe the cycles of nature.

My own experience at the Cresset Farm made me realize why organic produce often looks more appealing than standard fare. It reflects all the care that goes into the growing and packing. After spending the night in one of the spare rooms at the farmhouse, I meet the crew of four harvesters at the barn at 5:15 A.M. Larry explains what needs to be picked for the CSA delivery, and we walk a huge garden cart past the chicken yard and into one of the vegetable fields. The sunrise lights up Long's Peak and Mount Meeker in the distance, while right below the field flows the Big Thompson River. Two meadowlarks warble, completing my impression that I've somehow stepped onto a movie set.

Except it's real: the rows of yellow crookneck squash, Swiss chard, mustard leaf, dill, spinach, green onions, and lettuce; the clear morning air, the pink sky, the faint, faraway smell of a skunk, and the abundant silence. Not a single engine or motor disturbs us as we collect five or six kinds of vegetables. Larry shows me how he harvests bunches of spinach: severing the stem right below ground level with a paring knife, then neatly packing them into boxes upside down, so the reddish-white stems display a bouquet of well-grown produce. Larry's student interns appear with bunches of basil, potatoes, tomatoes, and broccoli, and each crop is carefully counted, weighed, and packed artistically in heavy-duty cardboard boxes.

As we work, I ask Larry to contrast his methods of planting and cultivating the crops with conventional methods. The picture becomes very clear as he explains it: In large-scale conventional farming, the end product is money, obtained with the use of huge machines, hybrid and GMO seeds, a cross-section of chemicals, large inputs of energy for machinery and shipping, processing and packaging, unpacking and marketing. In Larry's version of farming, the end product is health.

At the pickup location later that afternoon, the subscribers pull up one by one after their workdays, their eyes lighting up at the abundance in each share of produce. The smell of fresh thyme, basil, and dill fills the air as they talk with each other about the week's produce and about the upcoming folk dance at Cresset. Each of them seems energized by the direct link between the farm and the upcoming week's meals. Somehow, they know the value of the effort we had put into the harvest that morning.

A Dry Sense of Humor
· JIM KNOPF'S WATERWISE GARDEN TIPS ·

"WE NEED TO LEARN to live with the natural precipitation and amount of irrigation water we have now," Jim Knopf comments as we tour his waterwise backyard—a semicircular, eclectic collection of flowers, shrubs, and trees that make the most of each drop of water.

It's May 7, and no appreciable amounts of rain have fallen on his property or anywhere else along Colorado's Front Range for months. Weather forecasters' favorite word seems to be "virga," a term referring to rain that evaporates before it ever reaches the ground. Forest fires in late winter and spring have already burned 10,000 acres in the high country, and newspaper articles compare the current drought to Dust Bowl days back in the '30s.

"Still, that doesn't mean we can't have beautiful landscapes," Knopf says. "For example, we can have some of the showiest flower gardens in the world because of our abundant, intense sunlight, low humidity, warm days, and cool nights. The expression 'floral fireworks' may not be an exaggeration."

The proof is right there in his yard, where various shades of yellow, gold, purple, white, red, and pink announce the arrival of spring. The fragrances of daphne, three-leaf sumac, viburnum, and Lewis's mock orange mingle in the enclosed space, to the great delight of bumblebees, butterflies, and humans. Knopf comments as we walk past the Three-leaf sumac in bloom, "This scent always reminds me of my Peace Corps nights in Nairobi."

Standing near the flowering dogwood, I get my own flashback—my childhood neighborhood in Larchmont, New York.

"The good news is, we haven't had a freeze yet this spring," Knopf says, seeing a silver lining even in the *lack* of clouds. This perspective could only come from a plant guy who knows that some plants (and not just desert species) are so drought hardy that they actually prefer dryness to rain. Knopf reminds me that the 1980s and 1990s were way *above* average in precipitation in Colorado and the Great Plains, and that regional landscaping habits had become sloppy as a result. "Bluegrass, for example, is definitely a plant with a drinking problem," he jokes. "By comparison, tall fescue can remain attractive with half the water, and with much less fertilizer, too. But for some reason, city landscapers put in miles of bluegrass median strips, which they irrigate with high-quality drinking water."

A landscape architect and educator, Knopf keeps track of water availability and usage throughout the Rocky Mountain region, noting that in Santa Fe, when all surcharges are added in, the cost of tap water is currently higher than bottled water sells for in nearby Albuquerque. "Pretty soon they'll be trucking bottled water up to Santa Fe and watering lawns with it," he jokes.

Knopf's fascination with western landscaping goes back to the 1970s, when he was teaching site-planning courses at Colorado University–Boulder. He and his students kicked around the concept: What kind of landscape should the Rocky Mountain region have to be successful? Even then, policymakers saw water as a constraint, but the prevailing opinion was that we could simply get more of it, with dams and buyouts of agricultural water.

But Knopf saw it differently. He knew that many extraordinary plants could thrive here without unnatural supplies of water and exotic soil mixes he calls "chocolate cake soil—black, fluffy, moist, and rich." We just needed to become informed and methodical—for example, by grouping plants together that have similar irrigation needs. While in the Peace Corps, he'd researched plants in South Africa that are genetically familiar with up-and-down, back-and-forth weather like ours. In research about the climate of the arid West, he documented temperature swings of 60 degrees in a single day in Colorado. In Browning, Montana, as Knopf records in *Waterwise Landscaping with Trees, Shrubs, and Vines,* the temperature once fluctuated 100 degrees F. on a single January day, dropping from 44 degrees to –56!

Yet, despite extremes like these, he remains optimistic that our landscapes can be full of color and also provide shade. His best advice is, "Don't get frustrated, get clever." His backyard is a series of experiments where plants from all over the world coexist (for the most part, peacefully). He grows several kinds of citrus in a small greenhouse that remains cold in the winter (40 to 45 degrees F.). His collection includes my own favorite citrus variety, the deliciously juicy 'Clementine' mandarin orange (*Citrus reticulata* 'Clementine') that originated in Algeria and has become well-known with recent winter holiday shipments from Spain.

Seven Xeriscaping Fundamentals

1. **Plan and design** for water conservation and beauty from the start.
2. **Create practical turf areas** of manageable sizes, shapes, and appropriate grasses.
3. **Group plants of similar water needs together,** then experiment to determine how much and how often to water for the specific site.
4. **Consider using soil amendments** like compost or manure.
5. **Consider using mulches** like woodchips, especially in high and moderate watering zones.
6. **Irrigate efficiently** with properly designed systems (including hose-end equipment), and by applying the right amount of water at the right time.
7. **Maintain the landscape appropriately** by mowing, pruning, and fertilizing properly.

From *Waterwise Landscaping with Trees, Shrubs, and Vines,* by Jim Knopf.

Observation is a primary tool of the waterwise landscaper, and Knopf routinely watches certain plants as indicators of overall thirstiness in the garden. "When the mock orange shows signs of wilt, I know it's time to water again," he says. He also watches the interaction of plants in both designed and natural landscapes, to see how much water the plants really require. He estimates that automatic sprinkler systems often apply five to ten times as much water as necessary, and suggests an interesting approach to downsizing a private lawn. "What if we decided to reduce the size of our lawn to about the square footage and shape that our hose sprinkler could cover? Then, what if we cut back on the water and fertilizer we gave the lawn, so we wouldn't have to mow as often?"

Another of his principles is to seek a second opinion about how to care for a certain plant. "Some garden books will tell you to 'water often,' but what exactly does that mean? Low humidity is a major factor in this region, especially when combined with intense sunshine and high summer temperatures. This makes annual precipitation comparisons with more humid regions almost meaningless."

Knopf has long been an advocate of precision. He believes that water consumers should know exactly what they're paying for water. "If a household observes their water needs in the coldest four months of the year, they'll be able to calculate how much additional water is used for irrigation by subtracting average winter use from summer use," he says. "Eventually, we'll have meters and computer readouts showing precisely how much water we're using in our landscapes."

He also advocates a color-coded system to make water requirements of plants easy to understand. Rather than prescribe exact amounts of water, he likes groupings that show a relationship to different types of grass. The green-colored high-watering zones characterized by bluegrass, pansies, and redtwig dogwood use 30+ inches of added irrigation per season, which typically consumes more water than is used inside a house. A yellow-coded category, characterized by fescue lawns, potentilla, and purple coneflower, consumes only half the water of the thirsty landscape—about 15 inches extra every year. The red, low-watering zone, with buffalo grass for turf and drought-demanding species such as rabbitbrush and Apache plume, uses only 4.5 extra inches of irrigation. The unirrigated purple zone, too dry for turf, supports tenacious species like piñon pines, rabbitbrush, and junipers.

"Retail garden centers might want to consider this coding system, to promote waterwise gardening and increase their own business," he says. "Professional designers and do-it-yourself homeowners can benefit by color-coding their landscape plans, too."

Knopf's greatest strength as a Zen Master seems to be his enthusiasm and sense of play. (He planted spring bulbs to spell out the word "spring," for example.) Gardening energizes and entertains him. "Gardening is best when it's something to be done, not done with," he believes.

To keep gardening enjoyable, he advocates low-maintenance strategies such as "Pick plants to suit the soil, don't change the soil to suit the plants." Rather than being obsessed with killing the weeds, he suggests a more proactive approach: "Plant things you want and let the plants battle it out. Plant lots of varieties and be amazed that anything has a great year in this wild climate," he says.

Knopf brings his expertise in waterwise landscaping to political forums like the parks board and opportunities for public comment. He's wary of potential bans on landscaping if the current drought continues. "The politicians sometimes don't understand that even the elevated, first-year requirements for getting Xeriscapes established are less than typical requirements of green-zone landscapes. If they pass ordinances that forbid any new landscaping, they're missing an opportunity for more sensible solutions."

No Expectations, No Blame
· PAT BAKER'S HIGH-ALTITUDE ROCK GARDEN ·

AS I PULL IN the winding country driveway, an unconventional scarecrow stands guard in Pat Baker's vegetable garden—a nine- or ten-foot-tall prairie woman who's a little scary even to me. (Don't step in the wrong places.) Right away, I notice many other distinctive, unconventional features about Baker's house and garden, nestled 6,800 feet up in the foothills northwest of Fort Collins. An artist whose landscape is an evolving work of art, she's placed wind chimes, antique farm implements, and stained glass in strategic corners of the garden. Her day job is teaching math at a private elementary school, but her passion is rock gardening.

"I like rock gardening because it extends the growing season on both ends," she tells me as we stand in front of her seed-starting area—a neat, partly snow-covered collection of 2-inch pots in which some of the hardy species have already germinated. It's late spring, and her landscape is just emerging.

"Rock garden plants start earlier in the spring, and when we get early snow in the fall, they just shake it off." Every inch an experimenter, she figures the best way to find out if something will grow in her garden is to try it. As a member of garden clubs like the North American Rock Garden Society, the Penstemon Society, and the Scottish Rock Garden Society, she has access to a wide variety of seeds that are traded among members. Then she starts the seeds herself in an outdoor nursery.

(She uses a mixture of one-half sand and one-half potting soil, with a top mulch of gravel.) On a teacher's salary, she has an opulent garden.

"For awhile I kept track of all the genera I grow," Baker says, uprooting a weed trying to blend in with all the colorful competition. "But I gave up at 500. In the spring, I have to relearn all the names of the plants, and in the fall I have to relearn all the students' names." Since she's "100 percent Lithuanian," she likes to find plants with names like *Campanula kolakowski* and *Draba klastersky*.

Sometimes she tries a plant one more time in a different location, even if it's failed the first few times. *Sibiraea laevigata,* which looks like something from the tropics, is one of those. "I guess I just like a challenge," she says. Another member of the cast has a shady background—the opium poppy.

"I have no restrictions based on what plants are currently in or out of fashion," she says. Clearly, Baker prides herself on not being a plant snob, and as proof, she points out two cousins of the common dandelion that are treated royally in her rock garden—a rose-colored variety and a white one. "A friend had the white-blossoming variety on a plane, but it wasn't in blossom. She said the passengers looked at her like she was crazy, carrying a potted dandelion."

She appreciates the toughness displayed by rock garden plants, whose origins are the wind-blown steppes of Asia, the craggy scree piles of the Alps, or the cold mountain meadows of the Rockies. "Sometimes plants don't look like much aboveground, but their root masses are huge. Like penstemons, which are great transplanters."

On a gardening day, she wears a narrow Japanese trowel in a sheath on her belt. The tool is half Bowie knife and half English trowel—perfect for working in the narrow crevices of her rock garden. Her kitchen counters and dining room table have neat stacks of books and journals about rock gardening, an adventure that grew out of her first vegetable-growing experiments. "I intended to dig a root cellar where the rock garden now is, but it was essentially undiggable—too many rocks." So she let the garden be what it wanted to be. Friends

Selected Rock Garden Plants for High/Dry Western Gardens

Plant Name	Height	Exposure	Soil Preference	Flower Color	Bloom Period	Remarks
Aethionema grandiflorum **Persian stonecress**	6–12 in.	Sun	Dry, sandy	Pink	May	Evergreen; matlike foliage
Alyssum montanum **Mountain alyssum**	4–8 in.	Sun	Dry, rocky	Yellow	April–May	Gray foliage
Arabis alpina **Alpine rockcress**	6 in.	Sun	Dry, rocky, poor	White, pink	April–May	Evergreen; matlike foliage
Armeria maritima **Thrift**	4–10 in.	Sun	Dry, well-drained	Pink, white, purple	May–June	Several varieties
Campanula carpatica **Tussock bellflower**	8 in.	Sun	Well-drained	White, blue, purple	June–July	Several varieties
Campanula rotundifolia **Bluebell**	8–12 in.	Part shade	Well-drained	Blue	May–Sept.	Bell-like flowers on slender stems
Delosperma cooperi **Purple ice plant**	2–3 in.	Sun	Well-drained	Purple	June–frost	Succulent foliage
Dianthus deltoides **'Brilliant', 'Zing Rose'**	6–8 in.	Sun to part shade	Well-drained	Red	May–Sept.	Foliage dark green; matted
Dianthus plumarius **Cottage pink**	6–12 in.	Sun	Well-drained	Red, pink, white	May–June	Several varieties
Gypsophila repens **Creeping baby's breath**	4–8 in.	Sun	Well-drained	White, pink	June–July	Matlike
Heuchera sanguinea **Coral bells**	6–18 in.	Sun to part shade	Well-drained	Red, pink, white	June–Aug.	Mounded foliage with taller bell-shaped flowers
Iberis sempervirens **Candytuft**	12 in.	Shade to part sun	Well-amended	White	May–June, repeats in fall	Evergreen foliage
Minuartia verna **Moss sandwort**	3 in.	Shade to part sun	Well-drained, poor	White	May	Mat-forming
Penstemon caespitosus **Creeping penstemon**	3–6 in.	Sun	Well-drained	Blue	May–June	Mat-like; dark green foliage

Selected Rock Garden Plants for High/Dry Western Gardens (*con't.*)

Plant Name	Height	Exposure	Soil Preference	Flower Color	Bloom Period	Remarks
Phlox subulata **Moss pink or creeping phlox**	6–8 in.	Sun	Well-drained	Pink, white, lavender	April–May	Several varieties
Potentilla x tonguei **Staghorn cinquefoil**	6–8 in.	Sun	Well-drained	Apricot with red centers	May–Aug.	Evergreen some winters
Saponaria ocymoides **Rock soapwort**	6–10 in.	Sun	Well-drained	Pink	May–July	Shear after bloom
Saxifraga spp. **Saxifrage**	Varies with species	Sun to part shade	Moist but well-drained	Varies with species	April–July	Many species
Sempervivum spp. **Houseleek, hen and chicks**	2–6 in., flower taller	Sun	Dry, gravelly	Gray-green	July–Sept.	Succulent, evergreen foliage in rosettes
Thymus pseudo-lanuginosus **Woolly thyme**	2–4 in.	Sun	Loose, well-drained	Infrequent, pink and purple	June–July	Woolly-gray foliage turns purplish in winter; ground cover
Veronica pectinata **Woolly veronica**	2–3 in.	Sun to part shade	Well-drained, fertile	Blue to purple	May–July	Gray, mat–like foliage turns purplish in winter
Veronica repens **Creeping speedwell**	2–3 in.	Sun to part shade	Well-drained, fertile	Blue to purple	May–June	Matlike ground cover; several varieties

have harvested some of the decomposed granite that forms the framework of the garden, and others have brought nutrients to the garden. Like the pond-bottom soil a neighbor gave her, to enrich the spaces so exotic species could make a living.

Rock gardens are not supposed to be pampered environments. The idea is to mimic the harsh conditions of mountain ecosystems, and Baker's gardens do that successfully. A rain gauge on one of the garden gates measures precipitation in hundredths of an inch rather than quarter-inches. Her water supply is limited by the spring that supplies it, so irrigation is sparse—an hour of hand watering in the morning and an hour at night is all that's possible, even in the height of the season. In typical form, she catches water off the roofs of the house and studio with artful whiskey barrels and sculptures, so it can gravity feed to the gardens. "English gardening gurus have to build dry alpine houses to keep the rain *off* some of the plants that get along in my lean soil with scant rainfall," she says.

The weight of a recent surprise snowfall has split a handful of shrub and tree limbs, including a few on the Jonathan apple tree she planted the day her father, Jonathan, died.

But the most vexing challenge she's faced over the years is deer. "We tried every strategy we could think of, from foul-smelling substances to motion detectors that turned on lights and set off loud noises. We tried gunshots, urine, aluminum foil, and rock throwing. We even got a dog and named it Natty Bumppo, after a character in *The Deerslayer.*

"But in the end, the only strategy that worked was a double row of seven-foot-tall fencing surrounding the property. They'll jump over one fence, but not a double fence." Except, that is, in one unexplainably attractive location, where the fences evolved into a triple thickness. "I call myself the Chicken Wire Christo," she says, referring to the artist whose fabric artwork, *The Running Fence*, stretched across the California coastal countryside.

One of her most Zen-like qualities is detachment from the disappointments that come up (or sometimes, *don't* come up) every year. Her slogan is "no expectations, no blame." But she asks, "If we don't allow ourselves to feel disappointment, is it fair that we should feel moments of great satisfaction and joy?" Without hesitation, I give her permission to feel joy, since she appears to have earned it.

While some gardens are regarded strictly as end products, Pat Baker's garden is about the process, and the sensory rewards, of working with soil and plants. "I was included in a garden tour one year comprised mostly of very elaborate, showy gardens—the kind where the homeowner writes a check and looks out at the garden through the window. The gardens are not only flawless but also very predictable, since the same landscape architects designed many of them. They don't have any personality, they don't tell anything about the person who owns the garden."

Baker prefers the alternative garden tours in somewhat the same way beer aficionados prefer the microbreweries. "The gardens on those tours are more eclectic and more funky, and the homeowners' hands are more likely to be soil-stained."

WIZARDS OF SEED
· KEN VETTING, THIRD-GENERATION SEED MERCHANT ·

WHEN IT COMES TO GARDENING, February in Colorado is mostly a waiting game. Gardeners wait, paging idly through seed catalogs and web pages. The ground waits, freezing and thawing like a man shifting his weight from one foot to another. And seeds wait patiently, too, filled with genetic instructions onboard and a love for the game. One cold but sunny day, I got sick of waiting and decided to visit one of my favorite places—Rocky Mountain Seed Company, a solid fixture of Denver's Larimer Square.

As I walk in, Ken Vetting, whose grandfather launched the business way back in 1920, is talking with a customer about what kind of wildflower seed to plant this spring. Don Williamson, with tweezers in hand, is meticulously performing a seed germination test, with 100 cucumber seeds lined up on a moist blotter like soldiers. More than 95 of those seeds will germinate in the next few days, but Don comments that seeds like asparagus and artichokes will be a little less forthcoming.

Michael Gunnish fills several large sacks with birdseed, one of the company's biggest winter products. "We make up our own mixes," he explains, "complete with the right proportions of oyster shells, salt, and iodine. The Rocky Mountain area is big on pigeon racing, and customers come in from Fort Lupton, Pueblo, and Casper—all over—to get whole truckloads of pigeon feed."

Upstairs in the old brick building, Dominic D'Amato, who's worked for the company since the Depression, is preparing seed racks for delivery to 120 garden centers throughout the state. I walk past a vintage seed-sorting machine that performs like a well-maintained antique car, even after years of continuous use. Old oak bins, drawers, and barstools in the retail area augment the sense of continuity, as do the antique radiators and the familiar monster pumpkins in the store's windowsill. "We've been in business for eighty years," says Ken. "I guess we must be doing something right."

The workers at Rocky Mountain Seed appear to be ordinary people at first glance, but after talking briefly with each of them, I realize they are actually superheroes—wizards of seed. Each brings a passion for horticulture to the business, evidenced by years of experience in greenhouse operations, extension service, and huge garden plots at home.

Ken maintains an acre-sized demonstration garden in his own yard, and has for the last ten years been a judge in the annual All-America Selections (AAS) competition that selects the year's best hybrid prospects. This year, for example, 'Indian Summer' sweet corn and 'Savoy Express' cabbage were chosen by twenty-eight national field judges as proven winners, along with a round zucchini called 'Eight Ball'. "Scoop out the seeds and pulp," suggests an AAS press release, "and use the skin as a serving bowl." (Or maybe prop up ten 'Delicata' squashes, and use the round zucchinis as bowling balls?)

Ken explains his interest in participating in AAS. "We want to make sure the selected seeds will work in Colorado's climate, from the short seasons of places like Granby to the longer seasons of Delta County and the Arkansas Valley. We're looking for a wide range of traits including earliness to harvest, yield, fruit taste and quality, and resistance to diseases and pests." Some of Ken's favorite selections of past years are 'Super Sugar Snap', an edible-pod pea, and 'Clemson Spineless' okra, a winner seventy years ago and still growing. To keep customers loyal, his company needs to provide variety, affordability, and most of all, results. Some varieties have been sold for decades, like Burpee's 'Big Boy' tomato and various kinds of peppers that do well in Colorado—'Big Jim', 'Pueblo Chile', and 'Mucho Gusto' among them.

In fact, Rocky Mountain Seed is like a candy shop for tomato and pepper lovers. The company has years of familiarity with forty different varieties of tomatoes and fifty different peppers, from mild to flaming hot. Ken travels all over the West to visit his suppliers and inspect the vigor of the parent plants. Forty different suppliers grow seeds for Ken Vetting, many of them from Colorado. "We buy a lot of our melon, cucumber, and squash seed from the Rocky Ford area, and we get dry beans and peppers in state, too," he says.

Another thing that keeps farmers—and gardeners like me—coming back is the store's policy about quantities of seed. "The more you buy, the cheaper it gets," says Ken. "That's the way we've always done it." Instead of buying colorful but seed-sparse packets, you can buy ounces or pounds of seeds in plain-looking but bulging envelopes and sacks.

I tell Ken about a few of my plans for the upcoming season—artichokes and large beds of cilantro. He reveals a little more of the wisdom he's stored over the years. "Plant cilantro after July 10," he advises, "because it's daylight-dependent. When the days get shorter, the crop won't go to seed as quickly." Concerning artichokes, he reports that if I start seeds early enough—like in February, indoors—I'll begin to get buds when there are more than eighteen leaves. I feel some degree of comfort buying seeds for risky crops like artichokes when I know other Colorado growers have gone before. Ken and his crew are careful not to get customer expectations up on crops like these, though. They caution that success depends on both the season and the soil.

One crop they have complete Colorado confidence in is onions. Ken's particularly fond of a variety called 'Ebenezer'. "Plant them as early in the spring as you can, and you'll get a sweet-tasting, long-storing onion," he says. As Ken talks, I see how much experience is stored in his head, almost like the genetic information contained in one of his seeds. And as I pack up the seeds I've bought and leave the shop, another thought occurs to me. If it's true that "we are what we eat," then certainly Rocky Mountain Seed has played an important role in what Colorado is.

GARDENS FOR PEOPLE, GARDENS FOR PEACE
· CONVERTING KNIVES TO GARDEN TROWELS ·

IN THE MIDDLE OF A CEREMONY to dedicate the Troy Chavez Memorial Peace Garden, gang members showed up in their "colors." Nearly one hundred neighborhood youth had already been killed in gang-related conflicts, and community leaders were afraid more blood would be shed that afternoon in the garden. But the ceremony continued, and the gang leaders listened and left.

"There was a tacit understanding that the new garden would be a violence-free zone," explains Michael Buchenau, a co-director of the Denver Urban Gardens. His organization has helped establish more than seventy community gardens in the Denver metro area. Buchenau and I walk through the garden, past two impressive works of art: a 10-foot-tall stone carving on limestone with an Aztec motif, and an 8 x 18-foot mural that spanned over the garden's walkway. Neighborhood residents chose each artist, and helped put the massive works into place.

"Each of these tiles commemorates the death of a child," Michael says somberly, pointing to a mosaic on the garden's stone walls. "But we've seen a turnaround in this neighborhood since the garden was built. There's a sense of pride and hope that the violence will stop." One of the colorful tiles proclaimed, "As we cultivate the garden, so we cultivate, nurture, and guide the youth!"

Buchenau tells me about the many activities that take place in the garden, year-round. "In the summer, you'll find gardeners harvesting peppers, onions, garlic, and cilantro to make salsa, and you'll see the older women teaching the younger women how to make tortillas. Aztec dances take place in the courtyard, too, but mostly the garden was built for the children—a neutral zone where they can come in the daytime." He explained that the garden has become part of the school curriculum. "They get their GEDs while they learn skills, and learn how to work in the community. One young helper liked to lay sandstone so much that he went to work for a stonemason."

The Peace Garden, located at 38th and Shoshone, may be the most poignant of the more than seventy Denver Urban Gardens, but it's typical in many ways. Like the Peace Garden, many DUG gardens are neighborhood rallying points and hubs of social activity. For example, the Clarkson Garden, built on a vacant lot at 2346 Clarkson Street, once attracted "mostly beer bottles, needles, and trouble," according to Mike Jackson, who lives right next to the garden. Jackson and his wife, Sandra, helped get the garden going five years ago, and now take part in food growing as well as other activities like block parties, yard sales, and potlucks.

At the Ashgrove Garden on South Holly, gardeners of all ages (from 3 to 82) and many different cultures work together on their common goal—making the garden beautiful, productive, and inclusive. "Gardening is a healing activity," said Ashgrove garden leader Arzella Duerksen. "I remember when my mother died, I unconsciously headed out to the garden to renew myself." She explained that her fellow gardeners include people from Iran, Turkey, Afghanistan, Sweden, and other countries. "Sometimes there are heated discussions because the gardeners' home countries may be at war with each other. But the garden is like a miniature United Nations—we settle our differences and get on with the work."

Like other DUG gardeners, the Ashgrove gardeners compost materials on-site, but they augment that supply with purchased compost in the spring and an ambitious leaf-gathering program in the fall. "We go up and down the alleys in October and November and gather bags of leaves from peoples' yards. After more than ten years of that, our soil is starting to get pretty rich."

Ashgrove gardeners pay fifteen dollars a year, a typical fee, for pooled efforts like buying compost. If community gardeners pay water bills too, the fees are slightly higher. What began with a few gardeners has now expanded to fifty active members, and more on the waiting list. Because the garden is located at Ashgrove Elementary School, there is active participation from children, especially when volunteers are needed to eat ripe cherry tomatoes. Kids are a central part of the activities at Crofton Ebert Elementary also. The neighborhood's expert grower, thirteen-year-old A. J. Adolph, has proclaimed himself the "king of squash." Somebody had to do it. But A. J.'s Victorian Garden, in the Curtis Park/Five Points neighborhood, has not always been so productive. When the gardeners first rehabbed the vacant lot, they had to cart off many truckloads of rock, syringes, and even a sawed-off shotgun. Now, it's become a place where they gather once a month for dessert and coffee.

Some 85 percent of the Denver Urban Gardens are located in low-income neighborhoods. For example, at the Cheltenham School Community Garden, at 16th and Irvin Street, more than 90 percent of the students receive reduced-price or free lunch. Nearly 70 percent of the students speak Spanish as their primary language. So the food that comes from that garden is put to good use, as it is at the Fairmont Elementary School Garden, whose gardeners sometimes share a single house with twenty others. Other gardens, especially large ones like Lowry Air Force Base Garden (it has 100 plots), supply produce to homeless shelters. "There are a lot of hungry people out there," says Denise Wanzo, one of the founders of the Montbello Garden, "and one of them may be your neighbor."

Drew Myron, writer/editor of DUG's *Underground News,* describes community gardening as "the ideal prescription for a weary neighborhood. Toil in a community garden and you'll walk away with more than fresh produce: the full-face grin of a child planting his first seed; the quiet patience of a veteran gardener sharing secrets and skills with an eager, novice gardener; the team of enthusiastic volunteers determined to transform a vacant lot. It is from all that a community garden emerges and a neighborhood grows stronger."

Of course, as Director Michael Buchenau can tell you, the gardens don't just pop into place. "We usually work on the design and the lease arrangements for months, before a single shovel is lifted." Even before that, Michael or co-Director David Rieseck—former classmates and landscaping students at Harvard—typically get a call from a neighborhood leader representing a small group. "Usually, there's a vacant lot or some space on the schoolgrounds, and they want us to help them create a garden like the one they've seen ten or fifteen blocks away," explains Michael. "We assess the lot and make sure it's not some big, attractive corner property that will be sold to build a house on. Since most of the gardens are leased—we only own a handful—we have to be careful with developable land. We try to get ten-year leases from private owners, city governments, schools, and companies, because we don't want to put a lot of effort into a garden that's not going to last."

Michael and his colleagues treat each piece of land as a blank canvas on which to create a work of art. They use durable, high-quality fixtures, like stone pavers that are too big to crack or be stolen. They look around for materials that have historic and cultural significance, too. One of the gardens incorporates part of the stone pillars that were used in Larimer Square close to a century ago. Almost every garden has benches with children's paintings on them and well-designed, customized compost containers.

There's a lot of work involved in the design and construction of a typical garden, and one of DUG's greatest strengths is finding partners and allies. The program's list of sponsors includes corporations—from AT&T and the Gates Foundation to Starbucks Coffee, communities, restaurants, and individuals. A typical strategy is to involve a volunteer crew of corporate employees in the construction phase of a garden, working side by side with neighborhood gardeners-to-be.

"We like to do a lot of prep work before the workdays, to make sure that the workers have a sense of progress," Michael explains. "If we're going to put a fence up, for example, we'll set in the posts the week before, so at the end of the day, there's a feeling of accomplishment." Other work crews might consist of people performing community service for the County Sheriff's Department, Americorps volunteers, or school parents and kids.

Michael has been especially impressed with the energy, enthusiasm, and skills of Hispanic participants. "Their culture seems to really take pride in working with their hands, and they have a great tradition of growing gardens," he says.

I ask him what DUG's long-range goals are. He replies after a little thought, "We'd like to reach the 100-garden milestone, and maybe spread out into the six-county region. And we're driven by a desire to have every one of our gardens be a very positive influence on both gardeners and their neighborhoods."

I share my own personal slogan with him: "A gardener's best year is always next year," and he adds, "Couldn't the same be said about a neighborhood? There's always room for improvement, and I feel fortunate to be involved in that process of making each neighborhood better."

RECOMMENDED READING

Ableman, Michael. *On Good Land: The Autobiography of an Urban Farm*. San Francisco: Chronicle Books, 1998.

Ackerman, Diane. *Cultivating Delight: A Natural History of My Garden*. New York: HarperCollins, 2001.

Bartholomew, Mel. *Square Foot Gardening*. Emmaus, PA: Rodale Press, 1981.

Brenzel, Kathleen Norris. *Sunset Western Garden Book*. Menlo Park, CA: Sunset Publishing, 2001.

Chotzinoff, Robin. *People with Dirty Hands: The Passion for Gardening*. Hoboken, NJ: John Wiley & Sons, 1997.

Colorado Nursery Association. *The Rocky Mountain Perennial Plant Guide*. Denver, CO: Colorado Nursery Association, 1995.

Cretti, John L. *Colorado Gardener's Guide*. Franklin, TN: Cool Springs Press, 2001.

Cutler, Karan Davis. *Burpee: The Complete Vegetable and Herb Gardener*. Hoboken, NJ: John Wiley & Sons, 1997.

Denver Water. *Xeriscape Plant Guide: 100 Water-Wise Plants for Gardens and Landscapes*. Golden, CO: Fulcrum Publishing, 1996.

Gershuny, Grace. *Start with the Soil: The Organic Gardener's Guide to Improving Soil for Higher Yields, More Beautiful Flowers, and a Healthy, Easy-Care Garden*. Emmaus, PA: Rodale Press, 1997.

Gussow, Joan Dye. *This Organic Life: Confessions of a Suburban Homesteader*. White River Junction, VT: Chelsea Green Publishing Co., 2002.

Hemenway, Toby. *Gaia's Garden: A Guide to Home-Scale Permaculture*. White River Junction, VT: Chelsea Green Publishing Co., 2001.

Hyde, Barbara. *Gardening in the Mountain West*. Boulder, CO: Self-published, 1993.

Jeavons, John. *How to Grow More Vegetables: And Fruits, Nuts, Berries, Grains and Other Crops Than You Ever Thought Possible on Less Land Than You Can Imagine*. Berkeley, CA: Ten Speed Press, 2002.

Knopf, Jim. *The Xeriscape Flower Gardener: A Waterwise Guide for the Rocky Mountain Region*. Boulder, CO: Johnson Books, 1991.

———, ed. *Waterwise Landscaping with Trees, Shrubs, and Vines: A Xeriscape Guide for the Rocky Mountain Region, California, and the Desert Southwest*. Boulder, CO: Chamisa Books, 1999.

Lappé, Frances Moore, and Anna Lappé. *Hope's Edge: The Next Diet for a Small Planet*. Los Angeles: J. P. Tarcher, 2002.

Moffat, Anne Simon, Marc Schiler, and the Staff of *Green Living*. *Energy-Efficient and Environmental Landscaping: Cut Your Utility Bills by Up to 30 Percent and Create a Natural Healthy Yard*. White River Junction, VT: Chelsea Green Publishing Co., 1995.

Olwell, Carol. *Gardening from the Heart: Why Gardeners Garden*. Logan, UT: Antelope Island Press, 1990.

Overy, Angela. *Sex in Your Garden*. Golden, CO: Fulcrum Publishing, 1997.

Shapiro, Howard-Yana, Ph.D., and John Harrisson. *Gardening for the Future of the Earth*. New York: Bantam Doubleday Dell, 2000.

Smith, Shane. *Greenhouse Gardener's Companion*. 2d edition. Golden, CO: Fulcrum Publishing, 2000.

Springer, Lauren. *The Undaunted Garden*. Golden, CO: Fulcrum Publishing, 1994.

———, and Rob Proctor. *Passionate Gardening: Good Advice for Challenging Climates*. Golden, CO: Fulcrum Publishing, 2000.

Stein, Sara Bonnett. *Noah's Children: Restoring the Ecology of Childhood*. New York: North Point Press, 2002.

Tatroe, Marcia. *Perennials for Dummies*. Foster City, CA: IDG Books, 1997.

Tompkins, Peter, and Christopher Bird. *The Secret Life of Plants: A Fascinating Account of the Physical, Emotional, and Spiritual Relations Between Plants and Man*. New York: HarperCollins, 1989.

Weinstein, Gayle. *Xeriscape Handbook: A How-to Guide to Natural Resource-Wise Gardening*. Golden, CO: Fulcrum Publishing, 1999.

Resources for Seeds and Supplies

Ecology Action—Bountiful Gardens
18001 Shafer Ranch Road
Willits, California 95490
707-459-6410
Fax: 707-459-1925
www.bountifulgardens.org/order.html
Seeds and supplies for biointensive gardening

TheGarlicStore.com
Yucca Ridge Farm
46050 Weld County Road 13
Fort Collins, Colorado 80524
1-800-854-7219
www.thegarlicstore.com
Hardy garlic for the high and arid West

High Country Gardens
2902 Rufina Street
Santa Fe, New Mexico 87507-2929
1-800-925-9387
Fax: 1-800-925-0097
www.highcountrygardens.com
*Supplies plants that do well throughout
the high and arid West*

Johnny's Selected Seeds
955 Benton Avenue
Winslow, Maine 04901
207-861-3901
1-800-437-4290
www.johnnyseeds.com
*Wide selection of quality vegetable,
flower, and herb seeds*

Organic Growers Supply
P.O. Box 520-A
Waterville, Maine 04903
Fax: 207-872-8317
www.fedcoseeds.com
*Member of no-frills, reliable
Fedco Seed Packing co-op*

PRAIRIE NURSERY
P.O. Box 316
Westfield, Wisconsin 53964
1-800-476-9453
Fax: 608-296-2741
www.prairienursery.com
*Native plants and seeds for
ecological gardening*

ROCKY MOUNTAIN SEED COMPANY
P.O. Box 5204
Denver, Colorado 80217-5204
303-623-6254
Fax: 303-623-6254
*Third-generation seed company
offering dependable seeds*

SEEDS OF CHANGE
Box 15700, Dept. H.O.
Santa Fe, NM 87506-5700
1-888-762-7333
www.seedsofchange.com
*Broad selection of 100% organic seedlings,
gardening tools, books, and organic foods*

STOKES SEEDS
1904 Stokes Building
P.O. Box 548
Buffalo, New York 14240-0548
716-695-6980
www.stokeseeds.com
Wide variety of seeds, trees, and supplies

INDEX

About the Author

DAVID WANN has written six books that all feature his general mantra: "Waking up from the American Dream and learning to use our hands, hearts, and heads again." His book *Affluenza: The All-Consuming Epidemic* (2001), about beating the plagues of over-production and over-consumption, was a finalist in the 2002 Colorado Book Award for nonfiction and has been translated into German, Russian, Hebrew, and South Korean. *Deep Design* (1996) and *Biologic* (1994) both explore how holistic, nature-based design can prevent damaging environmental and social impacts. *Superbia!* (2003) examines the potential for reinventing America's existing suburbs to make them more sustainable.

A recent recipient of the Timothy Wirth Sustainability Award, David has worked for ten years at the Environmental Protection Agency, writing articles, producing videos, and helping implement the Pollution Prevention program. He has produced more than twenty videos and television programs about sustainable lifestyles and technologies, including "Sustaining America's Agriculture: High Tech and Horse Sense," narrated by Raymond Burr.

David began gardening in the early 1980s in the foothills near Denver, at 7,000 feet. He coordinates a community garden in a "living community" (cohousing) in Golden, Colorado, where wind, drought, heat waves, and cold snaps often converge on the same day.